Sport and Moral Conflict

Sport and Moral Conflict

A Conventionalist Theory

William J. Morgan

TEMPLE UNIVERSITY PRESS
Philadelphia • Rome • Tokyo

TEMPLE UNIVERSITY PRESS
Philadelphia, Pennsylvania 19122
tupress.temple.edu

Published 2020

Library of Congress Cataloging-in-Publication Data

Names: Morgan, William J., 1948– author.
Title: Sport and moral conflict : a conventionalist theory / William J. Morgan.
Description: Philadelphia : Temple University Press, 2020. | Includes bibliographical references and index. | Summary: "This book explores the dominant theories of ethics in sports, concluding that a conventionalist model is most defensible. It roots its inquiry in the collision of sporting ideologies in the early twentieth century's Olympic games where English and American ideas of sportsmanship highlighted differing approaches to fairness in sport"—Provided by publisher.
Identifiers: LCCN 2019029971 (print) | LCCN 2019029972 (ebook) | ISBN 9781439915394 (cloth) | ISBN 9781439915400 (paperback) | ISBN 9781439915417 (pdf)
Subjects: LCSH: Sports—Moral and ethical aspects. | Sports—History. | Sports—Sociological aspects.
Classification: LCC GV706.3 .M66 2020 (print) | LCC GV706.3 (ebook) | DDC 175—dc23
LC record available at https://lccn.loc.gov/2019029971
LC ebook record available at https://lccn.loc.gov/2019029972

♾ The paper used in this publication meets the requirements of the American National Standard for Information Sciences—Permanence of Paper for Printed Library Materials, ANSI Z39.48-1992

Printed in the United States of America

9 8 7 6 5 4 3 2 1

For Bob Simon,

in memoriam

You ask me what all idiosyncrasy is in philosophers? . . . For instance their lack of historical sense. . . . They imagine they do honour to a thing by divorcing it from history *sub specie aeterni*—when they make a mummy of it. All the ideas that philosophers have treated . . . have been mummified concepts; nothing real has ever come out of their hands alive.

—Friedrich Nietzsche, *Twilight of the Idols*

We must not begin by talking of pure ideas—vagabond thoughts that tramp the public highways without any human habitation—but must begin with men and their conversation.

—C. S. Peirce, *Collected Papers of Charles Sanders Peirce*

Contents

Preface and Acknowledgments ix

Introduction: Sport as a Kind of Moral Laboratory 1

1 The Fight for the Moral Soul of Modern Sport: Dueling Amateur and Professional Conceptions of Sport in the Early Modern Olympic Games, 1896–1924 9

2 Formalism and Sport 29

3 Broad Internalism, Moral Realism, and Sport: The Metaphysical Version 62

4 Broad Internalism, Moral Realism, and Sport: The Discourse Version 96

5 What a Conventionalist Ethical Theory of Sport Does Not Look Like: The Case against Coordinating, Deep, and Constitutive (Surface) Conventions 124

6 A Conventionalist Ethical Theory of Sport 155

Epilogue: Sport, Moral Progress, and Moral Entrepreneurs 193

Notes 203

References 215

Index 221

Preface and Acknowledgments

The main ideas and arguments of this book have preoccupied me for well over a decade. I have tried out initial, provisional versions of them at several conferences and invited talks and in various published writings. The book you are reading, however, is very much a new work that departs in important ways from my previous presentations and writings on this subject. It thus contains my latest, most developed thoughts on what a conventionalist ethical theory of sport rightly understood looks like and what it might offer in the way of ethical insight regarding the moral controversies and crises that continue to plague sport at all levels seemingly at every turn.

I could not have written this book, of course, without the help of my fellow workers in the philosophy of sport vineyard, who first drew my attention to the ethical questions I entertain here, made compelling arguments about how they might best be answered, and spurred me to seek my own answers to these questions that challenged their answers. In this regard, I owe a special debt of gratitude to Bob Simon and John Russell. It was Bob Simon who coined the term broad internalism (interpretivism) and who first sketched out an ethical theory bearing its name in his important essay "Internalism and Internal Values in Sport" (2007). He went on to refine the theory in several publications that helped make it the leading ethical theory in the literature. It is with profound gratitude for all his impressive work in this and other areas of the philosophy of sport that I have dedicated my book to him. I only wish he were still with us to read the finished work and offer his characteristic trenchant responses to it—always rendered, I hasten to add, in a gracious manner that typified his congenial and generous spirit. In short, Bob was not only a wonderful philosopher but an even more wonderful human being. John Russell's impressive writings further solidified broad internalism as the go-to ethical theory of sport; in fact, his seminal essay, "Are Rules All an Umpire Has to Work With?" (1999), was a major inspiration for Bob's first formulation of broad internalism. In subsequent publications, John developed his own powerful version of this ethical theory. I have learned more from John than I can put into words. And like Bob, he has always been gracious in his contributions to our debates over the years on this subject.

I also owe thanks to the different audiences I have presented my work to, because I profited from their challenging questions. Thanks also go to all those who have responded to my earlier iterations of conventionalism in my published writings and who helped me clarify my position and strengthen my arguments. I am indebted as well to two anonymous reviewers solicited by Temple University Press; they offered many helpful comments and suggestions that proved valuable as I prepared the final draft.

Further, I thank Ryan Mulligan, my editor at Temple University Press, for his initial interest in my book and for his expert advice and encouragement throughout the review process leading up to its publication. I could not have asked for a better, more helpful editor. Finally, I owe an important debt of gratitude to my copyeditor, Vicki Adang, for her expert editing of my text.

Sport and Moral Conflict

Introduction

Sport as a Kind of Moral Laboratory

Sport has often been likened to a moral laboratory. One way to understand this idea is that because sport typically puts people in competitive, emotionally charged situations in which the stakes for participants and spectators alike are uncommonly high (athletic accomplishment, community pride, etc.) even though instrumentally benign (athletic outcomes seldom translate into substantive real-life benefits like a rise in general social welfare), it tests, among other things, their moral mettle. Although it is relatively easy to treat people with moral respect when everyone's emotions are held in check and they are not competing with one another for a highly prized goal, it is not so easy to do so when conditions are fundamentally otherwise, as they commonly are in competitive sports. The moral part of this test looms more largely in sport than it does in many other spheres of contemporary life, since notions like fairness are widely recognized as central to genuine athletic accomplishment (the sport public's widespread and visceral moral condemnation of doping in sport is but one example).

The notion that sport is a kind of moral laboratory can also be understood in another sense. I have noted how our understanding of athletic excellence depends on our understanding of basic fairness or equality. As Mika LaVaque-Manty nicely puts it, "Something can only count as excellent against some basis of equal comparison" (2009, 190). This suggests that our changing conceptions of athletic excellence often give rise to new conceptions of fairness and equality, not to mention new moral ways of how sport should be done. Women's sport and disability sport are cases in point.

Each introduced a new rendering of the meaning of athletic accomplishment in which the difference of gender or disability could no longer be equated with a lack of talent, in which the idea that athletic excellence is the exclusive province of biological males or able-bodied persons could no longer be countenanced. That opened the way for, among other things, sex-segregated sports for women who would otherwise be denied an opportunity to showcase their athletic prowess and sports for the disabled that capitalized on what they could functionally achieve, rather than not achieve, given their different physical and cognitive capacities.[1]

It is to this latter idea of sport as a moral crucible in which different conceptions of the point and purpose of athletic endeavor and of the meaning of athletic excellence are up for grabs, and with them the different moral ways they suggest sport should be done, that I intend to make the main focus of my inquiry. But before I outline just what different conceptions of sport I want to single out, I should clarify that to call sport a moral laboratory is not to hold it up as a paragon of moral virtue. Far from it. More often than not, athletes and their enthusiastic followers fail the moral challenges they face in athletic contests and end up behaving very badly. That, however, does not count against the idea that sport is a moral laboratory; rather, it is evidence that sport remains one of the few places left in contemporary society where people's moral resolve is challenged rather than assumed, where the easy and comforting presumption that most of us can be relied on to do the right thing when it really matters—because at bottom we are all basically good people—is put to the test rather than passed off as a given.

I want to zero in on the conflicting accounts of the aim of athletic endeavor and of the meaning of athletic excellence, as well as the conflicting ways they suggest people should morally comport themselves in sport, specifically in one historical period of the Olympic Games, spanning roughly from the 1906 Athens games to the 1924 Paris games. I have chosen this particular historical period for my moral inquiry into sport for several reasons. First, during this period we saw the dramatic ascendance of the national and international prestige of the Olympic Games as a major social, cultural, and political event, which catapulted sport itself on to the world stage as a cultural and moral force to be reckoned with. Second, the central moral issues and problems that arose during this period were an omen of the morally stormy days ahead for present-day sport in which winning increasingly became the be-all and end-all of athletic competition. Third, the resolution of these newly emergent moral issues about how sport should be conducted proved to be incapable of piecemeal moral reform, of resolution on a case-by-case basis, but called for a more systematic approach, a moral theory of sport capable of dealing with the increasingly complex and vexing moral terrain of athletic endeavor.

However, the central factor of why this particular historical period of sport stands out morally speaking is because it was punctuated by an epic battle for the "soul" of modern sport, waged between two athletic factions that held markedly different conceptions of sport and athletic excellence. This dispute was fiercely and openly contested in full view of what was then the international sporting public, mainly Western Europe and the United States. The two rival camps and conceptions pitted a predominantly English version of gentleman-amateur sport against a predominantly American version of professional sport. The basic terms of this dispute will be familiar to contemporary readers because traces of it survive to the present. But after we get to the heart of what these two athletic camps were arguing over, the debate takes on a less familiar ring to us contemporaries because it had much less to do with the privileges of social class and the propriety of paying athletes than we have been led to believe.

On the gentleman-amateur side of this equation, the moral standards that were regarded as integral to honoring the purpose of sport and achieving athletic distinction were derived from the view that sport should be pursued for the love of the game itself rather than any tangible instrumental benefits that might be obtained by engaging in it. Of course, that ruled out pay for play as well as any attempt to pass off sport as a professional occupation. Further, the idea that sport was an avocation rather than a vocation worked against trying too hard to win, which, it was thought, would detract from the sheer pleasure of competing; this view also discouraged the adoption of rationalized training methods based on the latest scientific advances and the use of professional coaches to improve one's athletic performance. This avocational take on sport also considered morally askance any single-minded focus on athletic brilliance at the expense of all-around athletic excellence and the use of strategic tactics to gain a competitive advantage (to include strategies in team sports in which, for example, members set the pace for teammates in a footrace or members of a cycling team attempt to box in opponents to aid their side, and, of course, strategic attempts to bend the rules to one's advantage).

By contrast, the moral norms of professional sport turned those of the amateur conception on its head, which accounts for the unalloyed seriousness in which its adherents pursued sport and treated winning as its unambiguous aim. The idea that sport is a serious occupation rather than a casual pastime gave moral sanction to athletes' efforts to become the most accomplished performers they aspired to be and, therefore, permitted them to adopt scientific training methods, seek the best professional coaching available, become strategically savvy in terms of in-games tactics and rule bending, and specialize to their hearts' delight.

What we confront, then, in this small slice of the modern Olympic Games are two diametrically opposed moral conceptions of the point and purpose of athletic endeavor and of the meaning of athletic excellence. Indeed, each camp regarded the other's approach to sport and commitment to athletic achievement as practically and morally repugnant. This raises the question of how we are to make our way morally and otherwise in such a fractious, polarized athletic environment. That general question, of course, begs a series of more particular questions that bear on the moral conduct appropriate to sport that continue to confound us to this day: What, exactly, are the relevant skills that athletic contests are supposed to test, and how much weight should be accorded each so that our moral evaluations track the right mix of desired skills? What motive(s) is (are) conducive to right actions in sport? What moral standards are justifiably called for to evaluate actions carried out in the heat of athletic competition? How should we think about the increasing reliance on strategies that involve rule bending or outright rule violations to gain a competitive edge? What level of effort and commitment to athletic excellence is morally acceptable?

I am only scratching the surface here, but I think I have said enough to back up my previous claim that the answers to such questions that are touched off by moral conflicts like the amateur-professional divide require nothing short of a comprehensive moral theory of sport responsive to our shifting views of what is the purpose of sport and how we should think about athletic excellence. In the extant philosophy of sport literature, two moral theories of sport have been developed that go by the names of, respectively, formalism and broad internalism (or, as it is sometimes called, interpretivism). After I spell out in greater detail in Chapter 1 the moral dispute that put the amateur and professional athletic communities at odds with one another, I devote the subsequent three chapters to a critical examination of formalism and two versions of broad internalism and argue that they fall short when confronted with a moral dispute of the conflicting kind and breadth that is seen in the transition from amateur to professional sport.

The formalist moral theory of sport holds that the purpose of sport and the kind of excellence it offers can be mostly read off of its founding rules. When moral questions or controversies arise, therefore, formalists instruct us to look to the rules for the guidance necessary to resolve them. The problem, however, as has been oft observed, is that many of these morally hard cases fall outside the purview of the rules, as can be seen in my featured amateur-professional example in which the argument touched hardly at all on the existing rules. This is not surprising because the rules of sport, not to mention the rules of most relatively sophisticated social practices, are not exhaustive. That is why we can expect situations to arise in which there is no applicable rule to handle them. The other problem with rules is that they are not self-interpreting, which means that even when there is an applicable rule, it is not always clear how it should be interpreted. For instance, in the late stages of athletic contests, such as basketball and hockey, rule violations are often ignored to ensure the flow of the game is not interrupted or is not decided on the basis of a called penalty. The question is whether such strategic rule violations should be regarded as punishable offenses deserving of our moral reproach or are simply costs paid for pursuing a strategy that is morally above board. The answer cannot be found by consulting the formal rules.

The second moral theory of sport that Simon dubbed "broad internalism" was designed to handle the above problems with rules. On this theory, there is more to sport, morally speaking, than the rules; that something more has to do with general principles of athletic conduct whose moral force and utility derive from the fact that they are presuppositions of sport on which the very intelligibility of the game depends. That goes for the signature rules of sport as well, which have the form that they do, it is claimed, because of these principles.

This theory comes in two variants, both of which claim to be versions of moral realism. John Russell (2007), the proponent of the first version, argues that the moral principles relevant to sport represent or correspond to actual intrinsic properties of sport, to real facts about athletic endeavor that are, therefore, independent of the vocabularies we use to describe them as well as the different perspectives we might bring to bear to understand and interpret them in different historical and social contexts. Two such nonmoral structural properties of sport, he argues, are crucial in this regard. The first is that athletic competitions have an unmistakable purpose, which is to exercise and display skills in overcoming rule-created artificial obstacles. The second is that players must voluntarily consent to overcome such obstacles. Russell accordingly derives two moral principles, which count as independent moral facts in their own right, from these two nonmoral facts about the nature of sport. The moral principle of sport that follows from its clear perfectionist purpose Russell labels the "internal" principle, which holds that "rules should be interpreted in such a manner that the excellences embodied in achieving the goal of the game are not undermined but maintained and fostered" (2007, 58–59). The moral principle he derives from the voluntary character of sport he calls the "external" principle, which holds that activities that are not or cannot be consented to by athletes fall outside the realm of morally permissible actions.

Robert Simon (2004), the proponent of the second variant of broad internalism, argues for a more modest version of moral realism, which, unlike Russell's account, is agnostic on the question of whether the moral principles of sport correspond to independent, certifiable moral facts about the nature of sport. Rather, he claims that moral principles like Russell's "internal" principle, which Simon vouches for in his own account, can be generated in a less metaphysically robust and controversial way by an ethical approach based on a discourse that puts all the onus on the back-and-forth exchange of reasons by which we commonly justify moral principles. The basic idea is simple enough: All views regarding how sport should be conducted are welcomed and evaluated according to the intellectual contribution they make to the discussion. As long as the reasons traded back and forth in such a discourse are considered strictly in terms of their intellectual merit—that is, in accord with standards of rational appraisal that are duly "independent of all cultural, linguistic, or pragmatic considerations" (Simon 2004, 125)—we can be confident that the arguments that survive such reflective scrutiny and that the moral principles adduced from them are justified and deserve our intellectual assent.

Obviously, broad internalism is a more sophisticated and supple moral theory of sport than formalism and is, therefore, a better guide as to how we should conduct ourselves in athletic settings. Nonetheless, it has its own particular shortcomings. The main problem, which besets both versions, is the level of reflective generality it insists moral inquiry, rightly understood, must achieve if it is to warrant the intellectual assent of all rational human agents concerned. For the heavy price paid by requiring moral principles of sport to be grounded either in timeless, nonmoral facts about the point and purpose of sport or in intellectual considerations concerning the nature of sport whose justificatory force is independent of all social or cultural considerations is irrelevance to the actual practice of sport. That is because the abstract moral principles they favor are too far removed from the social and historical contexts in which sport is actually played to meet the two criteria any moral theory worth its salt must satisfy—namely, that it be action guiding and motivating.

In Chapter 5, I distinguish the kind of ethical conventions that underwrite my own forthcoming conventionalist ethical theory of sport from three other kinds of conventions canvassed in the philosophical literature. These other kinds of conventions include David Lewis's (2002) well-known account of what he calls coordinating conventions and Andrei Marmor's (2009) account of what he calls deep and surface conventions. I claim that although these conventions figure in sport as they do in the rest of our social lives, they do not figure in any important sense in the ethical life of sport. My claim that the ethical conventions that play such a vital normative role in sport are to be distinguished from Marmor's deep conventions represents a major departure from my previously published writings on this topic, in which I held they are one and the same. I now realize that was a mistake after taking a longer look at Marmor's discussion of deep conventions, which I thank Eric Moore for persuading me to do. I detail in Chapter 5 just why conflating Marmor's notion of deep conventions with my new, Hegelian-inspired notion of ethical conventions was a mistake, and a serious one at that. For now, it suffices to say that a conventionalist ethical theory of sport worthy of the name cannot take its lead from either Lewis's or Marmor's renderings of coordinating, deep, or surface conventions.

In Chapter 6, I sketch out my own conventionalist version of broad internalism, in which I propose a Hegelian, historicist conception of ethical conventions. Ethical conventions refer to the shared background understandings internal to forms of life like sport at particular times and places. Because these conventions are responsive to "the way things are done around here," they put us in touch with the conceptions of athletic excellence that inform, for example, the amateur and professional conceptions of sport. It is their responsiveness in this regard that, I claim, accounts for their action-guiding and motivational force, which abstract moral principles like the internal principle coveted by broad internalists decidedly lack.

But does my proposed conventional corrective, a critic might retort, not go too far in the opposite direction? Although it does go a long way toward narrowing the wide gulf between abstract moral principles like the internal principle and what actually goes on in sport, it also seems to bring our moral principles too close to the actual action and, therefore, too beholden to the athletic status quo to serve as the critical check that is also a trademark of any moral principle worthy of the name. Moral principles, after all, are not supposed to be rubber stamps but critical checks and counsels.

Getting too close to the action in our moral deliberations about things like sport undeniably poses special dangers that can deprive the moral principles we come up with of the sharp edge they need to have to be action guiding in the sense intended. However, I argue that the ethical conventions that inform the inner understandings and norms of athletic forms of life, of "the way we do things athletically around here"—whether it be amateurs or professionals or some other athletic community of similar stature and composition—avoid this problematic consequence. For while the phrase "the way we do things athletically or otherwise around here" sounds like a carte blanche endorsement of the *dominant* ways things are done in any given society, which are mostly, as Foucault took pains to show, owed to the machinations of power rather than the force of the better argument, that inference should be resisted. That is because the phrase can be understood in a contrasting and more compelling way that harkens back to how Hegel employed the phrase to draw critical attention to the ethical ways of living within the main social practices and institutions of his time—what he famously called the *Sittlichkeit* of a society or culture. These ethical forms of life warranted serious consideration, Hegel argued, because they acted as a critical check on the questionable power wielded by dominant parties in their effort to make modern German society serve their narrow needs and interests at the expense of their less powerful members. The same, I argue, is equally true today in which the ethical conventional understandings and norms of social practices like sport, rightly conceived and deployed, can and often do act as a critical check on the similar effort by dominant parties (in market societies like our own, typically those with the requisite cash to lord it over the rest of us) to remake society in their own narrow self-image. And the fact that Hegel thought these socially embedded ethical ways of living could play their critical role without resorting to impersonal moral standards or submitting to some universalizing test to certify their moral bona fides is all the more reason why I model my own ethical conventional athletic version of the *Sittlichkeit* after his.

In the Epilogue, I try to make the case that a conventionalist moral theory of sport of the kind I argue for must make room for what Richard Posner calls "moral entrepreneurs" (1999, 7–8). If there is one thing that moral entrepreneurs are not, it is conventionalists. Indeed, their express moral task is to break the crust of the reigning ethical conventions, to push beyond the conventional confines of our present moral vocabularies and principles, and to pry open new logical space (new reasons) and moral space (new moral vocabularies) in which we can reason together as to how we should live. We need moral entrepreneurs because if there is one thing we should have learned from the major social movements of the twentieth century (the civil rights and women's movements), it is that our moral horizons need to be constantly expanded. Sport is certainly no different in this respect, which is why it has experienced several revolutionary moral breakthroughs in the last century. For it, too, was transformed by both the civil rights movement and the women's movement, both of which defied our conventional understandings of black athletes and women athletes, who were formerly excluded from the going concept and practice of sport. The more recent disability movement has also sparked a revolutionary (anti-conventional) reconception of athletic bodies and sports. But our need for moral entrepreneurs to speak and agitate against the grain of conventional moral thought should not make us chary of moral conventions themselves. After all, what distinguishes successful moral entrepreneurs from failed ones is that the former, unlike the latter, are able somehow to convert their trademark metaphorical redescriptions of sport into conventional ones; that is, they prod a sufficient number of people to take up their new conceptions of sport and construct a new moral vocabulary to accommodate them so they can argue with one another anew as to how sport should be morally conducted in these newly conventionalized terms.

1

The Fight for the Moral Soul of Modern Sport

Dueling Amateur and Professional Conceptions of Sport in the Early Modern Olympic Games, 1896–1924

As I remark in the Introduction, the resumption of the modern Olympic Games at the turn of the twentieth century was notable not just because it was an important contributing factor to the remarkable ascendance of sport as a major social, cultural, and political force across Europe and North America but because it set the moral tone for sport for the rest of the twentieth century and beyond. Its outsized significance in this latter regard can be traced to the epic battle for the moral soul of modern sport that was waged during this historical period; the conflict pitted a mainly English gentleman-amateur conception against a mainly American professional conception of athletic endeavor. My ultimate aim in critically probing this epic clash over the point and purpose of athletic endeavor and of the moral outlook suited to its full blossoming is to show what crucial role ethical conventions of sport play in its moral reckoning. But for present purposes I first want to establish how wide and deep this split between these two factions of the international athletic community was; I also want to show what light it sheds on the possibilities and limits of moral argument and moral progress in and, by implication, outside of the world of sport. There is much to be learned, or so I claim, when communities of inquiry and the norms they rely on to make moral sense of valued social practices like sport are so at odds with one another that they are at a loss of how to morally adjudicate their differences because they cannot see eye to eye on the purpose and value of sport itself.

A Genealogy of the Gentleman-Amateur Conception of Sport

The seedbed of the gentleman-amateur conception of sport was, as oft observed, the English public schools, which, for those of us on the other side of the pond, were what we called and still call private schools and are reserved mainly for the youth of the upper-class elite. This fact is, of course, why we often think of amateur sport as a predominantly aristocratic concoction defined by patrician virtues and a contemptuous disdain of the working class. Much has been made of this public-school origin story and of the social snobbery it traded in and exploited to exclude manual laborers and their kind from its precious athletic ranks. Too much, in my estimation. For if amateur sport were nothing more than a public-school phenomenon confined to the well-bred and well-heeled, then its account of sport would be little more than a faint blip on our athletic radar screen. That it counted for considerably more than this had to do with its enthusiastic embrace by an ascendant professional middle class that owed its elevated social status to the rise of capitalism.

This new middle class of rising professionals took to amateur sport because of its meritocratic character, which fit nicely with its unfavorable view of landed wealth (and its favorable view of active, movable capital), and of an aristocratic patronage system that shunned open competition and disparaged merit based on achievement rather than social status. The fusion of upper-middle-class and aristocratic elements led to a redefinition of the gentleman, "away from the rural squire or courtly fops of the eighteenth century prominence and towards a more broadly responsible, self-disciplined, functional elite capable of retaining the leadership of a more 'modern' society" (Baker 2004, 4). This redefinition of the gentleman, as might be expected, prompted a redefinition of the gentleman-amateur athlete, in which the notion of sport as a competitive practice in which merit had to be earned rather than bestowed, rubbed off the harder elite social class edges of the older amateurism. On the American side, as Mark Dyreson notes, the cause of amateur sport was further advanced by a "new group of progressive, professionally oriented, college educated Americans," whose numbers made up the bulk of the American Olympic team that dominated the early games (1998, 40).

Why this emerging liberal and professional elite found amateur sport more to its liking than professional sport, given the great pride its members took in their own professional training and expertise, is often chalked up to their contempt for the working class and/or to their view that sport was too trivial an affair to be undertaken in a professional, meritocratic manner. But as Norman Baker and others have pointed out, while the residual influence of aristocratic practice still had a grip on this new professional class, its affinity for amateur sport likely had more to do with its own early development, in which it saw its professional acumen in commerce and trade as more craftlike than businesslike—that is, as more of an art than an applied science (2004, 8).

It should be apparent from what has been said thus far, then, that the idea that gentlemanly amateur sport was some sort of monolithic conception made up exclusively of aristocratic features and distinctly patrician virtues is, at best, a myth and, at worst, a blatant falsehood. Rather, it was an amalgam of aristocratic and middle-class professional aspirations and values that put stock in honest competition and meritorious athletic accomplishments. This coupling of the old elements of the aristocratic outlook and the new elements of the professional retained the former's endorsement of the classical ideal of the beauty of the well-proportioned body in motion and the greater aesthetic value of the all-around performer over the specialist.

Amateur Sportsmanship

At the core of the gentlemanly creed of sportsmanship was, as is well known, an implacable opposition to any form of financial remuneration for athletic engagement. To be sure, that entrenched wariness of the monetary motive in amateur athletic affairs was, in its earliest aristocratic iteration, an unmistakable form of social class snobbery intended to keep "menial" laborers from infiltrating its ranks. But in its more mature phase, as observed, social snobbery mostly gave way to genuine concern on the part of devotees of amateur sport of the morally deleterious effects of mixing money and athletic accomplishment. As one American enthusiast of Anglophile sport of the time smartly put it, "The social status of the [athlete] is not important except as it concerns his ethics." That means, he continued, that competing in sport "must always be open to all who show they are qualified; no social snobbery can be tolerated, yet it is very important to realize that a certain class of men, non-amateur in spirit and action . . . must either be educated or barred" (Crowther 1907, 502). This latter grouping of nonamateur athletes was singled out for moral derision, not for being born into the wrong social class but for harboring motives for participating in sport that were considered unsporting because they were unethical.[1]

Just what all those who lacked the amateur athletic spirit were to be educated about to render them temperamentally fit for sport—or expelled from sport for being uneducable—was, of course, the ideals of gentlemanly sportsmanship. The central ideal was that of taking up and pursuing sport for the sake of sport itself. The only motive and reason thought suited to athletic engagement by amateurs was for the sheer pleasure and "fun" of it (Crowther 1907, 502). That meant that there was not only no place for mercenaries in amateur sport but no place for any instrumentalist types who conceived and pursued sport as a means rather than an end in itself. This is, to say the least, a strong view, since even the mere presence of extrinsic motives and reasons in the, to borrow Bernard Williams's phrase, "subjective motivational sets" of would-be amateur athletes was deemed morally disqualifying (1981, 102).

The inauguration of the modern Olympic Games was an attempt to breathe new life into the amateur ideal of sport for the sake of sport itself. By the last decade of the nineteenth century, the profit motive had already begun to exert an appreciable influence on the motives and actions of social actors to include, of course, athletes. Mindful of this incipient upsurge of economic motives in and outside of sport, enthusiasts of the modern Olympics hoped that the games would serve as a purifying force, that they would, in Dyreson's apt words, "set new standards for sport by replacing the scramble for the 'almighty dollar' with the quest for the simple olive branch" (1998, 39). Of course, this hope that the Olympics might reset our moral compass by pointing us in the direction of sport for sport's sake explains why these international athletic contests became such an important moral flashpoint for amateurs who saw as their mission to save sport from the professionals in their midst and, as we shall soon see, for professionals who sought to do the same with regard to their amateur foes.

Being educated in the ways of amateur sport also required being educated to act as a gentleman on and off the field. To play sport like a gentleman was to play in a composed, disciplined, and virtuous way. Emotional outbursts or acts of violence were strictly forbidden. Excess enthusiasm for sport was, unsurprisingly, likewise frowned on and considered dangerously monomaniacal, if not borderline fanatical. Naturally, then, the gentleman athlete was supposed to "be generous in victory" and gallant in defeat (Whitney 1908a, 766). Being considerate to one's opponents was a moral imperative. The same, of course, went for the rules, which were not to be tampered with or exploited to one's advantage. But this respect for the rules, for abiding by their letter and spirit, reflected no rule fetishism on their part. As Samuel Crowther declared, "We have rules enough; sport is not made by rules" (1907, 502). Rather, to amateurs' way of thinking, sport is made by the gentlemanly manner in which it is taken up, in which how one acquits oneself in the game is of at least equal importance to the demonstration of athletic brilliance itself. To be called a true sportsman, then, "does not refer to the quality of the play but to the quality of conduct in play" (Whitney 1908a, 766).

Winning from an Amateur Perspective

That amateurs prided themselves on engaging in sport for the sheer intrinsic joy of the game itself, and in a gentlemanly fashion that discouraged overzealous efforts to come out on top, should not be taken to mean that trying to win was of no concern to them, that the emphasis on the quality of one's athletic conduct made athletic striving irrelevant, even ethically odious. On the contrary, amateurs competed vigorously and intensely. But in doing so, they maintained what Baker calls "a contained competitiveness" (2004, 1), the basic idea of which is plain enough to see: "Anything carried to its extreme becomes its contrary" (Collier 1898, 386). Victory thus counted for something to amateurs, but it did not count for everything or, notably, the most important thing. As one contemporaneous spokesperson of the amateur athletic scene pithily put it, "As for victory, it is regarded as a pleasant possibility but by no means an essential of self-respect" (Corbin 1901, 3).

One important reason why amateurs cautioned against putting too much emphasis on winning is that they attributed the "obsession" over it to the influx of money in sport (Whitney 1908a, 766). The allure of monetary prizes in sport, they claimed, encourages athletes to fixate on the outcome of the contest rather than the actual competition itself (Crowther 1907, 501). Money corrupts sport, therefore, because it interjects, as Anthony Trollope, the well-known English novelist of the Victorian era, wrote, "a desire to follow too well a pursuit which to be pleasurable, should be a pleasure" (quoted in LaVaque-Manty 2009, 99). These amateurs were fully cognizant that the joy of competition itself requires at the very least that they try to win and that pleasurable competitors have to strive to outdo their opponents rather than merely indulge them; however, they also understood that when money rides on the outcome, the desire for pleasurable competition is too often overridden by the desire for victory. Because the desire to win fueled by money typically weakens, if not supplants, rather than strengthens the desire to engage in sport for the sake of the game itself, amateurs regarded it as an alien desire that should not be allowed to upend the intrinsic pleasure sport provides when rightly pursued.

The principled, measured manner in which amateurs regarded winning, of course, was reflected in their ethical regard for their fellow opponents. This was true especially of their strict notion of and adherence to fair competition. The gentleman athlete was not someone, it was proudly proclaimed, who would intentionally break the rules or entertain "tricks" that might rattle or otherwise put their opponents off their game. And as was the case with practically everything amateurs of this era said, they not only "talked" a good game in this respect but "played" one as well. Just how strictly they insisted fair play be interpreted and observed in sport can be gleaned from a hypothetical example floated by Price Collier, one of their chief spokespeople. Imagine, Collier asked his readers, a tennis player who accidentally drops his racket in the middle of a contested point: "What gentleman athlete," he exclaimed disapprovingly, "cares to make his point against a helpless antagonist?" (1898, 387). Lest anyone think this example is more so expressive of a single, privileged sport, tennis, rather than of amateur sport as a whole, I cite another well-known exponent of the amateur point of view who instructed scullers in their races at Henley that if any of their opponents happened to run into the "piles," the only fair thing to do was to wait for them to recover rather than to exploit their misfortune by opening a big lead over them (Whitney 1908b, 248). We can thus be assured that what went down for fairness in amateur sports like tennis and sculling also went down for premier amateur athletic events like the Olympic Games, because the games put amateur virtues like fairness under an enormous spotlight that made any deviance from them that much easier to detect and so censure.[2]

Amateurs' measured approach to winning is further apparent in the relaxed way they trained and prepared for competitions. Obviously, excessive training does not comport with the idea of restrained athletic striving. Indeed, elite English track athletes of this early modern period typically trained three or four days a week and on other days went for long strolls (Corbin 1901, 34). Such a scarcely taxing regimen is uncharacteristic of not only contemporary elite athletes but also so-called contemporary workout "warriors," who put in long hours of hard training just for the sake of basic physical fitness and health without any thought of testing their athletic mettle. This amateur aversion to overtraining was also meant to ensure the athletic body was "not wrenched out of its natural rhythm and forced into extreme patterns" (Holt 2006, 366), not turned into, as one admirer of amateur sport at the turn of the twentieth century colorfully put it, "a distorted animal machine" (quoted in Dyreson 1998, 39). "Everything in moderation" nicely sums up the amateur outlook not just on athletic success and training but on its overarching athletic ethos.

Amateurism, Instrumental Reason, Strategy, and Specialization

It is not just excessive training, however, that offended the amateur sensibility but rationalized training methods designed to boost athletic performance by incorporating the best available scientific evidence and the latest technological developments. Obviously, such a rationalized scientific approach to sport is incompatible with amateurism's restrained approach to winning and overzealous athletic effort. But it is also incompatible with the amateur suspicion of what we today call instrumental reason. Instrumental reason is, roughly speaking, a means-based rather than ends-based form of rationality. That is, it is the view that ratiocination is essentially a matter of discovering and selecting the most efficient means to achieve ends like winning; these ends are not themselves said to be amenable to rational analysis or evaluation because they merely express our preferences for certain kinds of outcomes. The enlistment of science to improve athletic performance is anathema to the amateur point of view not only because it reflects an untrammeled concern for winning but also because it further reflects an overly narrow and technical view of athletic endeavor itself.

This wariness of scientific and technological interventions in sport touches on another cardinal tenet of amateurism—namely, its privileging of broad competence over narrow technical expertise both on and off the field. The roots of this idealization of broad competence run deep in amateurism. Indeed, they are grounded in both the aristocratic and liberal professional strands of the amateur outlook in which members of the former attributed their self-proclaimed capacity to be "natural leaders of society" to their breadth of vision that was supposedly unavailable to the narrowly focused and trained (Baker 2004, 9); members of the latter attributed their rapid ascendance in society as the twentieth century dawned to their wide learning as further evidenced by their perhaps more well-known ideal of the liberally educated citizen (LaVaque-Manty 2009, 100). The amateur misgivings about the wholesale application of science to sport can thus be traced to its valorization of all-around knowledge and proficiency.

The amateur loathing of instrumental reason, however, extended well beyond scientific and technological efforts to enhance athletic performance and targeted as well the use of strategy in sport. Strategy was a particularly attractive critical target for devotees of amateur sport because it was considered not just another variety of instrumental reason but an especially slick and pernicious one that introduced all sorts of trickery and deceit into athletic contests. Indeed, to amateurs the true sporting spirit is one devoid of any trace of "calculation," of tactics and strategies that are nothing if not "calculated" efforts to use one's opponents and the rules to one's competitive advantage (Hibbard 1900, 601). As noted, tactical efforts to rattle opponents and throw them off their game were maligned by amateurs as ungentlemanly. But amateurs were similarly dismissive of strategies in sports like cycling in which teammates try to box in their opponents to give their lead rider an edge and in footraces in which teammates do the same or set a pace for one another to ensure one of them crosses the finish line first. Such seemingly innocuous in-competition tactics, to our present-day eyes at least, were condemned by amateurs as egregious forms of "collusion," as not true competitions at all but dodgy athletic simulacra (Whitney 1908b, 248). In other words, they were far too calculating to qualify as sporting to amateur athletes. Indeed, to their way of thinking, strategy was not a bona fide athletic skill because it was not what competitive sports were supposed to test.

Professional coaches were further condemned as interlopers in sport because what they added to the athletic mix, according to the amateur point of view, was little more than a bag of slick tricks to coax victory out of defeat precisely by applying their strategic acumen. To be sure, the main knock against professional coaches was that they were paid to ply their craft. But because their craft was essentially one of devising clever tactics to improve their charges' chances of winning, they were similarly rebuked for practicing a craft that had no rightful place in amateur sport. Of course, the fact that coaches were paid for their strategic wizardry is itself a given for the amateur crowd, since it regards the profit motive as the source of all such tactical tomfoolery, as a market creation that has managed to insinuate itself into the heart of not only athletic affairs but practically all human affairs. And because the coaches' tricks of the trade were indeed tricks, their effectiveness required they be kept secret from their competitors. So it is no surprise that American observers of the English rowing scene in the early decades of the twentieth century were dumbstruck regarding, as one American commentator of that time wrote, the utter "absence of any secrecy or attempt to deceive as to time trials, test rows, style of rowing, or rigging of boats" (Withington 1914, 104). That English athletic competitions were entirely an open book affair, in which practically everything was shared with opponents and the public alike, was attributed by this same commentator to the fact that English coaches were not hired hands (105).

The amateur valuing of broad competence over narrow technical brilliance also explains its strong opposition to athletic specialization. Such specialization was frowned on in amateur circles, not just because of its narrow focus but as well for its aesthetic unbecomingness. Amateurs were very much aesthetic connoisseurs of sport, which, as previously remarked, derived from their admiration of the ancient Athenian ideal of beauty and its central notion of proportionality. Proportionality applied as much to the well-proportioned body, as opposed to the heavily muscled specialized body, as it did to the athletic all-arounder, who played a variety of sports well, as opposed to one dazzlingly (Holt 2006, 364). The amateur disdain for the athletic specialist, then, was as much a product of his lack of broad competence as it was his lack of aesthetic regard for sport, of his failure to have the good aesthetic sense to develop as many of his athletic capacities as possible and engage in as many sports as he could manage.

Amateurism and Game Officials

The remarkable respect players and coaches were enjoined to accord game officials charged with safeguarding the fairness and integrity of athletic competitions further distinguished the amateur conception of sport from its professional rival. What was remarkable in this regard was that not only were challenges to their rulings and calls considered beyond the pale, but they were to be accepted without complaint of any kind, even if wrong. The high regard afforded referees and umpires under the amateur code of conduct was not primarily owed to their knowledge and grasp of the rules or to their technical competency in discharging their adjudicative responsibilities, but rather to the crucial ethical role they were obligated to play in upholding the integrity of the game. To be sure, unknowledgeable and/or technically incompetent game officials were not kindly looked on in amateur circles; they were banished if not at least minimally knowledgeable and competent. But ethically challenged game officials were another matter entirely, since even minimal lapses in their ethical judgment were considered unacceptable. Their main task in ensuring the ethical integrity of athletic contests meant that the decisions they rendered had to be in keeping with the central interests of the game itself (Baker 2004, 2). Further, because amateurs were of the firm conviction that paying athletes corrupts sport by introducing a monetary motive that fuels an excessive concern for winning and all manner of deceit and trickery, it is unsurprising that they held the same conviction regarding paying game officials. They thus insisted that game officials take up their adjudicatory duties voluntarily out of love for the game. As long as the officials played their role out of fidelity to the game itself, and acted in good faith, players were obligated to accept their rulings without exception, even when wrong. Furthermore, any attempt by players or coaches "to bulldoze umpires and judges out of making decisions unfavorable to you" or to work officials to get more favorable calls later in the game was strictly verboten (Whitney 1908a, 766). This confirms yet again that the amateur conception of sport put ethical concerns regarding the integrity of sport over any conflicting technical or instrumental concerns motivated by the desire to win.

Amateurism Summarized

In summary, amateurism is a complex notion made up of a number of historically contingent interrelated parts that defy easy categorization. Above all, it extolled a gentlemanly athletic life in which the point of sport was to wring as much pleasure out of athletic engagement as individuals could muster. That required they focus their attention on the joy of athletic struggle itself rather than any satisfaction they might derive from having bested their opponents. That also required their motive for taking up sport be principally about pursuing sport for the sake of sport itself and free of any ulterior motives and purposes. Sport, then, was not to be sullied by money or overseriousness or an excessively strenuous pursuit of victory. Further, fair play was paramount; instrumental designs on sport were greatly discouraged; strategy was abhorred; professional coaches were ostracized; moderation and a sense of proportion in all things athletic were valorized. The thread that runs through all of these various strands of amateur sport was a keen awareness and wariness of the corrupting effects of money, of the professional pay-for-play athlete. The worry professional sport posed for devotees of amateur sport was not mere social classism or a concern that they could not compete successfully against their paid opponents in the Olympic Games and other competitions; it was what they adjudged to be a profound existential threat to a gentlemanly way of life that they thought absolutely crucial to ethical sport, to an athletic form of life that showcases our better angels as athletes and human agents. A letter penned by Dr. Edmund Ware, former headmaster of Eton, captures well this deep amateur apprehension regarding the growing influence of money in sport and of the encroachment of the professional athlete into the heretofore mainly amateur English athletic world: "I do earnestly desire that our amateur [athletes] . . . be preserved from the deadly inroad of professionalism, which is already making a business of so much that ought to be pleasure, and threatens to crush the life out of the sports of 'merrie' England" (quoted in Corbin 1901, 6).

A Genealogy of the Professional Conception of Sport

The emergence of the liberal professional middle class in the late nineteenth century saw a great increase in people working in commerce as clerks and office workers, in civil service, in retail businesses, in management, and in the administrative ranks of trade unions (Holt 2006, 354; Baker 2004, 5). Their rapid ascendance triggered a profound social and cultural shift in the respect afforded people who earned their living by competing in the market, who made their mark by the sweat of their brow rather than the patronage of others. This shift further touched off a no less profound social and cultural shift in sport itself and, thus, a newfound respect for athletes who, by the dint of their hard work and effort, were able to accomplish unprecedented levels of athletic excellence. Earnest competition then became the norm in sport.

Because social and cultural shifts of this grand scale and significance in and outside of sport never happen overnight, their initial emergence often makes for strange bedfellows. Such was certainly the case with respect to disciples of professional sport, who at first looked kindly on amateur sport and the idea of engaging in sport for sport's sake. To accommodate the amateur creed, they simply redefined the notion of a gentlemanly athletic way of life to make room for their evolving competitive, meritocratic ethos. But this accommodation proved to be short-lived because it was racked from the outset by a deep tension that would eventually and inexorably consign it to the dustbin of history. It soon became obvious to serious, achievement-oriented professionals that the unserious, relaxed manner of gentleman athletes was manifestly unsuited to their athletic aspirations. If they had any hope of realizing their professional athletic aspirations, they now correctly surmised, they would have to become serious, very serious, about all things athletic and work diligently to achieve athletic success. This remarkable change in athletic outlook ensured that these serious-minded athletes would be duly recognized and rewarded for their achievements on the field.

The era of professional sport thus bore witness to a fundamental reconceptualization of sport, of its main point and purpose, in which it went from being a leisurely pastime, a paradigmatic avocation, to a serious undertaking worthy of our utmost commitment and effort, a paradigmatic vocation. This reconceptualization meant that the amateur view of "contained" athletic striving could no longer be countenanced because it could no longer be regarded as intelligible. Indeed, from the professional vantage point, nothing less than unstinting athletic striving was acceptable. But it would be a grievous error to interpret this athletic reconceptualization as a transformation from a moral notion of sport to an amoral, or even immoral, one. Rather, as we shall see when we discuss the professional version of sportsmanship, it actually amounted to a moral transformation in which the ethics of amateur sport that constrained competitive fervor and an all-out pursuit of athletic excellence was replaced by an ethics of effort and merit in which serious intent and a wholehearted pursuit of athletic excellence became both performatively and ethically de rigeur. So not giving one's all in sport was reconceived in professional athletic circles as a concerning ethical lapse.

This reconceptualization of the proper aim of athletic endeavor wrought by professional sport was occasioned as well by a fundamental transvaluation of the value of amateur and professional sport. In the case of the former, the value of amateur sport and its practitioners morphed from widely admired lovers of sport to scorned, at best semi-competent, at worst incompetent, dabblers in sport. In the case of the latter, the value of professional sport and its practitioners morphed from loathed athletic mercenaries to highly skilled and accomplished athletes celebrated for their competence (LaVaque-Manty, 2009, 100–101). The previously esteemed amateur all-arounder, good at a number of sports but not great at any one sport, was no longer to be venerated but castigated for his athletic dilettantism. In turn, the formerly frowned-on professional athletic specialist was no longer to be ostracized but venerated for his athletic brilliance.

Professional Sportsmanship

At the core of the professional creed of sportsmanship lies a deeply felt and strongly valued ethics of hard work that placed a premium on the desire to excel and, therefore, on seeking meritorious athletic achievement. Such athletic striving, previously morally reproached as an especially pernicious vice by the amateur athletic community, was, as a consequence of the transvaluation of values effected by the rise of professional sport, morally reconstituted as a sterling virtue of a life well led. As one op-ed favorable to the professional cause boldly put it, "Competitive sport is hard work and its crowning glory is achievement" ("The World" 1912, 638).

What deeply offended the professional athletic sensibility in this stunning reversal of moral outlook was the lackluster attitude of amateur athletes who cared more about having a pleasurable experience than achieving athletic distinction. From the professional perspective, not giving one's all to one's sport was a moral affront, a regrettable trivialization of sport and of modern life itself. So it should come as no surprise that devotees of professional sport decried the English ideal of sportsmanship that instilled in would-be athletes "a lack of desire to do [their] best" (Corbin 1901, 5). John Corbin, the author of these words and an exponent of American professional sport, declaimed further that "there is something peculiarly displeasing . . . that makes sportsmanship a young man's ideal, and then permits, even encourages, him to do less at it than he reasonably and honorably can" (5). The problem with such a languid regard for sport, as far as the ascendant professional class was concerned, was not just a practical one that threatened future achievements in and outside sport but a moral one that threatened the very vitality of the human spirit itself, of our noble desire and special capacity to make the world over in our own self-image. Corbin's lament of the danger the amateur ethos posed for athletes and the general public is wholly representative of the modern professional perspective: "To teach that transient personal convenience is better than thoroughness and devotion is, in any modern philosophy of life, the depth of immorality" (6).

This reconceptualization and valorization of professional sport thus played an important role in the elevation of the strenuous life above the pleasurable life favored by amateur sport as the life most worth living, as the proverbial good life. Indeed, strenuousity in all human affairs of consequence became the preeminent reigning moral ideal of twentieth-century life. In the case of sport, however, this new ideal did its moral work not just by encouraging would-be athletes to pursue athletic excellence with gusto but also by discouraging athletes from taking that pursuit too far to the point that it became a troubling obsession.

To begin with the second point first, the strenuous life midwifed by professional sport had to contend with an emerging unbridled conception of winning fanned by capitalism that threatened to turn the passion for athletic distinction into the passion for the almighty dollar. As Casper Whitney warned at the time, the "get there" spirit responsible for strengthening modern sport in particular and our major American institutions in general needed "direction . . . [and] requires control in our sport as it does in our business" (1908a, 766). What sort of direction it needed, Whitney continued, was something that would ensure that "the slickness which enters into high finance" and that "has a tendency to creep into our athletics" was not allowed to have its way with our athletic affairs. For when it did intrude into our athletic affairs, he concluded, it would incite a "mad passion for money-making . . . as the highest expression of one's endeavors" (766). The professional ideal of athletic strenuousity provided moral direction and counsel; it coupled its charge that athletes do their level best with the assertion that they do so in keeping with the meritocratic spirit of sport itself. The point of sport, its professional spokespeople never tired of pointing out, was to pursue athletic excellence, not the money and materialistic values that the market sometimes bestowed on such excellence that far too often pushed athletes to do untoward things. So on this first iteration of professional sport, the worry regarding the corrupting power of money persisted despite its weakening of amateurism's unyielding opposition to paying athletes.

The strenuous athletic striving sanctioned by professional sportsmanship served not only as a moral antidote for slaking the mad passion for money but, in addition, as a moral antidote for checking the slothful tendencies of excessive consumerism, the other bugbear of the market. Because capitalist economies have to ensure they attract enough consumers who are able and willing to consume the products they peddle, the search for new and larger markets becomes increasingly important as their productive capabilities develop. Already by the 1890s, the national economy of the United States had become a mass consumer economy made possible by rising incomes and increased leisure time (Rader 2004, 126). As a consequence, many Americans began to think of themselves as consumers as much or more than they did as producers, in which the spending rather than the making of money became a major preoccupation. In an ironic twist, the professional class, after having successfully installed the ethos of the strenuous life and, in the process, making short work of the indolent life of the gentry—and along with it the lethargy of amateur sport—found themselves confronted by a new, market-based indolence centered on passive consumership. This new idol of mass consumption included the consumption of commercialized sports. It was against this very consumer backdrop, however, that members of the professional class could proudly point to and tout professional sport as one important and widely admired form of life in which the strenuous life in all its glory and grandeur had survived relatively unscathed, despite the large wads of cash thrown at it by sport entrepreneurs. They were able to single out sport in this regard not by turning a blind eye to its own commercialization, but by pointing out that the masses that flocked to them were, regardless of their ostensible reasons for watching sport, treated to a vivid display of physical prowess that could not help but impress on them the values of an active, intensely physical life. We should not be surprised, then, that the professional playing fields of America and the vision of the athletic good life (sportsmanship) its proponents claimed they modeled became the rallying cry for the virtues of a strenuous life, one that exemplified, to their minds, a qualitatively higher way of living than the mere making or spending of money.

No account of professional sportsmanship could be complete, however, without remarking on the indispensable role fairness or equality played in it. Fair play was as integral to amateur sport as it was to professional sport. What is more, in each case it obligated athletes to honor the letter and spirit of the rules. Whereas the letter of the rules was in most instances one and the same for both athletic communities, their spirit was anything but. And therein lies the major difference that distinguished the moral meaning and force of fair play in each realm. In amateur sport, fairness mandated that athletes temper their competitive fervor to accord with the norms of the gentleman, while in professional sport, it mandated athletes put their whole heart and soul into their athletic pursuits to accord with the norms of professional competence and excellence. What often gets glossed over or left unremarked in the professional case, however, is how tight the weld was between equality and the kind of excellence it trafficked in. It mattered very much in professional sport that one achieved athletic acclaim fairly. As Mika LaVaque-Manty nicely puts the point, "conceptions of excellence have always presupposed a baseline of equality" (2009, 190). So while professional sport obligated athletes to give their all to sport, it also obligated them to fairly pursue their athletic dreams if their achievements were to count as genuine achievements at all. As professional sport became more and more focused on maintaining and surpassing standards of excellence, on realizing its meritocratic aspirations, it also sought, not always consistently or successfully, to become more egalitarian. Its enthusiasts were well aware that if its athletic practices became less egalitarian, they would, per necessity, have to concede that they were less about athletic excellence than they claimed to be.

Winning from a Professional Perspective

American devotees of professional sport placed a much higher premium on winning than their English amateur predecessors. As an op-ed piece in 1912 exclaimed, "The greatest pleasure of all is winning . . .and the sensible man is he who takes all reasonable and legitimate means to that end" ("The World" 638). Any effort "to lessen the seriousness with which American [athletes] take [their] sport," is, therefore, to be resisted (Whitney 1907, 488). That is not to say anything goes in this regard. After all, winning counts as a genuine achievement in professional circles only if it is achieved, among other things, fairly. Winning becomes problematic in their view only when it is trumped by the financial rewards that redound to winners and is, as a consequence, transformed into a mad passion for the almighty dollar. What was not questioned, however, was the will to win itself. Indeed, the "get there" spirit of American athletes to achieve athletic acclaim fairly was widely heralded by admirers of professional sport as no less than "the spirit of the land that made us [Americans] what we are—a spirit which, let us hope, will never be quenched" (Whitney 1908a, 766).

Because the will to win in professional sport was regaled as the main reason for America's growing dominance in the larger world, it was only natural that American successes in the Olympics were regarded as proof of America's superior standing in that world. The games, of course, were a perfect venue in this respect, fielding a who's who of nations all competing for top athletic honors that were widely covered by the local, national, and international presses. The Americans seized on the opportunity to demonstrate their athletic superiority by concentrating their main focus and energies on track and field, or what in those days was simply called "athletics," the premier event of the Olympics. And it paid off in dividends as they racked up one success after another, dominating not only their main rival, the English, but the rest of the world in the 1896, 1900, 1904, and 1906 games.[3] Much to the consternation of the English, the Americans proudly touted their athletic accomplishments with great fanfare and nary a trace of humility. They also made no bones about the fact that their athletic dominance was directly owed to their indomitable desire to win (Whitney 1908a, 766).

Professionalism, Instrumental Reason, Strategy, and Specialization

The emphasis on winning in the professional athletic community gave rise to a corresponding emphasis on the training and preparation for athletic competitions, not to mention in-game strategies and the necessity and importance of athletic specialization. Professional athletes were under no illusion that their strenuous pursuit of athletic distinction alone could get them to the athletic promised land unless informed by intelligent preparation, planning, and action. So in addition to long, arduous training that would make their amateur forebears blanche and greater attention to detail in practice, everything leading up to and including the actual competition was subjected to rational analysis. By rational analysis and intelligent planning and action, the professional athletic community meant the full deployment of instrumental reason, of carefully divining and incorporating the most efficient means to achieve athletic distinction in which the goal of athletic distinction was a given requiring neither rational scrutiny nor evaluation. Unlike amateur athletes, professional ones were not in the least allergic to instrumental reason; indeed, they were on the constant prowl for whatever means they could discover or conjure up to aid them in one-upping their opponents. Their willingness, nay eagerness, to seek out every competitive edge they could reflected the pragmatic tenor of the times, in which intelligent action was widely viewed as the panacea for solving the problems of contemporary social life.

It was in this rational, analytic vein that scientific expertise and knowledge became an important element of professional sport. To produce winning teams, it was now thought essential that people with scientific expertise be recruited to the cause of sport. The days of amateur athletes training on their own, unassisted by paid coaches and the like, was no longer tenable, let alone coherent, in the drastically changed professional athletic landscape. So it was no coincidence that paid coaches, physical trainers, and even nutritionists soon became staples of the new athletic order. Nor was it a coincidence that these recent recruits to the athletic scene, especially coaches, began to think of themselves more and more as body management experts and less and less as educators, least of all as moral educators. The role of these coaches and cadre of athletic experts was quite clear: to win games, not to instill moral character. As Donald Mrozek avers, this ushered in a new understanding of athletic achievement that "depended less on the character of the man than on the management science of the new experts who regulated his life" (1983, 102).

Whether enlisting science in the effort to produce winning teams and, in the process, sidelining amateur-based ethical concerns to give its trained experts full scope to work their magic was a good idea or not was quickly and unequivocally answered in the affirmative as American successes in the Olympic Games piled up. So James Sullivan, a prominent leader of the American Olympic Committee, was not just whistling in the dark when, following the Americans' overwhelming dominance in the 1896 Athens track-and-field events, he gushed, "Our men were trained scientifically. We go into athletic sport with an earnestness that other nations cannot understand; and our methods of training and practices were simply revelations to the foreigners" (quoted in Dyreson 1998, 132).

By playing the instrumental reason card, the Americans also opened the door to in-game strategies and tactics that the amateur athletic community had previously dismissed as unethical forms of collusion. Now boxing in one's opponents in cycling or footraces, or having one's teammates set the pace to improve a fellow teammate's chances of winning, were viewed as not only sound tactics but ingenious ones. The same went for trick plays, which required secret practices so as not to give away carefully contrived strategic innovations (Mrozek 1983, 77). The English were openly critical of the Americans' strategic turn, writing it off as "second rate" because it merely showed they "could only win by 'tactics'" (Whitney 1909, 643). But winning by tactics, the Americans rebutted, was nothing to be ashamed of, since strategy is an important part of the mix of skills sports were designed to test. Indeed, from their professional perspective, honing one's strategic skills is as integral to athletic achievement as honing one's physical skills. If the English could not grasp this simple but crucial fact about athletic competition, they should simply admit, the American athletic establishment argued, that they are operating with an impoverished understanding of sport they would do well to jettison.

The Americans' incorporation of strategy into sport signaled a new understanding of and approach to the rules that put it at further odds with its amateur predecessors. They were well aware of the means-limiting function of rules and were no less steadfast than amateur enthusiasts in their insistence that the rules be fairly enforced and observed by all athletic parties—though what they meant by fair play was not the same thing, since the Americans' understanding of fairness was, as one critic put it, "sadly lacking . . . in the gentler feelings" (Crowther 1907, 499). But in accord with their own instrumental outlook, they viewed rules as "instruments for achieving their athletic goals" (Dyreson 1998, 145). That opened the door for a strategic approach to the rules, in which, among other things, looking for loopholes to exploit for competitive advantage became not only fair game but smart game. Sport thus became a battle of strategic wits that pitted coaches and players eager to exploit any gaps or ambiguities they found in the rules to their advantage against rule makers' and rule enforcers' intent on closing any such gaps and squeezing as much ambiguity out of the rules as possible to prevent such exploitation (Mrozek 1983, 77). Such strategic rule probing and rule bending is evidence of the shift in the regard for the rules encouraged by professional sport, in which rule violations were increasingly viewed as a price to be paid for following a strategy rather than a punishment leveled for doing something wrong. That shift has become a mainstay of our contemporary athletic practice as Robert Simon (2007) and others have persuasively shown.

The push toward athletic specialization in this context requires little in the way of explanation. After all, as winning became the preeminent goal of professional sport and the standards of athletic perfection rose sharply given this new emphasis, achieving athletic distinction became a much more difficult matter requiring specialization in a particular sport. So long as simply doing well in sport was the aim, as it was for amateurs, it's easy to see why the amateur community venerated athletes who could do a number of sports well rather than one or two exceedingly well. But when professional sport ushered in athletic perfection as the aim of sport, athletes, per necessity, trained their focus and energy typically on one sport. This substitution of the professional athletic specialist for the amateur all-arounder, however, was not just a practical necessity but a moral one as well. For if, as Kant famously claimed, "ought" implies "can" in moral affairs, professional athletes could likewise be held morally accountable for their actions on the field only in terms of their single-minded focus on the particular sport they chose to excel in. Holding them to moral account for taking such a single-minded focus—that is, for taking sport too seriously and strenuously, as those of the amateur persuasion did of their athletes—is a nonstarter in the professional case because that was not anything they could plausibly be asked, let alone commanded, to do.

Professional Sport and Game Officials

Professional athletes were no different than amateur ones in their insistence that game officials enforce the rules honestly and fairly. But if one were to surmise that the technical competence of umpires and referees became more important in professional sport given the emphasis on athletic excellence, one would be correct. After all, bad officiating can lead to bad competitive outcomes that undermine athletic excellence. That is why professionals, unlike amateurs, were not hesitant to take game officials to task for their errant calls; nor did they feel any need to constrain their emotions in doing so. Whitney was persuaded that this tendency of professional athletes "to kick at decisions"—that is, "to protest adverse decisions" of game officials—was a quintessentially American disposition (1908a, 766). It should also be said that American athletes were not above strategically "working" the referees, a practice in which a coach or player vociferously protests calls early in the game in order to get more favorable calls later in the game.

But it would be a mistake to gloss over the fact that professional athletes were also ethical sticklers that umpires and referees get their calls right. For the professional emphasis on winning entailed that winning only counted for something if it was achieved fairly. The famous finish of the 1908 Olympic marathon held in London is instructive in this regard. When the lead Italian runner Dorando Pietri entered the stadium on the final lap but collapsed short of the finish line, only to be subsequently carried across it by British officials after they had given him a shot of strychnine to rouse him to action to no avail, the Americans launched a formal protest that resulted in Pietri's disqualification and the awarding of first place to the second place finisher, the American John Hayes (Dyreson 1998, 141).[4] The Americans' protest was made in a fit of ethical pique, outraged they had to go to such formal lengths to overturn the initial official awarding of victory to Pietri under such unfair circumstances. This shows that ethical concerns were very much a part of the American professional athletes' disposition to, as it were, "kick at" the errant decisions of game officials.

What to Morally Make of the Amateur-Professional Sport Divide

My reason for featuring this dispute between the amateur and professional athletic community over the purpose and moral import of sport as the starting point of my own moral inquiry is that it sheds important light on the formidable obstacles that stand in the way of giving sport the full moral accounting it warrants. Disputes of this conceptual and moral magnitude and of this concrete, on-the-ground kind test the limits of moral argument, of our capacity to persuade others of a different cast of mind how sport should be done. When we breach such limits, moral argument often gives way to bald moralizing, to moral recriminations traded back and forth between the relevant parties. We should not be surprised, therefore, that this is precisely what happened between the amateur and professional camps. The English charged the Americans, among other things, for being "boorishly serious and mechanically over prepared" (Baker 2004, 12); the Americans charged the English, among other things, for their smug contempt of professional sport as "half" owed to "prejudice, one quarter" owed to "ignorance, and the remaining quarter [to] stupidity" (Whitney 1909, 646).

Lurking behind these recriminations lies two fundamental moral questions for my purposes. First, disputes this deep and pervasive raise important questions about the limits of moral argument itself, about whether they can be successfully resolved by rational inquiry, not to mention questions about the moral theories in which such arguments and rational inquiry are couched. Second, disputes of this kind also raise important questions about moral progress in social practices like sport, since they seem to call into question the very possibility of such moral progress, given that the history of sport is nothing if not the history of significant breaks or ruptures in what was considered morally acceptable conduct from one period to the next. The amateur-professional conflict in sport forces us to confront the issue of what a moral theory of sport must have going for it if it is to successfully navigate such a major divide in our views regarding the point and value of sport and if it is to serve as a substantive guide not only to judging right actions in sport at a specific point and time but also to evaluating future changes in our moral conceptions of sport.

It is with these two questions in mind that I proceed next to tackle the present moral theories of sport on the books—specifically the theory of formalism and the two iterations of broad internalism—to gauge how they measure up on both of these scores.

2

Formalism and Sport

Formalism is not a single theory of sport but, as Robert Simon (2007, 36) astutely notes, a "family" of theories of sport that define various game-derivative notions in terms of its formal structural features. What counts, therefore, as winning an athletic game (G), as playing G, as a move in G, as an instance of G, is in each case determined by the formal (abstract) properties that define games and sports. I emphasize the formal properties of sport here in the plural to make clear that formalist accounts of game and sport are not, as some like Fred D'Agostino claim (1981, 7), solely restricted to their formal rules. Indeed, my take on formalism follows Bernard Suits's (2007) well-known and well-respected formalist account, unquestionably the most cited and developed formalist account of sport in the literature, which persuasively argues that game and sport are defined by several formal elements in addition to their rules. With particular respect to the rules, however, because sport formalists have also relied extensively on John Searle's (1969, 1995) much discussed distinction between constitutive and regulative rules and, though less so, on H. L. Hart's (1997) distinction between primary and secondary rules, I would not be giving sport formalism its due were I to leave them out of the discussion. But I have two additional reasons why I think it is important to include their respective analyses of game rules. The first is that Searle's version of the distinction between constitutive and regulative rules is at odds with Suits's version, which has led to much confusion in the literature regarding the precise role played by constitutive and regulative rules in games. The second is that Hart's account of game rules—in particular, what he calls their secondary rules—adds an important element to Suits's account that provides Suits a limited defense against one of several important criticisms brought against his formalist theory.

My discussion of sport formalism proceeds as follows. I begin by sketching out the four main elements of Suits's account of games; I make these the centerpiece of his account of sport because Suits maintained in most of his writings that sport is a species of games that differs from other kinds of games principally in the central role ascribed to the demonstration of physical skill.[1] When I discuss the third, and perhaps most important, element of his definition of sport, its rules, I incorporate both Searle's and Hart's respective accounts of game rules. I next entertain the main criticisms leveled against sport formalism, several of which I argue that formalism can satisfactorily answer but the remaining criticisms of which I argue that it cannot. I conclude that despite its many strengths, sport formalism is plagued by several major problems that warrant its rejection as an adequate moral theory of sport.

Definitional Inquiry and Conceptual Analysis

Before I begin to unpack the main elements of Suits's formalist account of sport, I want to first discuss the conceptual approach he follows to come up with his definition of sport and its main elements, which serves as the normative backstop for both Suits's and his formalist compatriots' moral view of sport. What is perhaps most notable about the conceptual path he takes in this regard is that if we dutifully follow it, he assures us, we will discover *all* of sport's necessary and sufficient conditions. This is a heady claim, to say the least, because that would mean that with respect to the concept of sport (and by implication games), there is a privileged context of definitional (logical) inquiry—privileged, as Richard Rorty nicely puts it, "by virtue of being the object's rather than the inquirer's" (1991, 96)—that we can access simply by abstracting its essential from its contingent social and historical properties. This assertion of a privileged definitional context would be hard to swallow for most concepts, but especially so for concepts like sport, since, after all, sport is a social rather than a natural kind—that is, a social artifact as opposed to a natural mind-independent, language-independent fact or thing. Whatever features sport possesses, we have put there ourselves. It is on this basis that we typically distinguish sport and its humanly contrived kind from natural kinds, such as mountains or lakes or giraffes, because these things are what they are and have the properties they do independent of how we think about or describe them. This is no small matter for someone like Suits who wants to define things like sport as opposed to things like mountains, because we must already know what the definition of sport is, given that we are responsible for its being the kind of thing that it is and possessing the particular features that it does. Evidently, then, there is nothing for us to discover about sport that we do not already know and so no reason to ask after its definition or try to divine its necessary and sufficient conditions.

Norman Geras aptly spells out the challenge Suits confronts in trying to define a social practice like sport in this logical, abstract way, pointedly asking him, "How can it be that games, a range of activities that we invent and name, are identifiable as a reality independent of our linguistic usages—such that one could say with Suits that there are things which are games as distinct from things which are called games?" (2009, 193).

Suits's answer to Geras's skeptical question is contained in Geras's own allusion to Suits's distinction between what *are* games and what are *called* games, in which Suits steadfastly insists that the question "What is common to all things that are games?" is a perfectly good philosophical question that gives us the definition we seek if only we are emboldened enough to make the effort. It is rather the second question—"What is common to all things called games?"—that is the bad philosophical question, as Suits sees it, because it preempts any definitional inquiry by needlessly confusing and confounding various metaphorical or careless or arbitrary or stupid uses of the word game for the "real" thing (2014, 199).

Most but, importantly of late, not all philosophers in the analytic mold would likely retort that Suits has it exactly backwards, that we cannot simply shove language aside in our investigation of the "objective" reality of sport or anything else for that matter. The reason why, as Ludwig Wittgenstein (1958) argued, using the very concept of a game to make his case, is because sport and everything else in the world is what it is only under some sort of linguistic description; that is, only with regard to some prior choice of a vocabulary do we find it useful to talk about such things.[2] But Suits thinks it is simply foolish, if not, frankly, dogmatic, to maintain that things like sport cannot be defined before actually trying to define them; if we try, as he himself did, we may well succeed, as many have thought Suits has in fact succeeded in defining sport. That suggests that, at least in the case of game and sport, there are objective properties to be discovered about them, notwithstanding the fact we made them, which, if smartly analyzed, can tell us what are their necessary and sufficient conditions and, therefore, by implication, what sort of normative and moral treatment best suits them.

What counts as a smart conceptual analysis for Suits is one that, first, focuses primarily on the reference of concepts and only secondarily on their use, since it is the former that mostly fixes the determinative content of our concepts. The problem of charting how words get used is that the features they call attention to inevitably smuggle in features that are not of sport itself but of our linguistic descriptions of sport.[3]

The second feature of a fruitful conceptual analysis, according to Suits, is one that draws its data for constructing a definition from the fact that we already have a concept of sport in our conceptual repertoire, which means that implicitly we already know what a sport (game) is; here Suits meets his antiformalist critic, who thinks sport's status as a social artifact, a social kind, obviates any need to define it, halfway, but not all the way. Indeed, because we already implicitly know what a game is, Suits argues, we can come up with the data we need to construct a definition of it, which involves identifying a "hardcore" class of games (golf, hockey, bridge, and the like); if these activities are not games, nothing is (2014, 200). This in-hand implicit conceptual grasp of sport further explains how Suits knew, before he defined games, that Ring Around the Rosie, commonly called a game, is not a game, and that the hundred-yard dash, not commonly called a game, is, in fact, a game.

The third and last feature of a sound conceptual analysis to Suits's way of thinking is one that seeks to make explicit our implicit grasp of a concept like sport by analytically breaking it down into its component parts. This requires that our working concept of sport be subjected to careful reflective scrutiny, one that drills down yet deeper into our concept of sport to unearth its intrinsic structural features. The important thing to keep in mind regarding each and every one of these features is that the evidence they provide Suits in his quest to define sport is of the conceptual, a priori sort rather than the empirical (broadly conceived) sort, because he was interested only in the essential properties of sport, not its contingent features.

The Definition of Sport and Its Four Main Elements

True to his own commitment to conceptual analysis, Suits's definition of athletic games of physical skill breaks it down into four elemental parts. The first two parts concern its goals and the means by which its goals are achieved, which, because they are relatively straightforward and their normative implications clear if limited, can be easily summarized. The goals of sporting games are two in number and consist of what Suits calls pre-lusory goals, which are the specific states of affairs aimed for in sport, and lusory goals, which when realized count as winning. Examples of pre-lusory goals include crossing the finish line first (but not necessarily fairly) and getting a ball into a cup (but not necessarily using a golf club); examples of lusory goals are, by contrast, fairly crossing the finish line first and getting balls into cups by, among other things, using golf clubs (2007, 10). It follows, therefore, that two different means can be used in sport depending on whether players aim to achieve its pre-lusory or lusory goal. If the former, pre-lusory goal, players can avail themselves of impermissible means (means not allowed by the rules), what Suits calls "illusory" means, but if the latter, players can avail themselves only of permissible means (means allowed by the rules), what Suits calls lusory means (11).

However, it is not until we get to the third element of Suits's definition, its rules, that we get a sense of what is most distinctive about sport and games, what distinguishes them from other kinds of means-goals activities, and the normative potential of formalist accounts like Suits. It is also where things get a bit muddied and complicated: muddied because sport formalists often invoke Searle's account of rules in their accounts, which they mistakenly run together with Suits's account of rules, and complicated because some sport formalists also invoke Hart's account of rules, which adds to the number and kind of rules Suits identified as relevant to athletic conduct.

Suits's treatment of game rules claims they come in three kinds. The first and clearly most important kind are what he calls their "constitutive" rules, which, as the adjective suggests, are what make athletic games games and, therefore, the challenging affairs they are. In short, without these foundational rules, there would be no sports or games to speak of, because these rules are responsible for their being such things in the first place. They make the game by ruling out more efficient means of achieving its pre-lusory goal in favor of less efficient means. That is, they place obstacles in the way of players' attempt to achieve the pre-lusory goal by proscribing certain useful ways of attaining it. So it is useful but proscribed to trip one's opponent in a footrace. Because these rules set out the conditions that must be met in playing a game, their violation means that one is, in fact, not playing a game at all (Suits 2007, 11).

In addition to constitutive rules, Suits identifies a second type of rule for which there are fixed penalties (2007, 11). Curiously, Suits never got around to naming such rules, but most of his formalist epigones did and simply called them "regulative" rules. An apt description, no doubt, because rules with penalties regulate but do not constitute games, which would suggest their role is limited to getting athletic games back on track when players commit one or more infractions. The only problem with calling them regulative rules is that on Searle's account, as we shall see, regulative rules are not rules with penalties. Nonetheless, calling them "regulative" rules comports nicely with Suits's own understanding and treatment of these rules, since on his analysis such rules operate within the space circumscribed by constitutive rules and are distinguished from the latter only by the penalties affixed to them. Suits does, however, say that penalty-bearing rules are "extensions" of constitutive rules (11)—the normative significance of which is discussed shortly, but that does not compromise or otherwise weaken the distinction he wants to draw here; games can be regulated in this sense only after they have been constituted—something that cannot happen unless the game's constitutive rules are already in place. That this is precisely how Suits intended his distinction between constitutive and regulative rules to be understood is something he makes clear in a later essay when he concedes that Klaus Meier's (1988) criticism of him, in his own words, "for using the offside rule in football and hockey as illustrative of a constitutive rule," is spot on because, again in his own words, "such rules are extensions of, or derivative from, a game's basic constitutive rules" (1989, 11–12). That this is what he had in mind in distinguishing penalty-bearing rules from constitutive rules is further borne out by the fact that he did not regard the violation of the former kind of rules as a failure to play the game. Indeed, on the contrary, he argued that violating rules with penalties counts "neither [as a] fail[ure] to play the game nor (necessarily) [as a] fail[ure] to play the game well, since it is sometimes tactically correct to incur such a penalty (e.g., in hockey) for the sake of the advantage gained" (2007, 11).

Before factoring Searle's different version of the constitutive-regulative rules distinction into the discussion, it is important to note one other rule Suits identifies with respect to games like sport. I am referring here to his notion of rules of skill, which he equates with such familiar injunctions as "keep your eye on the ball" or "never trump your partner's ace." Rules of this kind merely specify useful cues for achieving game goals. So understood, they, too, are parasitic on constitutive rules, which further means that like regulative rules, they operate within the space marked out by constitutive rules. This also means that violating a rule of skill counts not as a failure to play the game but rather as a failure to play the game well (Suits 2007, 11).

I now turn to Searle's account of constitutive and regulative rules, which I have been intimating is at odds with Suits's in certain key respects, despite its frequent invocation by Suitsian-inspired formalists. Searle gives us an initial clue that he might have something different in mind by a constitutive rule than Suits does by giving it a formulation that is nowhere to be found in Suits's analysis. That formulation is the deceptively simple one of "X counts as Y in C," which any rule that warrants the constitutive designation for Searle must conform to (Searle 1995, 44). The way to understand the formulation when applied to sport is as follows. The X term names some physical action or movement (kicking a ball into a net); the Y term confers a "status" on the X term that goes beyond its sheer physical features (what Searle calls an institutional social status); and the locution "counts as" attaches a function to that status by way of a collective agreement that also goes beyond the sheer, brute physical functions that could be assigned to this physical action (kicking a ball into a net counts as scoring a goal in soccer) (44). The "counts as" feature of the formula is perhaps the most distinctive and crucial feature of a constitutive rule for Searle, because the function it attaches to the status conferred by the Y term is not anything that can be derived, let alone fulfilled, by the intrinsic physical features of the action (the X term) itself. That is why it requires our general agreement that the function has indeed been accomplished (48), that, to stick with our example, a soccer goal has been scored. And once this imposition of a status function "becomes a matter of general policy," a constitutive rule has been created, and with it a new normative status, because once the rule is created the possibility of it being abused is now introduced (48).[4]

Searle's formulation of constitutive rules is in one sense more elaborate than Suits's, given the new, more nuanced formula in which Searle frames and presents it, but also less fine-grained, given that Searle is interested in not just the constitution of games but the constitution of a whole range of institutional activities and facts such as money, marriage, and the like. That is why Searle's formula makes no mention of means-limiting rules, which is, of course, for Suits the signature feature of the constitutive rules of games. But that Searle paints with a bigger brush than Suits does in this respect is no knock against his account of constitutive rules, at least in terms of its applicability to things like games. Suits's own characterization of a game's constitutive rule fits quite easily and nicely into Searle's formula, since crossing a finish line by running around the track instead of across the infield does indeed confer both an institutional status and function on the sheer physical action of running it would not otherwise possess, and "counts as" winning in the context of the game. However, because Searle thought his formula could be put to use to make a much larger cut between all institutional actions and facts and all sheer natural, physical actions and facts, rather than between games and other kindred institutional fare, he ends up with a much less sharply delimited conception of constitutive rules than Suits does and, as a consequence, a conception of regulative rules that is not only significantly different from Suits's conception but at utter odds with it.

To see and appreciate just how different and incommensurable their notions of regulative rules are and, therefore, how different and incommensurable their respective accounts of the distinction between constitutive and regulative rules are, requires I now say something about Searle's conception of regulative rules. But one thing should be clear from our discussion of Searle's constitutive rule formula as to how he generally treats regulative rules; Because Searle argues constitutive rules are alone responsible for the existence of whatever institutional activities and facts populate and figure in our social lives at any one time and place, regulative rules cannot have any comparable institutional role to play. So whatever functions Searle tasks regulative rules to perform necessarily and exclusively have to do with the natural physical side of our lives rather than the institutional side. The consequence is that Searle's regulative rules, unlike Suits's, can only do their work outside of rather than within the institutional space circumscribed by constitutive rules. This is precisely the way Searle characterizes regulative rules as descriptions, specifications, and causal claims regarding natural physical actions and facts. As an example of such brute actions and facts as they relate to sport, he cites the case of fishing and the fact that "sometimes fish bite at worms but very seldom at empty hooks" (1969, 37). Because regulative rules are only relevant to the natural and physical domain, Searle further argues, they do not create any new forms of behavior but only regulate already existing pre-institutional actions and facts. That is why the descriptions and specifications of actions they provide could have been given "the same description or specification (the same answer to the question 'What did he do?') whether or not the rules existed, provided the description or specification makes no explicit reference to the rule" (1969, 35). In other words, if we ask what someone did, we can reply that she kicked a ball into a net, and this same sheer and brute description of her physical actions can be given whether or not the institutional practice of soccer ever existed.

That Searle's notion of a regulative rule does not square with Suits's should now be apparent. The one thing a regulative rule is not for Searle is a penalty-bearing rule, whereas the one, indeed only, thing a regulative rule is for Suits is a penalty-bearing rule. However, that Searle and Suits do not see eye to eye on what is a regulative rule follows from the fact that they also do not see eye to eye on what is a constitutive rule. For Searle, any rule that plays a part in the institutionalization of an action or fact, no matter how peripheral, gets assigned to the constitutive category. In the case of an institutional game like baseball, the constitutive rule category for Searle includes both rules that have a direct hand in its creation and the new forms of action they make possible (pitching, batting, fielding, base running), as well as rules with penalties that have an institutional role to play only after the former rules are in place (that proscribe such things as illegal bats, base runners interfering with fielders and vice versa, and the like). For Suits, constitutive rules include only the former, narrower institutional class, things such as pitching, batting, and the like, as opposed to rules that penalize things such as illegal bats and base-running interference. Because Suits's constitutive rule column is much shorter than Searle's, he was forced by Meier's previously mentioned criticism to retract his "careless" claim that the offside rule in football is a constitutive rule. Of course, it goes without saying that Searle would have justifiably waived aside any such criticism and requested retraction, because for him the offside rule and all of its penalty-bearing instances are, given their institutional lineage, genuine constitutive rules.

It is safe to say, therefore, that Suits and Searle are about as far apart on their respective takes of game rules as they could be. Indeed, they disagree about everything important—specifically what is a constitutive rule, what is a regulative rule, and where to draw the line between them. All of which raises an obvious question: Why did sport formalists think not only that Suits's and Searle's accounts were compatible but that their use of Suits's account could be backstopped by Searle's? Surely they could not have been this massively misinformed to run these two accounts together. Well, misinformed they were, as R. Scott Kretchmar (2001, 167) was the first and only, as far as I know, sport philosopher to point out.[5] However, their mistake can be traced, as Kretchmar further noted, to their perfectly plausible but, alas, still mistaken reading of a key phrase in Searle's account: "Regulative rules regulate antecedently or independently existing forms of behavior" (1969, 33). Formalists interpreted this to mean simply that rules with penalties only come on the scene after the game has been created by its constitutive rules, the familiar formalist dictum that games must first be constituted before they can be regulated. But if that is so, then it follows that regulative rules also have a part to play in the institutionalization of sport, but only a secondary one. Whereas for Searle, as argued, regulative rules are matters of natural as opposed to institutional fact, such as the natural fact that sometimes fish bite at worms but hardly ever at empty hooks. Because they operate outside the bounds of any institution they figure in, facts and actions like these can be understood and appreciated on their own.

The last kind of rules that play an important role in social practices like sport are what Hart calls secondary rules, which he distinguishes from primary rules (which in this case would include constitutive rules and regulative rules—but only of the Suitsian variety). Secondary rules "are all concerned with primary rules," specifically with "the ways in which the primary rules may be conclusively ascertained, introduced, eliminated, varied, and the fact of their violation conclusively determined" (Hart 1997, 94). Thus, secondary rules supplement primary rules by, among other things, establishing formal procedures to deal with doubts that may arise about what the relevant rules are, how they should be interpreted, and what is their appropriate scope. Secondary rules can do these things typically by authorizing certain people (league presidents, officials) to make such decisions and by authorizing certain texts (rulebooks and the like) to serve as their guide. That is, they empower particular agents (legislative agencies) to modify existing rules or create new ones (rules of change) and empower other particular agents (officials of various stripes) to apply, interpret, and enforce the rules (rules of adjudication).

The fourth and last structural feature of athletic games has to do with what Suits calls the "lusory attitude." This shift from features of athletic games themselves (ends, means, rules) to a specific attitudinal feature of those who play them is necessitated, Suits claims, to explain what is most distinctive and, at least from our everyday instrumental perspective on life, what is most perplexing if not odd about game playing—namely, in games we voluntarily abide by rules that require we forsake the most efficient means for reaching our goals. Most of the time doing something in a deliberately less efficient way is simply irrational. However, there are occasionally situations outside of games where it is quite rational (instrumentally speaking) to refrain from using the most efficient means at our disposal to accomplish our goals. Suits's telling example is the decision to use conventional rather than nuclear weapons in a military conflict, because doing the latter rather than the former is likely to make us worse off and lead to a catastrophic result (a nuclear holocaust) (2007, 12). But that is not the reason game players follow rules that make the accomplishment of their goals decidedly harder, since tripping one's opponent in a footrace is likely to lead not to some disastrous outcome but only to one's defeat for violating a game rule. So the reason game players refrain from using such highly efficient means as tripping one's opponent to gain a competitive edge is simply "because there is a rule against it" (2007, 12). Accordingly, Suits aptly characterizes the lusory attitude as "the knowing acceptance of constitutive rules just so the activity made possible by such acceptance can occur" (12).

Formalism as a Moral Theory of Sport

Having accounted for the major structural features of athletic games divined by formalists such as Suits, Searle, and Hart, we are now in a position to assess what can be said on behalf of formalism as a moral theory of sport. The standard answer given to that question by its many critics is not very much. Critics have made a number of powerful arguments that cast doubt on the moral credentials of formalism. In general, however, their main gripe with formalism is that what it has going for it as a definitional account of sport—its mostly successful effort to tease out the main features of sport—it sadly lacks as a moral account of sport; it fails to say anything of moral significance regarding sport beyond the inference it draws from its logical incompatibility thesis that cheating is wrong. That thesis claims that one cannot win a game by violating its constitutive rules, because such rule violations mean that one is no longer playing a game, and one cannot win a game unless one actually plays it. Thus, cheaters cannot win games because cheating at very least involves breaking one or more of its rules. If one values winning athletic games, therefore, one should not cheat.

However, this simple, single moral injunction against cheating that formalists manage to squeeze out of the logical incompatibility thesis is no substitute for the comprehensive and robust moral theory a complex social practice like sport deserves. What is worse, critics maintain formalism is itself plagued by a conceptual flaw that threatens its account of the rules and, therefore, the moral utility of the logical incompatibility thesis. Because these same critics of formalism are already on record in claiming that the only element of Suits's definition of games and sport that has anything going for it, morally speaking, is the rules, their criticism amounts to a wholesale rejection of formalism as a viable moral theory of sport.

Formalism as a Moral Theory of Sport Defended

I am mostly sympathetic with the critics' indictment of formalism as a moral theory, which is why I, too, think it leaves much to be desired in this regard. However, I also think that formalism has more going for it as a moral account of sport than its critics have given it credit for—though not enough, of course, to reverse my critical reservations concerning its moral facility. I am persuaded that there is more than meets the eye here for two main reasons. The first is that I think the formalists' moral injunction against cheating, at least a certain reading of that injunction that takes its cue from a certain reading of its constitutive rules (the Suitsian reading), is completely persuasive and can defeat the main objection critics have raised against it. Second, I further think that two other structural features of sport identified by formalists—the lusory attitude and secondary rules—have something morally important to contribute to the discussion of how sport should be conducted that the critics have simply missed. Before I take up the objections to formalism that I think it cannot satisfactorily answer, I want first to defend formalism against several criticisms made against it that it can successfully fend off, which is why I am persuaded, notwithstanding its significant shortcomings, that formalism deserves a more sympathetic moral hearing than it has so far received.

Perhaps the main objection leveled against formalism's moral utility has to do with the simple observation that most games involve rule infractions of some sort or other.[6] This point is forcibly pressed by D'Agostino in his impressively argued essay "The Ethos of Games" (1981), in which he observes that it would be a very odd game indeed if none of its rules were broken. Why games typically involve rule violations poses a moral problem for formalism because its claim that cheating is wrong is based entirely on its thesis that breaking the rules, in effect, breaks the game; a game in which such violations occur is no longer a game at all. However, if, as D'Agostino claims, rule infractions are, no pun intended, the "rule" rather than the exception, then games are "only very imperfectly realized in their alleged instances" (65). The formalist reliance on the logical incompatibility thesis thus commits it, according to D'Agostino, to a certain Platonist take on games, which make them out to be ideal types (Platonic forms) that are seldom, if ever, realized in their alleged real world, nonideal instances. The same goes, of course, for the moral injunction against cheating, because in most games the ideal of perfect adherence to the rules is seldom, if ever, achieved. That implausibly suggests that most instances of games are not games at all and that most game players are cheaters.

D'Agostino argues further that a Platonist account of the kind endorsed by formalists is especially pernicious in the case of games in two important moral senses. In the first sense, what is troublesome about treating games as ideal types is that the only justification for doing so, morally and otherwise, is if the behavior in actual games approximates more and more the ideal itself as the players become more adept at playing them. But in the case of games, D'Agostino claims, the very opposite is true, because while it is true that as players become more skillful, they commit fewer unintentional rule violations than novices, it is also true that as players become more skillful, they typically commit more intentional rule violations than novices (65). It would thus appear that as players' level of play improves, as they become more excellent in their game-playing ways, they further depart from, rather than more closely approximate, the formalist ideal of a game free of any rule infractions. In the second sense, D'Agostino argues that the formalists' Platonist treatment of games effaces an important distinction between playing a game and playing it fairly. After all, if breaking a rule means the perpetrators are no longer playing a game, then why penalize their rule-breaking ways (65)?

D'Agostino readily concedes there is an easy and predictable way formalists can beat this Platonist charge. All they need to do, he writes further, is to distinguish constitutive rules from regulative rules in the Suitsian penalty-bearing sense and argue that only if one breaks one or more of the constitutive rules of games can one justifiably be charged with no longer playing a game. So if rules can be distinguished in this way, such that a rule is either a constitutive or a regulative rule but not both (he calls this the "dichotomization thesis"), then so long as only rules of the latter penalty-bearing kind are violated in a game, we have no reason to doubt it is indeed a game and no reason to doubt why it should be penalized—because although the violators are still playing a game, they are playing it unfairly.

However, D'Agostino does not think this "easy" fix completely protects formalists against his Platonism charge, but rather only limits their vulnerability to it. That is because the so-called dichotomization thesis glosses over the important point that the constitutive rules of games implicitly refer to the regulative rules of games. To see why this is indeed an important point, he poses the following hypothetical that raises the question of how we can ascertain what constitutes a move in a game and its consequences (e.g., whether the successful execution of an action, kicking a ball into a net, qualifies as scoring a goal), reminding us that, for formalists, such determinations are allegedly the work of the constitutive rules alone. Suppose a soccer player successfully kicks a ball into the net but in doing so violates the offside rule (68). Even though no apparent constitutive rules have been broken, we are prevented from saying a goal has been scored because a regulative rule has been violated. In commonplace examples like these then, to determine if a goal has been scored requires we take into account both the relevant constitutive rules and the relevant regulative rules. But if that is so, D'Agostino argues, we should be suspicious of any account that would have us believe we can make a clean separation between these two kinds of rules. For it seems that regulative rules, at least in instances like these, play both a constitutive and regulative role.

If D'Agostino is right that game rules cannot be strictly dichotomized in this fashion, then the formalist moral stricture against cheating collapses like a house of cards, and along with it the logical incompatibility thesis that supposedly supplies the glue that holds it all together. But I think the formalists' moral case against cheating and the logical incompatibility thesis on which it rests can be salvaged on Suits's rendering of it. For he readily concurs with D'Agostino's observation that constitutive rules do indeed refer to the regulative rules and says as much when he explicitly notes penalty-bearing rules are "extensions" of constitutive rules (Suits 2007, 11). I suspect, however, that D'Agostino was convinced that Suits was guilty of the Platonism charge because he never elaborated what, precisely, he meant by saying regulative rules are extensions of constitutive rules. I argue, by contrast, that if D'Agostino had taken the trouble to flesh out Suits's claim here, as a philosopher influenced by Suits did, he would have recognized that Suits is no Platonist. In claiming such, I am not asserting that Suits has a knockdown argument to handle every hard case and borderline example that a critic like D'Agostino might throw at him—for neither moral inquiry in particular nor philosophic inquiry in general are amenable to such knockdown, that-settles-the-matter-once-and-for-all arguments. Rather, I am claiming something much more modest but, nonetheless, more than adequate to meet the argumentative challenge D'Agostino poses here—namely that Suits's account of game rules gives a clear and persuasive answer to the question of whether a particular rule in a hard, borderline case is a constitutive or regulative rule and, therefore, whether a game is being played at all or whether it is being played fairly in such instances.

Before I show how a Suitsian formalist can successfully rebut D'Agostino's Platonism charge, I first want to show why a Searlean formalist cannot. Searle makes no distinction in *kind* between constitutive rules and rules with penalties, but simply lumps them together under the constitutive category. His rationale for treating all game rules as constitutive has to do with his view that game rules always come in clusters or systems and that the entire system is responsible for games being the distinctive social enterprises they are (1969, 36). However, Searle does make a distinction in *degree* between and among constitutive rules, arguing that although all play a part in the constitution of games, some play a more central part than others. That is why Searle is convinced that a "slight change in a fringe rule doesn't make it a different game, or a non-game" (34). He also holds that the violation of such "fringe" constitutive rules does not make the game in question a different game or a nongame.

Searle's claim that all rules contribute to the constitution of games, but some subset of them makes a greater contribution than others in setting out the conditions that must be met in playing them, does at first seem to give him a plausible defense against D'Agostino's Platonism accusation, at least with respect to so called "fringe" rules. Most players and observers of games would happily grant Searle's point that violating a "trivial" rule, such as pitchers taking too long between pitches or Professional Golf Association (PGA) tournament players carrying too many clubs in their bags, are hardly game-wrecking infractions and, therefore, give us no reason to fret over whether the former are still playing baseball and the latter golf. However, things get decidedly less clear and decidedly less intuitive on Searle's account when other apparently less trivial, more central rule-bearing penalties are broken. In a sport like basketball, for example, how many travelling offenses, three-second violations, and hacking calls would it take for Searle to be convinced a basketball game is no longer being played? The same question could, of course, be asked of any sport, since Searle is committed to saying that as these rule violations pile up, at some point they will undermine the games in which they occur. But given the fact that these kinds of penalties are committed fairly often and sometimes for deliberate strategic reasons—indeed, a game free of all such witting or unwitting rule violations would assuredly be an odd game—I do not see how Searle can tell us with any confidence whether we are witnessing merely a sloppily played game or something that is no longer a game at all. Obviously, if the rules are violated on every play, then we can uncontroversially claim no game is being played. I would argue, however, that such wanton disregard of the rules destroys the game precisely because it entails the violation of what Suits would call the game's constitutive rules (dribbling, passing, shooting, and the like). Aside from such noncompliance with the rules and from the violation of "fringe" rules, I think Searle has no satisfactory response to D'Agostino's Platonism objection when it comes to commonplace, middling cases such as, to reference yet another sport, false starts or offside penalties in football. And the reason why is directly attributable to his insistence that all rules, including those with penalties attached, are responsible in some fashion for the constitution of games.

It thus follows that the only way to avoid the Platonist trap D'Agostino sets for formalists is to make a qualitative cut in kind between rules that constitute games and rules that regulate them. As we have seen, once we move rules with penalties into the constitutive category, a whole class of mostly uncontroversial rule infractions (ones we can be reasonably confident, both argumentatively and intuitively speaking, that do not destroy the game) becomes far too often controversial ones raising unfounded doubts (Platonist-backed philosophical ones, to be specific) that the games in which they figure might not be games at all.[7] That Suits proposed just such a qualitative cut in game rules is why I think he gets the better of Searle on this crucial matter and why I further think he is better able to shake off the Platonism accusation. The only rules that get the constitutive designation on his rendering are those that have a direct hand in creating the contrived challenges and ends that define games and, therefore, the perfectionist ways in which those challenges, and the skills and excellences they are designed to excite, can be accomplished. In baseball, that means the rules that establish such action categories as pitching, fielding, hitting, base running, and the like; in soccer, the rules that establish different kinds of kicks (scissors, corner) to advance the ball downfield, to pass, or to score goals, or actions like heading the ball and the like; in hockey, rules that govern the use of sticks in certain prescribed ways to pass the puck, score goals, and the like. Because these rules literally make the game, it is not hard to see why breaking them does indeed break the game. So intentionally throwing at batters' heads is not pitching; intentionally using one's hands to put a ball into a net is not soccer; and wielding one's stick in hockey to assault an opponent is not hockey. In all such cases, violating the constitutive rules of these games destroys them. And in claiming such actions amount to cheating and thereby deserve our moral censure, Suits cannot be so easily dismissed, or so I argue, as a raging Platonist.

A critic might rejoin that I have conveniently ignored the fact that all of the transgressions of the constitutive rules of various sports I have just cited elicited a specific penalty. This omission is significant because it gives the false impression that constitutive rules do their work independently of regulative rules, when, in fact, their respective constitutive and regulative roles, as D'Agostino insisted, seem to be closely intertwined, so closely that it is difficult to see how their roles could be distinguished from one another at least in actual games as opposed to ideal ones. Such a critic might further argue that Suits's own claim that regulative rules are extensions of constitutive rules confirms the suspicion that both kinds of rules are involved in the constitution of games. If true, that would put Suits in the same Platonist bind as Searle.

But I think my hypothetical critic is wrong on both counts. On the first, the fact that constitutive rule infractions give rise to penalties confirms rather than disconfirms Suits's distinction. For the whole idea behind his distinction is that games must be constituted before they can be regulated, in which constitutive rules do the former and rules with penalties the latter. So constitutive rules establish what are legitimate moves in a game, and regulative rules prescribe specific penalties to ensure the constitutional design of the game is protected and/or to ensure fair conduct. The key point is that their close interaction and working in tandem with one another is parasitic on their performing different functions not, as the objection suggests, the same ones. And the fact that they complement one another as well as they do can also be chalked up to the different functions they perform in games.

What, though, of the second point, Suits's thesis that constitutive rules are extensions of regulative rules, which, unlike the previous objection, does seem to open the door to the possibility that violating a regulative rule might, under certain conditions, be rightly construed to be game destroying. Here the critic is indeed on to something, but it is not as damaging to Suits's position as it might initially seem. The conditions that must occur for this to be true are as relatively rare as they are clearly disruptive of the games in which they occur. It is not Suits who spells out these conditions but Edwin Delattre, a sympathetic interpreter of his work, who argues that violating a rule that warrants a penalty proves to be game destroying if and only if the violation is committed "knowingly" and the violator does not "incur the penalty" or "ignores it" (2007, 199). According to Delattre, "To ground a club in golf or to commit a foul in [straight] pool is not to cease to play the game. But to ignore the penalty imposed by the rules surely is, and it is this sense that we understand rules with penalties as extensions of constitutive rules" (199). I think Delattre is right about this and that Suits would have concurred with Delattre's elaboration of his "extension" thesis, but only on the condition we clear up an ambiguity in Delattre's formulation. The ambiguity concerns the second condition, that the knowing violator of the regulative rule is obligated "to incur" or to not "ignore" the penalty meted out for the offense. Not incurring a penalty is not necessarily the same thing as ignoring it, and the confusion about whether he means the former (calling a penalty on oneself) or the latter (which could simply mean refusing a called penalty by a game official) stems, I think, from the particular sports he features in his account. Golf and pocket billiards are both largely self-policing sports, unlike sports such as football and cricket in which game officials are charged with calling and enforcing the rules. Thus, many violations of the rules in sports like golf require the players, rather than some second party, to call the violations on themselves and to impose (incur) the requisite penalties. Whereas in a sport like football, the game officials call and impose the penalty, which if ignored (in the sense of not accepted) by the violators similarly undermines the game.[8] I am not at all sure Delattre would accept my interpretation of his position, but I am convinced that it is necessary both to avoid any confusion as to whether the second condition of when a violation of a penalty-bearing rule counts as a constitutive rule violation has been met, and to comport better with our intuitions that requiring players to call penalties on themselves to preserve the constitutional integrity and fairness of the game has normative force mostly or only in self-policing games as opposed to officiated games.[9]

Everything considered, then, I am persuaded that the critics' first major knock against formalism's moral utility, that its moral sanction against cheating is undermined by its reliance on a badly flawed logical incompatibility thesis that commits it both to an untenable distinction between constitutive and regulative rules and a pernicious Platonist account of games, is unsuccessful. Provided, as argued, that that moral sanction is based on Suits's account of game rules as amended by Delattre's elaboration of those rare instances in which violating a rule with penalties proves to be game destroying.

However, the issue of game penalties raises yet another apparent normative conundrum for formalists, but this time specifically with respect to officiated sports. This objection comes as well from D'Agostino's pen in which he poses yet another hypothetical example of rule breaking with one simple twist. The example this time begins with a player who scores a goal (for example, successfully kicking a ball past the goalie into the net in a soccer game), but whose success is a consequence of the fact that said player was offside. The complication he adds is that the game officials for some unspecified reason missed the rule infraction and allowed the goal to stand. Is this alleged instance of a game, D'Agostino pointedly asks, a "genuine instance" of soccer (1981, 68)?

From an intuitive perspective, he argues, the answer depends on the reasons why the officials wrongly credited the kick as a goal. If the reason is because they accepted a bribe, then he thinks this is clearly not a genuine instance of a game. However, if the reason is they simply made a mistake, then he thinks this is just as clearly a genuine instance of a game. After all, such honest mistakes are inevitable, since no game official can plausibly claim to possess papal-like infallibility in discharging their officiating duties. Games in which such (inevitable) errors never occur would be odd games indeed. Further, claims that games in which such errors do occur are not real games would be odder still because they simply beggar the imagination. However, and here is the rub, according to D'Agostino, from a formalist perspective it makes no difference what the reasons might be for the officials' errant calls, because if the (primary) rules define what is an instance of a game, then game officials who make mistaken calls are sanctioning (by omission or commission) actions that are not in accordance with the rules and, therefore, are not genuine games (1981, 69). So formalism, he concludes, has a problem when it comes to such cases that call into question its normative bona fides.[10]

This is a fair criticism of Suits's formalist position because he confined his attention to the primary rules of games, but it is not a fair criticism of fully fleshed-out formalist positions that pay attention to both the primary and secondary rules of games. Secondary rules include those that authorize particular agents (legislative bodies) to modify or change existing primary rules (rules of change) as well as rules that authorize particular agents (rules of adjudication), in our case game officials, to interpret, apply, and enforce primary rules. D'Agostino's hypothetical, of course, speaks to the adjudicative feature of secondary rules, which even though he makes no explicit mention of this feature or the secondary rule that authorizes it, he does implicitly acknowledge that game officials are empowered to oversee and enforce the rules. When we factor such secondary adjudicative rules into the equation of what is or is not a game, and importantly the two different kinds of normative attitudes that attach to such rules, we see that D'Agostino's criticism of formalism's supposed disregard of the reasons behind referees' mistaken calls does not go through.

The two kinds of normative attitudes I am referring to are *de re* normative attitudes and *de dicto* normative attitudes.[11] *De re* normative attitudes are those held by an athletic community that concern the *right* of game officials to apply and enforce the primary rules. The presence of these attitudes means the members of an athletic community recognize and accept that game officials are normatively entitled to apply and enforce the primary rules, even if they disagree with the calls they make and even if they are unaware of the particular governing rules invoked by these officials (as is the case with obscure and complex rules in sport that most people have little to no knowledge of). By contrast, *de dicto* normative attitudes are those held by an athletic community that concern game officials' application of and enforcement of the primary rules—that is, the calls they make in executing their adjudicative role in maintaining the fairness and integrity of games they preside over.[12]

The presence of these attitudes means the members of athletic communities are normatively entitled to hold game officials accountable for their mistaken calls and may criticize them when their errors put in question the fairness and integrity of the games in which they occur.

What the secondary adjudicative rules of games and the different normative attitudes appropriate to them add to the formalist picture is a way to theoretically shore up rather than, as D'Agostino alleges, contravene our intuitions that mistaken calls owed to corrupt officials are not genuine instances of games, whereas those owed to simple mistakes are genuine instances of games. How so? Well, the *de re* attitudes that attach to the right of game officials to apply and enforce the (primary) rules is contingent on that right not being abused, which is unmistakably the case when referees accept a bribe or are otherwise corrupted.[13] So a full-blown formalism that incorporates such secondary rules and *de re* attitudes into its normative portfolio is not vulnerable, as D'Agostino alleges, to the charge that the corrupt reasons that lie behind such abuses of regulative authority have no bearing on the determination of whether the games in which they occur are or are not genuine games. On the contrary, they provide formalists all the normative ammunition they need to deny games adjudicated in such corrupt, abusive ways are real games.

On the other side of this normative coin, the *de dicto* attitudes that concern game officials' mistakes as opposed to corrupt calls once again confirms rather than defies our intuitions that such honest, though unfortunate, errant calls are not game destroying. As noted, these *de dicto* attitudes do not indemnify game officials from the critical wrath of the athletic community when they make such mistakes. On the contrary, they justify such criticism, especially when these errant calls have a decisive impact on the outcome, notwithstanding their inevitability. So game officials' bad (mistaken) calls are not beyond critical reproach, because the applicable *de dicto* attitudes normatively entitle members of athletic communities to render such criticisms—assuming, of course, that the mistakes were evident to players and observers alike—a safe bet, given instant replays and media accounts that revel in such visual confirmations of dubious officials' calls.

Perhaps the most striking example of such criticism was a call made by first base umpire Jim Joyce, who ruled that a Cleveland Indians batter had safely reached first base on an infield grounder with two outs in the ninth inning, which spoiled a perfect game by Detroit Tigers pitcher Armando Galarraga on June 2, 2010. Joyce determined the base runner had beat the throw to first base by a whisker. However, watching the replay after the game, Joyce realized that the runner was actually out by a whisker and, in admitting his mistake publicly later, tearfully apologized to Galarraga. Unfortunately for Joyce, millions of fans had also seen the replay, thanks to the sport's media replays of it in the days that followed, which led to a public outpouring of sympathy and support for Galarraga and scorn and disdain for Joyce. Expecting the athletic public to give a critical pass to Joyce or other game officials in such circumstances is obviously not in the cards, and rightly so. After all, he blew a call that cost a pitcher an opportunity to pitch a perfect game, a rare feat in baseball.

But while such honest (uncorrupt) mistaken calls warrant public criticism, they do not warrant challenging the right of game officials to apply and enforce the rules. That right has to do with the *de re* rather than the *de dicto* normative attitudes of the athletic community. These former attitudes speak to the normative authority of referees to make calls, correct or incorrect, which is enshrined in the secondary adjudicative rules of games. That normative authority is binding no matter the *de dicto* attitudes of athletic communities, so long as it is not abused. Although the baseball community's criticism of Joyce's errant call is entirely justified, any effort on its part to deny Joyce's *de re* moral authority to make such a call (good or bad) is decidedly not justified. If I am right about this, then the players' compliance with the officials' decisions and the athletic community's acceptance of them, even when wrong, cannot be written off as evidence of their mere acquiescence in the official power that game officials hold over them, or as evidence of any instrumental calculation on their part that challenging officials' calls would be technically counterproductive because of, among other things, possible further sanctions. Rather, their compliance and acceptance is required by virtue of the normative authority vested in game officials by the secondary rules of sport and by the corresponding *de re* normative attitudes they call for on the part of athletic communities.

The third and, for my purposes, final criticism of formalism on moral grounds that I find lacking in persuasive power is based on the fact that the only structural feature of games identified by formalists that has anything going for it normatively speaking is its rules, and mainly its constitutive rules. In fact, my own defense of formalism to this point could itself be said to confirm this criticism, since if I have shown anything, it is only that both the primary and secondary rules should be given their normative due in games, not some other feature of games. The criticism then is that formalism's narrow focus on the rules severely narrows its normative scope, showing that it is not equipped to deal with normative conflicts that are not rule-centered ones. I disagree, however, and argue that Suits's notion of the lusory attitude of games also has something to contribute normatively to formalism that enables it to adjudicate moral controversies that go beyond the purview of the rules. Before I make this argument, however, I must first consider the argument that the lusory attitude is just another normatively vacuous feature of games.

Recall that on Suits's earlier account of the lusory attitude before the publication of his magisterial book, *The Grasshopper*, he characterized it as "the knowing acceptance of constitutive rules just so the activity made possible by such acceptance can occur" (2007, 12). Many sympathetic readers of Suits seized on the "just so" part of his characterization and interpreted him to be claiming, in effect, that games are intrinsic goods that enjoin players, on pain of not being game players at all, to play them as amateurs do for the sheer love of the game itself. That is, they took him to be saying that there is one and only one acceptable normative (lusory) attitude for abiding by the rules of games and the contrived challenges they create, which is to make possible the very activity of pursuing the contrived challenges they put on offer. For when played with no ulterior nongame purpose in mind, their true nonmoral value as endeavors worthy of our commitment and effort, and their moral value as enterprises in which moral virtues such as fairness, respect for people, and the like are crucial to the achievement of genuine athletic excellence can find their rightful expression. What is more, as Thomas Hurka insightfully points out, the lusory attitude not only facilitates the intrinsic good of playing games by accepting the rules that make the achievement of their goals more difficult but, further, adds to the intrinsic value of games by engaging in them precisely for this good-making (difficulty-inducing) feature. For if pursuing difficult athletic goals is itself intrinsically good, then "the positive attitude of loving it for the property that makes it good . . . is also, and separately, intrinsically good" (2007, 27).

Had Suits left matters there, no argument would need to be made that his account of games has more normatively going for it than mere rule adherence, because Suits's initial explication of the lusory attitude would already have made that case in terms of its just-noted contribution to the intrinsic value of games. However, in *The Grasshopper* Suits modifies his original interpretation of the lusory attitude to meet a possible objection it poses for his definition of games. That objection is that on his first rendering of the lusory attitude, professionals and other instrumentally like-minded players would, in fact, have no place in his game-playing universe. So although he acknowledges his sympathetic readers' interpretation of his pre-Grasshopperian notion of the lusory attitude is a "reasonable" interpretation of the crucial phrase "just because," he favors another "equally reasonable" interpretation. On his preferred interpretation, the "just because" phrase is to be read as this is "the only reason [players] must have in playing a game, but it is not the only reason [they] may have" (2014, 156). This rendering allows the lusory attitude to fraternize with several other clearly instrumental attitudes and reasons for playing games without somehow jeopardizing or corrupting them. These other extrinsic, nongame attitudes and reasons run the gamut, Suits helpfully elaborates, from those who play (use) games "to decide an issue ('Let's play a hand of poker to decide who goes into town for a beer'), to those who play (use) them to achieve the greatest good for the greatest number ('You know how I hate bridge, but since you need a fourth I'll play this once'), to those who play (use) them to gain approval ('Percy joined the football team because Gwendolyn fancies football players')," and, of course, to those professionals who play (use) games to make a living (154–155).

The criticism that the lusory attitude is a normatively vacuous feature of games is based on Suits's second interpretation of it. Such a criticism, however, has to contend with what at first looks instead like a normative gain rather than a normative loss for the lusory attitude. After all, on this interpretation, unlike the first, the normative portfolio of games is expanded to include a whole host of instrumental social and moral goods on top of its positive contribution to the intrinsic value of games. However, according to this criticism, what looks like an expansion of the normative range of games to include their instrumental value is not what it seems because it comes allegedly at the expense of its vaunted intrinsic value. Two arguments lie behind this claim.

The first argument is that while Suits's account of the lusory attitude in *The Grasshopper*, on one hand, does accommodate those few true amateurs left among us who play sports for the sheer love of the athletic challenges they present, on the other hand, it denies any normative or moral priority be given to the intrinsic regard for sport that is the signature feature of amateurism, even as a moral ideal to aspire after. That is because in allowing the lusory attitude to associate with other instrumental attitudes people might have for accepting the rules of games without impugning the integrity of such games, Suits's interpretation is morally agnostic as to how games should be played so long as at least one of the reasons people accept the means-limiting rules of games includes a reason actually to play them (2014, 156). Whatever gain in the instrumental value of games, not to mention in definitional precision, Suits achieves by interpreting the lusory attitude in this conceptually expansive way, according to this argument, he loses in normative terms by downgrading its value as an intrinsic good. For when all is said and done, his accounting of this pivotal attitudinal feature of games would have us believe that the only reason why game players should not avail themselves of the most efficient means at their disposal for achieving their athletic purposes (say, by tripping their opponent in a footrace) is "because there is a rule against it" (2007, 12). There is thus no longer any suggestion that playing games as amateurs do is morally de rigeur.

The second argument targets, naturally enough, the instrumental side of Suits's interpretation of the lusory attitude, specifically the claim that it expands the scope and variety of social and moral goods potentially served by sports. There is, of course, no denying that his amended interpretation of the lusory attitude does just that, allowing, as it does, games to be used to procure any number of goods, both noble and ignoble moral and political ones among them. Indeed, the founding idea behind the modern revival of the Olympic Games, for instance, was to stage athletic events to spread international goodwill and thereby encourage world peace. In short order, the games became, as I observe in the Introduction, a prominent way for representative nations whose athletes fare especially well in accumulating Olympic gold to demonstrate their moral and political superiority on the international stage, further testifying to the instrumental range of goods and ends games can effectively serve. The rub, however, is that as the instrumental value of games becomes ever more dominant, their intrinsic value becomes not only less so but in danger of being lost altogether. That means that Suits's second accounting of the lusory attitude, which, in effect, validates such instrumental use of sport, not only downgrades the intrinsic value of games by denying its moral priority, as the first argument suggests, but potentially puts in jeopardy its very status as an intrinsic good, as the present argument suggests.

To see why, we need to remind ourselves, *pace* Hurka, that the prelusory goals of games are "intrinsically trivial." Putting pucks into nets, as hockey players aim to do, or little balls into little holes, as golfers aim to do, counts for so little as far as human goals go that any genuine value or meaning that can be imputed to them must have to do with "the process of achieving" them (Hurka 2007, 28). Hurka skillfully showed that the inherent triviality of such game goals, the fact that in themselves such goals have no independent importance or value, makes them paradigmatic examples of intrinsic goods. To locate the value of games, we have to look inside them to their internal features that determine the manner in which their goals are to be achieved. However, when the achievement of these prelusory goals becomes, in effect, synonymous with the achievement of national prominence and prowess among the nations of the world—when getting more pucks into the net than any other players from other competing nations in hockey and other sports is regarded as proof of the superiority of a nation's way of life and/or political system, as it commonly is in the Olympic Games and other international sport competitions like the World Cup—these heretofore inherently trivial goals become instrumentally important in their own right. When this happens, we tend to locate the value of games by looking outside of rather than inside them by considering what extra-game value and meaning they have rather than what intra-game value and meaning they have. All of which suggests these prelusory goals are independently good and valuable quite apart from and even in contravention of the internal process by which they are achieved (which would explain the higher incidence of cheating and rule breaking in elite sports both on the international and national scene). When prelusory goals, therefore, are conceived of and treated as independently valuable, as opposed to intrinsically valueless, in these ways, actions in games "if successful, will be instrumentally good, and this can seem the most important thing about them" (Hurka 2007, 28).

What is especially worrisome about this eclipse of the intrinsic value of games by their instrumental value is that when games prove to be no longer useful in these manifold ways, people might think there is no longer any reason to engage in games or to take them seriously. Suits himself was well aware of this possibility, noting with regard to his own more quotidian examples of how games get used up that if beer drinkers discovered an overlooked case of beer, they would gladly forsake a hand of poker, or if an enthusiastic bridge player appeared on the scene, the reluctant fourth would happily defer, or if Gwendolyn started to fancy sedentary types, Percy would quit football (2014, 155). The same would be true if professionals suddenly inherited a fortune; they might well abandon their athletic pursuits seeing no other (intrinsic) value for further participation in them (155).

I think there is much merit in this criticism of Suits's amended rendering of the lusory attitude. Nevertheless, this criticism of Suits is not entirely fair. That is because what this criticism glosses over is that Suits's rendering of the lusory attitude entails not just that players accept the rules "just so" they can play the game—either for the sake of the game itself or for the sake of some other ulterior purpose—but further that the reason for accepting the rules is also a reason to value and pursue the lusory goal of the game. In other words, it is not enough to accept the rules and abide by them, but equally importantly to do so with the intent of trying to win the game. This feature of the lusory attitude comes out in Suits's discussion of triflers at games, who, despite the fact that they typically obey all the rules of games, do not have the slightest interest or intent in trying to accomplish their corresponding lusory goals (2014, 49). Their odd behavior of accepting and abiding by the rules but not striving in the least to win them can be explained, according to Suits, by the fact that they have some other purpose in mind, say, in tennis, trying to see how long they can keep a volley going with another player or focusing on how they look when executing tennis skills rather than on trying to hit the ball. And while their behavior starkly contrasts with cheaters', because triflers place no value and extend no effort in trying to win games, whereas cheaters place too much value and extend excessive effort in trying to win, what they share in common with cheaters is that their reason for accepting the rules of the games does not include a reason to play them. So what Suits's lusory attitude adds to the moral picture of sport that goes beyond what its rules contribute is that one can fail to play a game not only by breaking its (constitutive) rules but by failing to value or pursue its lusory goal.

What makes this later Suitsian take on the lusory attitude an important normative addition, however, is that it is not restricted to the admittedly bizarre athletic conduct of triflers, who as a group are not only odd game players but conspicuous outliers, given the present sports-crazed world in which we live. For in contemporary elite athletic circles, it is unfathomable to think there are any athletes or game players who suffer from a deficit of zeal in trying to win the games they play. If there is a moral problem with sports today, it is that winning is greatly overvalued, not undervalued. But, oddly enough, it is precisely because winning is too much valued in sport today that players for certain strategic reasons not only, like triflers, lack zeal in accomplishing their lusory goals but, quite unlike most triflers, deliberately try to lose athletic contests.[14] I am not referring here, for example, to a well-known and despised game type much chronicled in the history of sport, involving players who throw games and fix matches for a pot of money (a recent example is the match-fixing scandals that have plagued men's professional tennis). Rather, I have in mind a more contemporary and more strategically minded game type, the kind that surfaced and caught the always-looking-for-a-scandal eye of the media in the 2012 London Games in, of all events, women's badminton doubles. Some of the top badminton players in the world from China, South Korea, and Indonesia were disqualified by Olympic officials for deliberately losing their matches to lesser opponents whom they should have handily defeated. They were not charged, however, with fixing or throwing their matches or with the kind of telltale lackadaisical behavior characteristic of triflers but, contrarily, with the kind of win-at-all-costs mentality we usually associate with cheaters. They apparently played to lose because having already advanced to the quarterfinals, they had nothing further to lose and everything to gain by losing the remaining games in the first round, because that would increase the likelihood they would face an easier opponent in the next quarterfinal round. In other words, they played to lose for purely strategic reasons because that would give them an easier path to winning the gold medal.

What makes this example relevant to Suits's interpretation of the lusory attitude is that it introduces another specimen of players whom we should expect to see more of in tournament play of the kind staged in the Olympic

Games and in the playoff system of many North American sports—in which how one fares in one athletic competition directly affects how one might fare in a subsequent athletic competition—and with it a new moral wrinkle that his rendering of the lusory attitude seems to offer just the right moral antidote for. We should expect both to see more of this kind of player and moral confusion and controversy to follow because, as noted in the previous chapter, of the important role strategy plays in sport, which first came to prominence in the early professional period of elite sport. Its importance has grown by leaps and bounds in part because of today's greater reliance on playoff systems to determine athletic success. While strategy used to be restricted to in-game tactics such as pacing in footraces and not telegraphing one's next move in an athletic competition, it has more recently ramified into a tactic for breaking rules at the most opportune moments of a contest (the so-called strategic foul), and yet more recently into the strategy for playing to lose as evident in the Olympic badminton example. And just as the advent of the strategic foul touched off a heated debate about its moral permissibility, the advent of the strategy to play to lose has touched off a similar debate about its moral permissibility. In this latest case, however, the controversy about what to make morally of this strategy regarding the lusory goals of games cannot be resolved, as it was with respect to the strategic foul, by appealing to game rules, specifically, to the distinction between constitutive and regulative rules; it must be resolved only by explicating what moral attitude should govern our pursuit of lusory goals. Hence, the relevance of Suits's notion of the lusory attitude.

Before I delve into the controversy featured in the badminton example, however, I first need to consider cases in sport in which teams deliberately take actions that lessen their chances of winning without running afoul of the lusory attitude.[15] There are several such cases that are not normatively problematic in this regard. Consider, for instance, a team that rests their best players at key times in the course of a season so they are better able to play at the top of their game over the long haul, or who simply rest them at the end of the season so they are fresh for the playoffs. There is the further case in which teams that have not fared well over the season and have no chance of making the playoffs opt to play their second-string teammates to size up their potential for the next season or, convinced they are already starting material, groom them for the following season (in intercollegiate circles this often means sitting seniors for underclassmen) or do both. Further, teams often find themselves not playing at full strength because one or more of their players has been benched for violating team rules or some such offense.

Now in each of these cases, I contend, lessening a team's chances of winning seems to be normatively unobjectionable in part because no violation of the lusory attitude occurred; indeed, in each and every instance the players who found themselves starting tried very hard to win. The only one that might be considered to be borderline is when teams that have already secured a playoff spot rest their best players at the end of the season to get them ready for the playoffs, and then find themselves matched against teams still in the hunt for the playoffs who would not dream of sitting their best players. By giving these wannabe playoff contenders less of a run for their money, they put other playoff-contending teams facing teams playing at full strength at a competitive disadvantage. But if this is normatively objectionable, then it is for reasons of competitive fairness rather than for violations of the lusory attitude.

What makes the badminton case different from these latter cases is that the players in question were most assuredly not trying to win the game because their actions were at odds with the lusory attitude. Indeed, as Hurka forcefully puts it, the badminton players were "working positively against rather than not just positively for the goal of the game."[16] That puts them in the same quasi–game player category that Suits put triflers in, who similarly lack the requisite lusory attitude, but for the very different reason that the badminton players had their eyes on the larger prize of Olympic gold. In this badminton example, therefore, formalists like Suits are committed to the view that because possessing a lusory attitude is a necessary condition for playing a game and because the badminton players clearly lacked this attitude, they were not really playing badminton but merely making badminton-like moves.

The referees of the badminton games under consideration also deemed the players' actions to be unsporting and, as a consequence, disqualified them, a decision that formalists like Suits would, I think, applaud. Many observers similarly applauded the game officials' decision, including some spectators at these matches who let their disapproval of the players' less than stellar effort and play be known by their loud booing and hissing. Like the officials, they were evidently appalled by the women's unsporting behavior and agreed they should be disqualified for demeaning the sport by not trying to play at their best. However, a not insignificant number of observers sided with the players, arguing that they should have been praised and rewarded rather than blamed and penalized for their strategic savvy. If any blame was to be handed out, they opined, it should be aimed at the organizers' ill-fated decision to arrange the matches in such a fashion that it made the strategy of playing to lose the smart and appropriate one.[17]

The reason I bring up this example, however, is not because it was controversial but because it shows, as I see it, that Suits's formalist position on such matters is a forceful one not easily dismissed. For the tactic of playing a game not to win does seem to be game destroying in the illusory attitudinal sense Suits explicates. What is more, because Suits's argument that playing a game not to win is normatively suspect targets not just the atypical and weird behavior of triflers, at best a small and offbeat subset of players, but also the increasingly more common and more widespread and worrisome strategic behavior of players in tournaments, it has more going for it normatively than is usually appreciated. For these strategy-savvy would-be badminton players, like cheaters, are too much invested in winning than on the effect their tactical behavior has on the good of the game itself. As winning becomes more and more important in athletic games and with it, strategic cunning and a heavy reliance on playoff formats to determine athletic excellence—the net effect of which is to diminish the importance of the more comprehensive in-season record of athletic accomplishment—we can expect such quasi-badminton behavior to occur on a more frequent basis.

If I have understood Suits correctly, I want to argue that there is indeed a normative dimension built into his notion of the lusory attitude. What his rendering of the lusory attitude shows, or so I claim, is that accepting the rules to play the game obligates players both to value game goals and to value the normative qualities (fairness and the like) that are central to their realization. After all, what is the normative point of accepting the rules if not that trying to realize the athletic challenges they create is a good thing.

Formalism Rebutted

I have been arguing at some length that formalism is a more powerful moral theory of sport than it has typically been given credit for. However, I also let it be known in the opening remarks of this chapter that I think it has serious defects that ultimately prove to be its undoing as an adequate moral account of sport. In the remaining section of this chapter, I discuss what I see to be its two most serious moral failings.

The first moral defect that formalist theories of sport suffer from is that their accounts of sport disregard its social and historical context, which means many of its moral prescriptions are too thin and abstract to do the normative work they are asked to do. That would explain why its morally authoritative guidance is mostly, if not wholly, limited to determinations of when a player can be said to be actually playing a game or not, to moral transgressions that are game destroying. More granular and fine-grained determinations of when players can be faulted for not playing a game as morally (not to mention aesthetically) well as it should be played, as opposed to not playing a game at all, are mostly beyond the reach of its abstract prescriptions. More fine-grained moral judgments of this sort require that we consider the social and historical context in which athletic games are played. By doing so, we can get a handle on something centrally important to our moral assessment of sport: The moral compass of amateur sport points in the direction of a gentlemanly take on athletic conduct, whereas that of professional sport points in the direction of a greater winning take on athletic conduct. D'Agostino had this general contextual point in mind when he faulted formalists for not being able to explain why in games like basketball, whose formal rules stipulate that it is a noncontact sport, the contemporary game is "filled with (one might also say consists of) incidents in which players (accidentally or deliberately) make contact with one another" (1981, 14). This led him to criticize formalists for not noticing that games have what he calls an "ethos," which he defines as "the unofficial, implicit, empirically determinable conventions" that govern how the rules are applied (69).

D'Agostino is clear that his criticism of formalist accounts of games for not taking into account their ethos is not intended to be, and does not amount to, a wholesale refutation of formalism as such. That is, he thinks formalism can be salvaged so long as it is supplemented by an account of the ethos of games (16). I think he is right about this. But that formalism can be salvaged in this way is, for my present purpose at least, beside the point. My beef with formalism is not that it cannot be salvaged, but that it cannot be defended on its own formal terms as a satisfactory moral theory of sport. Supplementing it with D'Agostino's notion of an ethos may be what the moral doctor ordered, but taking this step means that our moral assessments of sport can no longer simply rely on its formal, structural features.

The second related major moral shortcoming of formalism directly concerns its crucial reliance on the rules of athletic games for determining how they should be played. In a nutshell, what undermines the moral force of rules, even when we add the all-important lusory attitude to the mix, is that they are neither exhaustive nor self-interpreting. As a consequence, the moral guidance they offer too often turns out to be both indeterminate and indecisive. This is one big reason, of course, why our moral reckoning of sport is best served by a contextual approach.

Just how incomplete and sketchy the moral guidance game rules provide was one of the central points to be gleaned from my retelling of the amateur-professional conflict. The main issues that sharply divided these two athletic camps had little to do with the rules of sport as such. Rather, they had mainly to do with their significantly different socially and historically freighted conceptions of the main purpose of athletic endeavor. So when Crowther insisted that "sport is not made by the rules" (1907, 502), he can be rightly considered as speaking for not just the amateur community but the professional community as well. In both communities, how the rules, when applicable, were to be interpreted, enforced, or simply ignored and, when not applicable, how athletic agents were to morally navigate the complicated athletic terrain they found themselves in, were determined by their respective overarching conceptions of sport. So even though they both were subject to the same "letter" of the rules of the Olympics and other international competitions they mutually engaged in, they were not subject to the same "spirit" of the rules, given their divergent contextual understandings of the purposes served by these rules. Leaving out of the account, as formalists do, that amateurs viewed rules as devices for cultivating a gentlemanly athletic way of life and that professionals viewed rules as "instruments for achieving their athletic goals" to certify their athletic competence (Dyreson 1998, 145) thus counts as a serious knock against formalism.

My criticism of formalism's heavy reliance on the rules of sport thus boils down to the important point that there is more to sport than the rules that define them—and that goes, of course, for the other formal features of sport Suits singled out. What, exactly, this more is will be addressed in Chapter 6. But for now it suffices to say that "more" has to do with what D'Agostino calls the ethos of sport and what I have been calling the social and historical context in which sport is played, understood, and interpreted. It is this ethos or larger historical context of sport that, for example, amateurs rely on to determine when following the rules suffices to check, in Anthony Trollope's memorable words, "a desire to follow too well a pursuit which to be pleasurable, should be a pleasure" (quoted in LaVaque-Manty 2009, 99), and that professionals rely on to determine when strictly following the letter and spirit of the rules suffices to demonstrate athletic excellence and when it does not, as when, for example, exploiting a loophole in the rules is the more strategically competent way to demonstrate athletic excellence.

Calling on the lusory attitude alone to bail out the rules in hard cases such as these when they provide little to no moral direction will not work. The lusory attitude is unable to fill this gap in the rules because it is too abstract for its own good, too detached from the particular context in which sport is played to make a difference. That is not to deny what I previously affirmed: that the lusory attitude does add something important to the moral repertoire of formalism—namely, that one must not only follow the rules but value game goals enough to try to achieve them to satisfy the normative requirements of formalism. It is what it does not tell us, however, that is the problem: how much should we value game goals, and, therefore, how hard should we try to realize them. That puts the lusory attitude in the same bind as the rules when it comes to settling controversies of the amateur-professional kind. The lusory attitude is in no better position to shed light on whether the amateur's moderate take on athletic competition that enjoins players not to try too hard to win if it gets in the way of a pleasurable athletic experience, or the professional's strenuous take on competition that enjoins players to try very hard to win if winning is to count for something worthy of our time and effort, is the better moral reckoning of competitive sport. We thus find ourselves once again in the same moral blind alley that formalists have steered us into before, in which we must remain mute as to whether amateurs were right to insist that in sport personal "transient pleasure" should trump "thoroughness and devotion," which makes doing the latter "the depth of immorality," or that professionals were right that "thoroughness and devotion" should trump personal "transient pleasure," which makes doing the latter the "depth of immorality."

The normative hole in game rules that I have argued the lusory attitude is unable to fill, given its same formal, acontextual character, has specifically to do with the fact that rules are not exhaustive. John Russell provides yet another example of the limited scope and applicability of the rules that touches specifically on the professional side of this dispute. The case he cited was an 1887 American Association baseball game in which a player who, after safely crossing home plate, interfered with the catcher, allowing two of his teammates to cross home plate as well. The relevant rule at the time stated no base runner may interfere with a fielder. The rub, of course, is that once the player crossed home plate, he was no longer a base runner when he interfered with the catcher (Russell 1999, 28). The strategic ruse failed, however, because the umpire disregarded the formal rule and called the two teammates out who crossed the plate after him. Whether this was the right call cannot be determined, Russell argues, correctly to my mind, by the extant rule, but by whether it speaks to the integrity of baseball itself, of the kinds of skills that are the point in a game like this—something that, in my view, depends very much on the particular social and historical context. But whatever the merits of the call, the main point is that it was made in spite of the rule, not because of it.

One might object, however, that such gaps in the rules pose at most a provisional problem for formalism. For over time, loopholes like this one will eventually be closed by adding new rules, which means at some future point umpires and game officials will be able to adjudicate any situations that may arise by simply citing the applicable rule. There is a grain of truth to this objection, but only a grain. For as our conceptions of sport, of its aim and what skills it is supposed to test, change as they have in the past and surely will in the future, it is inevitable that new, unanticipated situations will pop up for which there is no applicable rule. So it is wishful thinking to claim that at some future time we will have come up with a definitive, inexhaustible list of rules that covers any and all contingencies that might arise on the playing field.

Even if we were somehow able to divine all the rules we would ever require to handle the contingencies that sport throws our way, formalism would still come up short as a satisfactory moral theory of sport. That is because formal features of sport like rules are not self-interpreting. Here context is all-important as well, because how we interpret rules depends very much on the social and historical context in question. So whether we insist on a strict interpretation of the rules or a less rigid one cannot be resolved by the rules themselves, no matter how scrupulously formulated, but rather by the conception of sport at hand that signals what interpretation is called for. So in the example of the interfering base runner, the amateur community would not only counsel the umpire to discount the rule and call the runners who scored as result of his actions out but would also hold the interfering runner morally culpable for his actions. That is, the amateur camp would regard his strategic ploy as a wrong that should be punished and not, as is the wont of the professional camp, as a cost for pursuing a strategy. The upshot is, therefore, whatever reading of the rules we settle on is very much an interpretive matter rather than a straightforward, mechanical application of a rule.

This dependence on interpretation to make the rules do real moral work in sport—which I hasten to add holds for the lusory attitude as well because it cannot be mechanically applied either—is the point Russell (1999) astutely makes in another hard case he cites in his essay that also features baseball. This latter example occurred in July 1983 in a game between the Kansas City Royals and the New York Yankees, in which Royal player George Brett hit a potentially game-winning home run with two outs in the top of the ninth inning. However, when the Yankees manager brought to the attention of the umpire that Brett's bat had pine tar resin (an adhesive substance used by batters to improve their grip on the bat) above the allowed eighteen-inch limit stipulated by the rule, the umpire called Brett out for using an illegal bat, which resulted in the Royals losing to the Yankees by one run. Though the umpire's decision was technically correct, the larger issue at stake is that the pine tar gave Brett no special advantage, and because it is a sticky substance, it might well have made his home run a greater rather than lesser accomplishment. The latter interpretation of the Brett episode most likely led to the decision by the president of the American League, Lee MacPhail, to reverse the umpire's call. Although MacPhail conceded that the umpire's decision was technically correct, in his view it was not in keeping with the "intent or spirit of the game itself" (1999, 30).

Perhaps the most important moral to be drawn from the Brett case is not only that rules give us no moral guidance unless they are supplemented by an interpretation that is itself not derived from the rules but, rather, as Russell once again smartly notes, that strict adherence to the rules may run afoul of the very "aims and purposes of the game itself" (1999, 33). That is presumably why MacPhail found it necessary to ignore the pine tar rule so the true aim of the game—demonstrating athletic excellence on the field—could be realized. In this case, therefore, the normative problem with the rule was owed to the rule itself, which if adhered to would have nullified Brett's batting excellence based on a minor technicality that in no way diminished his athletic accomplishment but most likely made it all that more impressive. Lest anyone think that the need to ignore the rules to honor the purpose of the game is at most an infrequently needed interpretive intervention, Russell further points out that sometimes it is a systematic requirement. His example is the constant expansion and contraction of the strike zone in baseball, which, while it violates the rule that stipulates its precise boundaries, was and remains necessary to set an appropriate standard to ensure the "contest between pitchers and batters is a meaningful one" (40). Such examples, he maintains, are not restricted to baseball but apparent in sports such as hockey and basketball, in which rule violations are not called so as not to disrupt the tempo and flow of the game.

The upshot of these criticisms—that formalism operates at too abstract a level, that its privileging of the rules too often proves to be a liability because too often the rules are not applicable or require interpretative unpacking or need to be discounted altogether in favor of considerations of the aims of the game—shows that formalism does not have what it takes to be a satisfactory moral theory of sport. They also show, I argue, that if we are to give sport its moral due, we need to cast our net wider to find a more adequate moral theory of sport, one that is keyed to principles derived not from the rules or other formal elements of sport but from considerations of the point and purpose of athletic endeavor and, therefore, from what kinds of athletic excellences are most germane to athletic contests. That will be the topic of Chapter 3 and of a group of philosophers who have developed just such a moral theory of sport that they call "broad internalism" or simply "interpretivism."

3

Broad Internalism, Moral Realism, and Sport

The Metaphysical Version

As I left things at the end of Chapter 2, I conclude that formalism leaves something to be desired as a normative guide to how we should act in sport in those hard cases when the rules, for various reasons, fail us and when appeal to what Bernard Suits called the lusory attitude proves unhelpful. It thus becomes apparent that we need to rely on other moral resources that go beyond what the formal elements of sport can provide if we are to navigate successfully its complex normative terrain. The moral theory of sport I discuss and examine in this chapter purports to do just that by invoking general normative principles of sport that are supposed to take up the slack when the formal elements of sport let us down. Robert Simon (2007), one of the main proponents of this theory that also includes Nick Dixon (2003) and John Russell (1999), dubs this new theory broad internalism. The title is apt because he, and they, claims that these normative principles are to be found within sport itself, and the moral guidance they provide ranges beyond that provided by the rules. What is more, all three proponents of broad internalism maintain that these normative principles are, in addition to being irreducible to the rules of games, also irreducible to the social conventions that typically accompany them. It should be noted as well that Simon sometimes calls his theory interpretivism, because he explicitly draws his theory from Ronald Dworkin's interpretive theory of law and argues, as Dworkin does with respect to the law, that sport contains normative principles of athletic conduct that are crucial to any moral reckoning of sport worthy of the name.

What all three proponents of broad internalism/interpretivism further share in common is a commitment to moral realism. However, the moral realism they embrace comes in two versions, each of which requires its own critical examination. The first version, which is the focus of this chapter, is a metaphysical one favored by John Russell (2007). The normative principles that figure in Russell's version are derived from a philosophical account of the nature of games and sport, of the intrinsic properties that constitute sport. By appealing to these intrinsic properties, which he argues are independent of our beliefs and the evidence we adduce for them, we can determine what normative principles are appropriate to guiding and evaluating athletic conduct. The second version of moral realism, favored by Robert Simon and Nick Dixon, which I take up in Chapter 4, adopts a discourse approach to sport. In this version, normative principles of sport are to be derived from a rational dialogue open to all comers, the aim of which is to divine intellectually warranted moral norms "that have a rational basis independent of cultural, linguistic, or pragmatic considerations" (Simon 2004, 125). Both Simon and Dixon are content to leave the metaphysical implications of their moral discourse position open because they do not think they have any important bearing on their main thesis that the justificatory force of moral reasons and arguments is not bound or otherwise limited by the social and historical context in which such discourse takes place.

The Basic Tenets of Russell's Metaphysically Grounded Normative Theory of Sport

As noted above, Russell argues for a metaphysically grounded form of moral realism of sport, or what he also calls "a non-reductive ethical naturalism" (2004, 144). The basic tenets of moral realism as he conceives it can be summed up as follows: (1) Moral claims are cognitive ones that are approximately true or false, in which their truth or falsity is independent of our moral beliefs, theories, and evidence for them; (2) moral concepts such as "good," "right," "fair," and "just" are natural facts about the world that supervene on and are constituted by yet more basic natural, biological, psychological, and social facts; and (3) everyday standards of rational inquiry are reliable methods for acquiring moral knowledge (144). In Russell's metaphysical view, then, the moral and nonmoral properties of sport are natural ones that reside "out there" in the real world of sport where all the action takes place. So to say, for instance, that fairness is a moral property of sport is to say that the property of fairness is a real feature of sport that is antecedent to and independent of our descriptions and conceptions of it as such. These natural nonmoral and moral facts about sport are thus, he contends, not Platonic forms or Moorean nonnatural facts or discoverable only by some esoteric human faculty like intuition (2012, 7). Moreover, he insists they are not what John Mackie famously called "queer" facts in the sense, as some moral theorists claim, that moral facts are inherently normative or prescriptive, that judging an action to be right (or wrong) *in itself* gives someone a reason to do it (or not do it). If moral facts were inherently normative in this way, they would be, Mackie argued, unlike all other mind-independent facts about the world (Russell 2004, 152). But Russell insists moral facts are just like all other mind-independent facts about the world, because the moral fact that fairness is a constitutive feature of sport does not *in itself* give someone a reason to act fairly or not.

What sort of evidence does Russell marshal for his morally realist take on sport? How can he be confident that the properties of sport he identifies are indeed mind-independent features it actually possesses, that they are instantiated in sport and not just features of our linguistic descriptions of sport?

He begins with evidence gleaned from the semantics of moral discourse about sport, with the way we talk about sport. Our moral views of sport are typically couched in simple declarative, fact-stating language (Russell 2004, 148). For instance, we say that the game was fair or unfair, that all the players morally respected or disrespected the game and each other, that someone was a good or bad sport. These moral claims "look straightforwardly realist" because they refer to actions that took place in the game, in which their truth or falsity can be assessed by whether they correspond to what actions did, in fact, take place in the game (2004, 148). Russell claims further that we often use moral explanations to give causal explanations of nonmoral events that occur in sport, that, to use his example, "it was the poor sportsmanship of the home fans that led to the unprovoked attack on the visiting fans" (2012, 3). And Russell observes that we often do the opposite as well and use nonmoral explanations to give causal explanations of morally freighted actions in sport, to cite his example again, "it was his win at all costs desire that led him to cheat" (2012, 3). What this semantic evidence shows, Russell opines, is that moral realism must be true because it confirms what we would expect to be the case if moral facts were indeed part of the real world around us (2012, 4).

The main evidence Russell adduces for his metaphysically based moral realist theory of sport, however, is derived from a philosophic account of the nature of sport, of its intrinsic properties that distinguish it from other human fare. He thinks this philosophic evidence is especially powerful for making the case for his particular brand of moral realism because it establishes that moral properties and the moral principles they put in play are essential properties of sport, that they make up a key part of its internal architectonic structure (2004, 158). The specific kind of philosophic account he has in mind here is one already discussed at some length in Chapter 2—namely, Suits's conceptual analysis of the necessary and sufficient conditions of playing a game. Russell thinks Suits's conceptual inquiry is ideally suited to his own metaphysical quest to discover the intrinsic moral properties of sport, because he thinks Suits's widely accepted successful definition of sport makes an important metaphysical contribution as well (2004, 158).[1] That is, he regards what Suits achieved in explicating the necessary and sufficient conditions of playing a game as nothing less than an explication of its real, mostly nonmoral properties that are responsible for it being the special human endeavor that it is. And by extending Suits's conceptual analysis of games and sport in a normative direction, Russell is confident that he can discover further the moral properties that are no less essential to the practice of sport that can tell us what moral principles should govern athletic conduct.

However, before I discuss Russell's Suitsian-inspired conceptual analysis of the essential moral properties of sport, I first need to consider a problem that using Suits's conceptual analysis of sport in this normative way raises, which we also encountered in Suits's own attempt to define the essential nonmoral properties of sport. I am referring to the problem that arises when conceptual analysis takes as the object of its inquiry a social kind like sport rather than a natural kind like mountains. The challenge that Suits faced in this regard was that it is one thing to analyze the concept of a mountain, whose basic properties are what they are independent of our descriptions and conceptions of them, and another thing altogether to analyze the concept of sport, whose basic properties are what they are only because we conceived, made, and named them. This made it difficult to see how we can distinguish, after Suits, between what *are* games and what are *called* games, between what properties belong to sport itself and what properties belong to our linguistic descriptions of sport. Russell's metaphysically oriented conceptual analysis raises much the same problem but seemingly in a more acute way. For, again, natural kind objects like mountains exist and have the properties they do independently of human agents, but social objects like sport exist and have the properties they do only because we have put them there ourselves. That makes it especially difficult to see how we can distinguish moral properties of sport that purportedly inhere in sport itself, that are mind-independent in the sense that their "facticity" has nothing to do with our moral beliefs and evidence for them, from moral properties of sport that are mind-dependent in the sense that they have everything to do with our moral beliefs and evidence for them.

To Russell's credit, he is aware of the problem and not under any illusion that sport is anything but a social artifact, a bona fide social institution. And he has a simple answer to the above question, which is that once we have created a social institution like sport we can simply step back and "meaningfully ask what it is we have created" (2011, 261). Once we take this step, he continues, we will find that "the nature of the institution of sport [possesses] . . . certain intrinsic purposes, including moral purposes" (268–269).

If a Suitsian-styled conceptual analysis is the key to unlocking the real-world moral features and moral principles of sport, as Russell contends, then the starting point of that analysis must be the same starting point from which Suits began his inquiry, and the analysis to follow must similarly follow Suits's preferred method of conceptual explication. That means we begin with our implicit, prereflective concept of a game and the group of "hardcore" games from which it derives its content, and we then conceptually mine this group of hardcore games "to get at its essence" (Suits 2014, 168). Russell's conceptual task is simply, as suggested, to follow Suits's lead, but this time to get at the moral essence of games and sport. However, he adds one caveat in this regard that concerns a fairly common temptation when it comes to inquiry into the moral properties of almost anything. And that is not to slight the moral properties we discover about sport by "resign[ing] them to a lesser ontological status" (Russell 2004, 158).

It is important not to confuse the kind of conceptual analysis Suits went in for to get at the nonmoral essence of sport, and Russell its moral essence, with the kind Ludwig Wittgenstein went in for that entertains no such metaphysical ambitions. This is especially so in two respects. First, whereas Wittgenstein treated concepts in general and the concept of a game in particular in terms of our use of words, in which he sought commonalities in what we *call* games, Suits treated the concept of games and sport in terms of their reference to objective things in the world at large. Suits was not interested in analyzing the word game, or the idea or concept or sense expressed by that word, but the thing referred to by that concept. It is no secret, therefore, why Suits's analysis of sport took as its point of departure our implicit concept of sport, because tacit concepts like these are our crucial portal to the outside world, our principal way of gaining cognitive access to objective, worldly things like sport and the objective properties that constitute them. Whereas our concept of sport represents it and its basic properties by referring to them, but, of course, does not and cannot instantiate them, the objective, worldly thing (sport) so referred to instantiates those properties but, of course, does not and cannot represent them. All of which explains why for Suits the sine qua non of conceptual analysis is the reference of concepts like sport rather than their sense, because his aim was not to discover the essence of the concept sport but the essence of sport itself.

The second important difference is that whereas Wittgenstein trained his sights on the surface resemblances of games, on their perceptible, observable features, Suits trained his sights on the deeper, structural features of games. Suits focused on the structural features of games because at the level of sensible appearance, cops chasing a thief look an awful lot like runners in a footrace chasing a lead runner. It is only if we drill down deeper into our concept of a game, if we abstract from surface resemblances and the contingences of time and place, that we can hope to uncover those objective properties that distinguish the different activity that cops chasing crooks is from runners chasing one another in a footrace. It is not that surface resemblances or considerations of the history of sport or the social contexts in which it occurs do not give us knowledge about sport and even a richer appreciation of its cultural pedigree and significance, but that it gives us the wrong sort of knowledge because it sheds no light on the essential properties of sport, on those properties without which it would not be what it most fundamentally is. So if we are after the essential properties of sport, rather than its incidental, nonessential features, then the only knowledge we need is already to be found in our implicit concept of a game, which it is the job of the conceptual analyst to make explicit. That is why Wittgenstein's empirical turn, his impressionistic observations of various games, takes us too far afield from the object of our inquiry. Only if we stick to the conceptual path that Suits has so carefully cleared for us can we hope to explicate our prereflective concept of a game and thus uncover the essential nature of games and sport. And if Russell is right, we will be further rewarded by following Suits's conceptual lead, because he thinks such conceptual probing will also reveal that "the nature of sport incorporates specific moral principles within itself" (2007, 54).

The Internal and External Normative Principles of Sport

I have been arguing that the conceptual analysis Suits uses to define sport serves as the conceptual template for Russell's moral analysis of sport. However, Suits's definition also furnishes the two fundamental nonmoral facts about sport that Russell, in turn, uses to derive his two general normative principles of sport, both of which are pivotal to the brand of moral realism he is peddling. There is no need to reprise Suits's full definition in this regard because these two nonmoral facts can easily be gleaned from Suits's shorthand version of his definition: "Playing a game is the voluntary attempt to overcome unnecessary obstacles" (2007, 14). The first nonmoral fact Russell takes away from this shorthand rendering is that sport has a clear underlying purpose, indeed clearer than most other social practices human agents go in for, which is to provide a context "for the exercise and display of skills in overcoming artificial obstacles" (2011, 264). The aim of sport, then, is quite simply to achieve athletic excellence, to attain athletic perfection. The second nonmoral fact he draws from this shorthand version is that it is paramount that would-be players seek to pursue athletic excellence by voluntarily trying to achieve the (prelusory) goals of games made difficult by the introduction of unnecessary obstacles. So understood, sport fails to be the perfectionist pursuit that it essentially is if would-be players do not consent to such pursuit and all that it entails. Of course, that both of these nonmoral facts are constitutive features of sport gives the two normative principles Russell derives from them the moral heft required by his moral realist theory.

From Suits's first nonmoral fact that sport has a singular, unmistakable purpose to demonstrate athletic excellence, Russell teases out what he calls the internal principle of sport. This principle, he tells us, is "the most general normative principle" of moral evaluation in sport (2007, 58), and he gives it the following formal rendering: "The rules should be interpreted in such a manner that the excellences embodied in achieving the lusory goal of the game are not undermined but maintained and fostered" (1999, 35). The normative force of this principle is as clear as the (lusory) goal of sport from which it is derived; after all, if sport does indeed have a single, overriding purpose or goal, then it follows that only certain ways of accomplishing that purpose will pass moral muster, will satisfy the athletic perfection necessitated by the nature of the athletic test itself.

More broadly speaking, Russell considered his internal principle as a necessary safeguard to protect the "spirit" and "integrity" of athletic endeavor, "to make a game the best it can be as a test of skill and competition" (2004, 147). In conceiving and putting it to work in this normative way to protect the perfectionist aim of sport, Russell directly linked his principle to the more general Aristotelian ideal of human flourishing.[2] For sport at its best is a form of human flourishing in which "certain physical, emotional, and intellectual excellences" are at play and at stake, often in high-pressure situations in which timely and decisive action are called for (2007, 61). Even though his formulation of the internal principle in this particular respect is abstractly and thinly appointed, he nevertheless thinks it contains all the determinate content required to make those difficult moral judgments to ensure athletic flourishing is given its due when the rules leave us in the lurch.

Just what sort of normative determinative content and guidance does Russell think the internal principle provides when we have no recourse but to seek its counsel? His answer is rather expansive, in which he claims a number of deontological commitments and duties follow from its invocation. To begin with, Russell argues the internal principle figures importantly in laying out the normative conditions that must be met in athletic competition by enjoining players to strive to win, seek competitive balance, and foster a general competitive environment in which athletic human flourishing can, well, flourish (2011, 265). He also claims the internal principle prescribes fair play and respect for the integrity and perfectionist point of competitive sport. Finally, Russell regards the internal principle as the primary moral force behind and main protector of sportsmanship and its highest ideals, especially of the kind of altruism sportsmanship requires out of respect for the game (2007, 61). For the absence of such altruism threatens to turn sport into just another egoistic endeavor in which the common, shared good of the game is sacrificed to the players' individual self-interests and private agendas. Such altruism, then, as Russell sees it through the lens of his internal principle, is not an adventitious feature of sport but essential to the athletic excellences that at its best define it (2007, 60).

From Suits's second nonmoral fact that the pursuit of athletic distinction must be voluntary, Russell divines what he calls the external principle. According to this principle, one is not a genuine participant in sport unless one consents to be such a participant and engage in all that follows from assuming such a role. That does not mean one cannot be forced to play sport, but it does mean one cannot be a fully engaged player and held duly responsible for one's moral actions in a game unless one has consented to do so (2007, 59). And just as Russell argued the internal principle is grounded in a more general moral ideal—namely, the Aristotelian ideal of human flourishing, he similarly argues the external principle is grounded in a more general moral ideal, in this instance the Kantian ideal of respect for people (2011, 256). Indeed, he thinks sport "has a more profound commitment to a Kantian consent principle" than most all other human fare, since one's very standing as a player depends on such consent (2007, 59).

The normative importance of the external principle is not to be underestimated in Russell's view because he thinks the consent it mandates from all would-be players does nothing less than set "the boundary of morally permissible conduct in sport" (2007, 59). So even though he acknowledges some of the external principle's normative work overlaps with some of the internal principle's normative work, such as upholding moral norms of fair play and impartial treatment, he insists the external principle does the majority of that work in cases of cheating. For the line that separates morally permissible and impermissible actions in sport in which the charge of cheating is warranted rests largely, according to Russell, on what players think they have consented to in playing a game. Those actions that they plausibly can be said to consent to when playing a particular sport, therefore, fall on the morally permissible side of this line; those actions that cannot plausibly said to follow from their consent fall on the morally impermissible side of this line.

Russell's example of "slashing" offenses in hockey, in which a player uses a hockey stick not to strike or intercept a puck but as a weapon to rein blows on the head or body of another player, is illustrative in this regard. When someone agrees to play hockey, one cannot plausibly be said to have agreed to be assaulted by a hockey stick. Any claim, then, that slashing is part of the game of hockey, Russell argues, should be soundly and roundly rejected in the name of the external principle, because that principle establishes that such acts unmistakably fall outside the moral boundaries of sport (2007, 59).[3]

Russell sees the external principle further at work in helping us to assess morally why certain rule violations, say, tripping one's opponent in a footrace, should be accounted as cheating because they could not be anticipated or plausibly held to follow from one's consent to engage in such a competition, while others, say, a strategic foul in basketball to prevent the clock from running out, should not be accounted as cheating but as accepted, credible parts of the game because they could be anticipated and plausibly held to follow from one's consent to play basketball. Consent is the crucial, overriding moral factor in cases like these, Russell maintains, because although tripping an opponent and strategically fouling an opponent both give the rule-breaking party an advantage they would otherwise not enjoy, only the strategic fouler is warranted in claiming such rule violations are a morally respectable part of the game given their consent to play it (2007, 60).

The same goes for altruistic acts in sport that have to do with respect for the people who engage in competitive sport. Here the external principle works in a complementary way with the internal principle in safeguarding the moral integrity of sport, which is a central concern and tenant of sportsmanship, but this time with the accent on respect for persons qua players. Russell's example in this case is the common practice in soccer of kicking a ball out of bounds so that an injured player can be attended to. This admirable respect that soccer players accord one another in cases where one of their members requires medical attention shows the altruism that respect for persons is and should elicit and Russell contends, is what players of this game plausibly consent to when they agree to play. Further, that the advantage sacrificed in this example is often not compensated by getting the ball back on the in-bound throw goes at least some way in quelling skepticism that such acts are not genuinely altruistic (2007, 61). However, sport proves to be no different than everyday life in this one particular moral respect because being a good sport, very much like being a good person, typically exacts a "prudential cost," where one as a matter of principle forgoes an individual advantage with no expectation or promise of recompense (61). In sport, however, such altruistic acts reflect the singular contribution the external principle makes to the moral evaluation of sport out of respect for persons qua players.

Russell's Coherentism

Before considering what Russell's metaphysical version of broad internalism has critically going for it over formalist theories of sport, I need to consider yet another methodological avenue he pursues to justify his robust moral realism. I am referring to what he calls coherentism, an epistemological method he employs to supplement his conceptual analysis of the essential moral features of sport. By a coherentist methodology, he has in mind something that is, in his own words, "akin to [John] Rawls's idea of reflective equilibrium, wherein theoretical commitments and considered judgments are traded off against each other to secure greater consistency" (2004, 155). This very same toggling back and forth between theoretical principles and considered judgments he also finds at work in Ronald Dworkin's interpretative approach, yet another important part of his epistemological repertoire. In Dworkin's particular interpretative take, which Russell considers "avowedly moral realist" (2007, 64), the moral principles of a community's legal system are played against its culturally influenced judgments and intuitions to ensure greater consistency in the legal decisions proffered in its name. In adding this coherentist piece to the methodological mix, Russell does not hide the fact that his intention in doing so is precisely because he considers it an "alternative to foundational approaches to justification and knowledge" (2004, 155).[4] Nonetheless, though an alternative to foundationalism, he thinks foundationalism has nothing over coherentism as a method to *acquire* moral knowledge of normative principles. What is more, Russell is also convinced that coherentism is an especially reliable method for *applying* that moral knowledge to ensure the normative principles it divines are relevant to the particular social and historical contexts in which sport is practiced.

Understood in the first sense as a method for acquiring moral knowledge of normative principles of sport, Russell views coherentism as a full-fledged "truth-tracking methodology" (2004, 154, 157). That is, he thinks coherentism is the epistemological equal to conceptual analysis when it comes to discovering morally true beliefs about sport, the very sort of true beliefs that make up and inform his internal and external principles (155). For such normative principles are only as good as the evidence that lies behind them. And because coherentism to Russell's mind is no slouch in generating such moral knowledge, it can tell us, he claims, when normative principles "may need to be amended, or even discarded" (2012, 8).

In the second sense as a method for applying already identified normative principles of sport, Russell claims coherentism is integral to ensuring the moral judgments that follow from the internal and external principles are relevant to the particular hard cases they are called on to resolve. This is no minor point because normative principles must be able to accommodate the disparate ways in which sport is played and conducted at different times and places. Otherwise, we will not be able to get right the inferential relationships that obtain between the normative first principles of sport (the internal and external principles) and the moral judgments made in their name to resolve these particular hard cases. That means, of course, that our appeal to the same normative principles may well yield substantively different moral judgments depending on the relevant social and historical circumstances (2004, 157).

Coherentism is further Russell's preferred method for unraveling the adjudication problems that face game officials owing to the indeterminacy of rules.[5] In claiming such, Russell once again reveals his debt to Dworkin's view of judicial adjudication in law. For legal decisions, as Dworkin sees it, are "interpretative judgments" because they cannot be read directly off the laws themselves owing to their open texture (indeterminacy). Further, what is most characteristic about such interpretative judgments, Dworkin argues, is that they "combine backward-and-forward-looking elements" to render the most comprehensive and coherent moral interpretation of past judicial decisions and thereby portray the law as it has developed to that point in the best possible light (1986, 225). Accordingly, Russell also argues that the decisions of game officials often call for interpretative judgments owing to the indeterminacy of game rules. What is most characteristic about such interpretative judgments in sport for Russell is, again like Dworkin, that they, too, combine backward-looking and forward-looking elements to put the best face on past decisions by game officials and thereby portray sport as it has developed to that point in the best possible light (1999, 35). Moreover, just as Dworkin maintains judges have the discretion to make decisions that may be at odds with existing laws so long as they comport with "the best interpretation of the community's legal practice" (225), Russell similarly maintains that game officials have the same discretion to clarify "ambiguities in rules, to add rules, and sometimes to overturn or ignore rules" so long as they comport with the best interpretation of the point and purpose of sport (1999, 28). In both the law and sport, therefore, judges and game officials may only exercise "weak" discretion because both are duty bound to abide by the normative principles of their respective social practices. That is why judicial decisions in law, Dworkin writes, should not be "too novel, too far divorced from what past judges . . . said as well as did" (1986, 248), and why game officials' decisions in sport, Russell writes, should not stray too far from what past game officials said and did (1999, 28).

Critical Appraisal of Russell's Metaphysical Version of Broad Internalism

There is no doubt that Russell's distinctive brand of broad internalism marks a considerable normative upgrade over formalist moral theories of sport. For it nicely fills in the normative gaps when the rules fail us in determining how we should think about and act in such hard athletic cases, whether these failings are owed to the absence of any applicable covering rule, to ambiguities in the rules, or to the fact that the rules steer us in the wrong moral direction. However, Russell's normative achievement in this respect is, I think, more modest than it might at first appear. The normative force of his internal and external principles is mostly limited to those instances in which there is broad agreement, and I underscore the adjective broad here, on what are the relevant skills, the right combination of those skills, the general athletic excellences in play, and the overarching purpose and point of competitive sport. But in the harder cases I featured in my previous accounts of the amateur athletic and the incipient professional athletic communities, in which there is significant disagreement on all of the above athletic counts, I think Russell's normative principles fare far less well, if not fail us altogether. I think they leave us morally rudderless when presented with disagreements of this breadth and depth because the metaphysical underpinnings of Russell's normative principles, to include the epistemological arsenal of Suitsian-styled conceptual analysis, coherentism, and Dworkian interpretivism he used to generate them, are themselves problematic in several respects. I want first, however, to comment on the normative advance Russell's broad internalism makes over formalist moral theories of sport.

Russell's normative contribution to moral inquiry in sport can be traced to the important normative work his internal and external principles do when the rules leave us unsure of how to think and act in certain athletic situations. Russell's class of hard cases all share these particular rule-defying situations, and his principles were designed to come to our normative rescue when these situations inevitably crop up by providing a reliable guide to right action. We have already come across some of these hard cases and Russell's resolution of them in Chapter 2. Perhaps one of the most memorable he dubbed the "Helping Out at Home" case (1999, 28). It involved a turn-of-the-twentieth-century baseball game, in which a player who had already crossed home plate safely proceeded to wrestle the catcher to the ground, thereby allowing two of his teammates on base to score after him. The rule at the time stated no base runner may interfere with a fielder, which meant that when the player in question crossed home plate, he was no longer, technically speaking, a base runner. Appealing to the internal principle, Russell reasoned the runners who scored after the aforementioned player pinned the catcher to the ground should be declared out because, after all, wrestling is not a bona fide skill of baseball or part of the perfectionist aim of this sport.

Russell culls a further example of a rule-challenged hard case from the history of professional baseball that occurred in a 1957 game between the Cincinnati Reds and the Milwaukee Braves. The situation once again involved base runners, in which the Reds' Don Hoak was on second base and his teammate on first (1999, 29–30). The Reds' next batter hit a ground ball headed straight for the Braves' shortstop that ordinarily would result in an easy double play. However, to the shortstop's astonishment, Hoak fielded the ball himself, thereby preventing the double play. Of course, by rule Hoak was immediately declared out for interfering with the shortstop. But the runners who advanced to second and first were allowed to remain on base because there was no rule to penalize an offensive player for interfering with a fielder to break up a double play. Appealing once again to his internal principle, Russell reasons that the runner who safely reached second base thanks to Hoak's interference should be declared out as well because Hoak's illegal fielding of the ball was not a legitimate skill of baseball or a part of the game's ostensible purpose.

I find Russell's moral judgments in both of these hard cases and the potentially other numerous cases that plausibly fall into this hard category completely persuasive. That is, I think the normative principles he fashioned precisely with such rule-defying examples in mind do just the moral job he asked them to do. And insofar as they did, and likely will continue to do in future rule-challenged instances of this kind, they clearly show that broad internalism is, as Russell set out to prove, a more powerful moral theory of sport than formalism.

However, we begin to see cracks in his argument for why broad internalism should be regarded as the go-to moral theory of sport in the same essay in which he discussed the above examples, specifically in another hard case he featured that we also canvassed in Chapter 2. The case in point was the Kansas City Royals' George Brett "Pine Tar Incident," in which Brett's home run was nullified, and he was declared out because the pine tar on his bat exceeded the eighteen-inch limit allowed by the rule. This resulted in a win for their New York Yankees opponents. Russell sided with the president of the American League, Lee McPhail, who overturned the umpire's decision and reinstated Brett's home run and then ordered the teams to replay the game from that point on. Russell also followed McPhail's reasoning that although the umpire's decision was technically correct, it violated the "intent or spirit of the game itself," something which, of course, Russell's normative principles are supposed to safeguard (1999, 30).

I find Russell's principle-driven interpretation of the pine tar case to this point at least as convincing as his interpretation of the previous two cases. It does seem compelling that the pine tar rule call nullified a genuine offensive skill of baseball that went against the purpose of the game. But when we add to this example the crucial but previously unremarked point that the New York Yankees' manager Billy Martin had much earlier in the season suspected Brett was using an illegally pine tar–smeared bat but had decided to wait to bring it to the attention of the umpire at the most strategically opportune time, Russell's interpretative judgment looks far less sure-footed. I say this not because Russell fails to consider Martin's gambit, for he not only factors it into his evaluation but even muses whether Martin's decision to use Brett's home run as the opportune occasion to notify the home plate umpire could it itself qualify as a reputable baseball skill and, therefore, rightly be considered a part of the game. Rather, my concern has to do with his immediate and categorical rejection of such a normative-friendly reading of Martin's decision, in which he ventures not only that baseball does not "set out to create a context for these sorts of [strategic] excellence to flourish" but more strongly that "they normally do their very best to anticipate and eliminate their possibility" (Russell 1999, 37).

What gives me pause about this part of Russell's interpretative judgment is that it gives short shrift to the various roles strategy has played or not played in sport at different times and places; the future role managerial tactics of the sort Martin dabbled in may yet come to play in sport, if they do not already, and be accepted as a legitimate part of athletic competitions. I do not know how else to assess Russell's categorical dismissal of the normative legitimacy such managerial gambits may play in sport now and forever more, except as a wholesale rejection of the importance of historical context in normative inquiry and, therefore, of the possibility that, because of a major change in the social and historical landscape of sport, Martin's actions might well warrant normative approval rather than reproof.[6]

Whether strategy more generally has any place in sport was, of course, one of the things the amateur and professional athletic communities fought over. This disagreement and the several other aspects of how sport should be done that they could not see eye to eye on is what distinguishes harder cases like these from the hard rule-challenged cases Russell cites. The central normative lesson to be learned from the differences between these two kinds of cases, or so I argue, is that when there is widespread agreement on the central purpose of sport and the appropriate mix of skills it is supposed to test, as there was in the hard cases Russell cites, then his internal and external principles can do the normative work he asks them to do. However, when there is widespread disagreement on these points, as there was in the harder amateur and professional cases I cite, his principles prove normatively unworkable. Why his favored principles prove normatively infelicitous in the face of such pervasive disagreement over the point and purpose of athletic endeavor, I argue, has to do with the metaphysically top-heavy moral realist commitments that lie behind them. I now turn my critical attention to these commitments.

The main metaphysical route Russell followed to come up with his normative principles of sport and the essential moral properties he uncovered with their aid was the same conceptual one Suits followed to come up with the essential nonmoral properties of sport. Just as Suits's interest in analyzing the concept of a game/sport was the referential access it provided to a group of games situated in the real world and the objective properties they share in common by virtue of their membership in that group, so Russell's interest in extending Suits's conceptual analysis of a game was the referential access it provided to games in the real world in terms of their objective moral properties that compose their moral essence. In Russell's realist conceptual lexicon, however, the essential moral properties of sport are one-and-all natural properties or facts that supervene on other more basic psychological, sociological, and biological facts about human agents. Like Suits's nonmoral properties of sport, however, Russell's naturalized moral properties of sport are alleged to be mind- and language-independent properties instantiated in its actual practice as opposed to descriptive- and belief-dependent properties attributable to the way we talk about sport.

If Russell is right that his internal and external normative principles of sport are "approximately true statements" of its basic moral nature (2004, 144), then it follows they furnish just the objective normative standards, the relevant normative facts, needed to evaluate moral conduct in sport. What has to be determined in morally analyzing athletic actions and conduct, therefore, is whether they comport with the basic nature of sport, with the purpose of athletic testing and the values that follow in its train. That task is made all the more easier in moral inquiry into sport, according to Russell, because sport has "a clear underlying purpose," which is "to provide a context for the exercise and display of physical skills in overcoming rule-contrived obstacles" (2011, 265). That perfectionist aim and notion of athletic excellence is enshrined in Russell's internal principle, as is the voluntary consent entailed by such pursuit of excellence enshrined in his external principle. We have already observed what such a moral realist inquiry has to say about Russell's own so-called hard cases in sport, where a player pinning a catcher to the ground, or base runners interfering with fielders, or picayune technical rules contravening genuine athletic excellences in baseball, are all adjudged to be morally problematic because they run afoul of the point of that game and the central skills it is designed to test. What remains to be seen, therefore, is what such a moral inquiry into the harder cases I bring to the normative table will have to say about the disparate normative notions of sport entertained by the amateur and professional athletic communities.

The first thing to be said in this regard is that Russell is confident that his realist internalist principles are up to the challenge such harder cases pose. He seems neither especially daunted nor fazed by the deep normative disagreement between these two communities, despite the fact that he is emphatic that his commitment to moral realism does not entail or even suggest that all such disagreements are in principle resolvable (2012, 10). But he is persuaded this particular normative conflict, and presumably normative conflicts similarly marked by pervasive differences in outlook, is resolvable. Even so, he largely splits the differences between them.

On the amateur side of the normative divide, Russell opines that his "realist internalist principles are consistent with the amateur view" (2012, 12). In particular, he affirms the amateur conception of athletic excellence, fairness, and sportsmanship, and considers them "fundamental elements of a defensible conception of sport" (12). He also seconds "amateur concerns about overvaluing competition," which he does think can normatively compromise the pursuit of athletic excellence and thus come into conflict with the internal principle (12). But in a negative note, he criticizes the amateur community's full-throated criticism of athletic strenuousity, accusing its proponents of overstating its moral dangers.

On the professional side of the normative ledger, Russell also has a generally favorable view of its conception of athletic endeavor, finding it, too, largely "consistent with the internal and external principle[s]" (2004, 156). In particular, he regards the professional community's embrace of strategy and tactics as bona fide athletic skills as not only consistent with these principles but, "quite possibly, a development of them" (156). This chimes with his previous criticism that amateurs exaggerated the morally deleterious effects of incorporating such strategies and tactics into sport on the grounds that they amount to little more than morally dubious tricks. However, Russell draws the line, as we observed, when it comes to managerial tactics like Billy Martin's timely disclosure of Brett's "illegal" bat to the game officials. And he reiterates his moral worry that professionals are not sufficiently cognizant of the moral perils of taking the desire to win too far.

What Russell's moral realist evaluation of both sides of this dispute gives us, then, is a decidedly mixed bag, one that in my estimation falls well short of resolving the differences between them. There are various reasons why I think his strong moral realist take on sport is unable to move the normative needle when confronted with harder cases like these. But I think the chief reason can be traced back to the moral authority he claims for his internal and external principles. His thesis that these principles capture the moral essence of sport, that they furnish us with an objective fact of the matter regarding how sport should be done that we can appeal to in determining what is or is not morally permissible, does not pass critical muster. That it does not should not be all that surprising, despite Russell's insistence that the metaphysical commitments that inform his realist principles are not excessive (2004, 145). After all, his claim to have uncovered the objective moral essence of sport is a strong claim and, more important, is based on a no less strong presumption that the referential path that leads from the concept of sport to the fundamental normative facts that constitute sport is a seamless one.

What is hardly seamless about this transition from the concept of sport to natural, objective moral facts about sport is that these facts supposedly bear no trace of the descriptive markers laid down by the concept of sport. But this is a fanciful claim at best. After all, there is no way sport is apart from our descriptions of what we purport it is, to include what we take to be the main purpose of sport, its essential properties, and central values—all of which reflect our various and ever-changing human interests in athletic endeavor. As Richard Rorty pithily explains, "We can only inquire about things under a description" (1991, 99). That means we can only speak of things like sport, of their nonmoral or moral essence, relative to the different ways we describe it and in terms of the different human interests that inform these descriptions. So it is pointless to inquire what sport might be or should be when we, per impossible, try to erase, to parrot William James, all traces of the human serpent over it. For what sport is or should be under no description at all is simply unknowable, if not unimaginable.

This is something we should have learned from Suits's own conceptual analysis of games because his analysis is hardly the *cause celebre* for metaphysical realism that Russell has made it out to be. To see why, recall that the data Suits tells us launched his own conceptual analysis of games were derived from so-called "hardcore" games, hardcore in the sense that if the things that fall into this class are not games, then nothing is. He thus included in this class such noncontroversial instances of games as "bridge, baseball, golf, hockey, [and] chess" (2014, 164). What he claimed next about these can't-miss examples of games is often overlooked but crucial to his entire account—namely, that all these things are "*called* games" (164; emphasis added). What is telling about Suits's remark should be obvious because it shows that the starting point of his conceptual inquiry was nothing other than a particular description of a game that depicts it as some sort of attempt to overcome unnecessary obstacles just so we can be about meeting the (in the case of athletic games, mainly physical) challenges they pose. Further, his interest in this particular description and idea of a game explains his decided lack of interest in another common description and concept of a game expressed in utterances like "don't play games with me." This familiar description of games as con activities that indulge our fancy for cunning and deception in our interpersonal relationships did not concern Suits in the least or figure in his analysis, except when he went out of his way to make it clear that the concept of a game he was working with was not the same concept Eric Berne of *Games People Play* fame was working with, which centered on just such con activities—a point to which Suits devoted an entire chapter in his *Grasshopper* book.

Because Russell's analysis of the essential moral properties of sport simply followed Suits's conceptual lead in this regard, we can safely assert he, too, took his normative marching orders from the very same description of games qua contrived challenges. That Russell's interest in sport so described was not to define it, but to unearth its normative features does not change the fact that it was indeed a description of sport he was operating with and not, as he claimed, its unadulterated, worldly essence. The objective moral properties of sport he claimed to have conceptually wrung out of Suits's definition, therefore, were descriptive-dependent ones, very much bound up with the vocabularies we use to talk about sport. For once again there is no way sport is under no description at all. Indeed, the only description-independent way to get at what sport really is, to discover what it is and what are its nonmoral and moral features under no description, "would be to find a language for describing an object [sport] which was as little ours, and as much as the object's [sport's] own, as the object's causal power" (Rorty 1991, 84).

That things in the world like sport cannot, as it were, speak for themselves, cannot mandate that they be described in certain terms (their own) or valued in certain ways (again, their own), puts in question the strong metaphysical claim Russell makes for his realist moral theory. That is, it suggests that because we cannot make a clean distinction between what is a feature of sport and what is a feature of the language we use to describe sport, his claim to have discovered descriptively unadorned, "approximately true" moral facts about sport, facts that reveal its moral essence, does not pass critical muster. The same goes for his main realist thesis that these so-called moral facts are true because they are more faithful to the nature of sport, because they supposedly bring us closer to what sport really is, to the nonmoral and moral reality of sport with a capital S (Sport). And it further suggests that we need to reject as well his assertion that his metaphysical version of broad internalism is superior to all rival moral theories of sport, to include the discourse version of broad internalism espoused by his fellow broad internalists Simon and Dixon, because it puts us in touch with the moral essence of sport (2004, 145).[7]

My argument that Russell has failed to deliver the moral essence of sport he has promised us—in particular, that he has overplayed, like Suits before him, the referential prowess of the concept of sport—suggests that we have something to learn from Wittgenstein after all. For his counsel that concepts are uses of words and, most important, that language is an integral part of our, to use his terminology, "forms of life" (1958, par. 43) help us see that language is not just a referential tool.[8] That is, it reminds us that the vocabularies we use to describe sport are woven into, and thus are inseparable from, the purposes, values, and nonmoral and moral properties we identify as central to athletic forms of life. That is why such vocabularies are crucial both to the continuance of existing forms of life and the invention of new forms of life (Searle 2010, 104). So the feminist objection to "ladies" and "gentlemen," to use Searle's example, was to the deontology such words commit us to. And the professional objection to "gentlemen" athletes was similarly a rejection of the deontology such a term commits us to. When we aim to change things, therefore, one of the first things we need to change is the language game presently in play, whether the point of the change is to alter gender relations or athletic forms of life or political regimes or whatever.

This tight weld between the vocabularies we use to describe sport and the purposes and properties we attribute to athletic forms of life suggests that we have something to learn from Willard Van Orman Quine's notion of "descriptive relativity." In his book *Word and Object*, Quine poses the example of a person he calls Oscar who happens to be both a mathematician and a cyclist (1960, chap. 6). He then asks what properties are essential to someone like Oscar: Is his being rational essential and his being two-legged incidental, or the other way around? The answer, opines Quine, depends on what interests us about Oscar. If it is his cycling, then his being two-legged is essential and his rationality incidental.

However, if it is his mathematical capability that interests us, then his being rational is essential and his being two-legged is incidental. But if we ask what Oscar's essential properties are under neither one of these descriptions, indeed under no description, we would, Quine insists, be unable to give any intelligible answer.

The normative relevance of Quine's descriptive relativity thesis to Russell's claim to have discovered the moral essence of sport is, I think, clear. What are or are not the essential moral properties of sport, contra Russell, squarely depends on what our interests in sport are at different times and places. In the specific case of the amateur community, its members' interest in sport was rooted in the notion of the gentleman athlete, which is why they regarded having no instrumental designs on athletic endeavor—that is, competing for the love of the game, not trying too hard to win, and eschewing rational planning and strategy—as essential properties of sport. Whereas for professionals, their interest in sport was rooted in the ascendant notion of the professional expert, which is why they regarded the serious pursuit of athletic perfection, incorporating scientifically informed rational training techniques, and employing well thought-out strategies as essential properties of sport. Based on Russell's internal and external principles and his normative appraisals of amateur and professional sport practices, it seems evident his interest in sport selectively borrows from both of these athletic communities and from a more updated, contemporary view of the point and purpose of competitive sport.

The important point not to be lost sight of in calling attention to the fact that these three different takes on sport are, in fact, simply three different descriptions of sport is that no one of them can legitimately claim normative privilege over the others. In other words, whatever normative standing each enjoys is derived entirely from its fidelity to the descriptive and evaluative vocabulary of a particular athletic community whose interest in sport it expresses. For that is the only kind of fidelity that any description of the aim of athletic endeavor is normatively entitled to. Russell's attempt to have it otherwise, to assert that one of these descriptions of sport, the philosophic account of the nature of sport he and his fellow theorists subscribe to, is not a description at all but an approximately true rendering of the moral essence of sport; by virtue of that fact, the objective standard bearer by which all other descriptions of sport that command a public following are to be measured and evaluated should thus be resisted. Giving normative license to any such description of sport to be the arbiter of all other descriptions of sport the public embraces or might embrace in the future is a surefire recipe for normative mischief because no one description has the metaphysical heft necessary to pull off this ambitious normative feat.

That Russell's moral theory cannot get us to the realist normative promised land, that it cannot do the normative work of evaluating harder cases where disagreement about how sport should be done is the norm not the exception, does not mean we find ourselves in this bind because we have no facts at our disposal to deal with such apparently intractable normative cases. Rather, it only means that the facts available to us are not, as Russell argued, natural facts but institutional facts. That follows, of course, because sport is nothing if not a human contrivance, a social rather than a natural kind. Now much rides on the instituted status of social practices like sport in this regard because institutional facts differ from natural, or what Searle calls "brute," facts in two important respects: (1) Institutional facts qualify as such only under a description, and (2) only under a description agreed to and accepted by a community (Searle 2010, 116). Take the sport of baseball, for example. Before the invention of this game, human beings had from time immemorial hurled and struck at objects in various ways and for various, but perhaps mainly, instrumental purposes. What they did they did naturally because neither their purposes nor their actions required or depended on some institution for their intelligibility or meaning. But what they never did or could do was throw a runner out at first base or pitch a one-hitter or hit a home run or score more runs than their opponent, all of which had to await the invention of baseball. Pitching a one-hitter, hitting a home run, and the like are institutional actions because they require and depend on an institution and, as a consequence, require and depend on the assignment of a purpose to make their actions intelligible to one another and to those who watch them. The assignment of an institutional purpose, in turn, introduces normative criteria of assessment, since to say something has a purpose is to say some ways of realizing that purpose are better than others, and therefore, that certain nonmoral and moral properties of sport are crucial to the realization of that designated purpose. As institutional facts about sport, therefore, none of them can be read off of or reduced to the natural physical actions of throwing or striking or whatever natural, preinstitutional actions we might cite. That is why these institutional nonmoral and moral facts about sport count as such only under a description and only if they are in concurrence with what the members of the relevant community believe about them.

What goes for the invention of a new sport goes as well for major changes in already instituted sports. Which brings us right back to the harder cases we have been discussing. When the changes in question are of the depth and scope as noted in the transition from amateur to professional sport, we see a significant change in the purpose assigned to sport and in the descriptive and evaluative vocabularies used to normatively monitor and assess this change and all it entails. So the relatively clear purpose of sport compared to other human endeavors that Russell claims made moral inquiry into sport a simpler task turns out to be not so clear; therefore, moral inquiry into sport is not so uncomplicated after all. Hence, when the professional community made changes to the aim of athletic striving and the sorts of skills sport is supposed to test that put them at odds with the amateur community, the institutional facts each had at their disposal not only were of no help but were the main obstacle to settling their normative differences. For the normative shelf life and reach of the institutional facts in dispute in such cases are no longer or no more extensive than the normative shelf life and reach of the particular community whose concurrence they depend on. The upshot is that the (institutional) facts each had to work with to make its normative case were not recognized by the other as (institutional) facts at all. They thus fell on deaf ears and led to the normative impasse previously discussed.

It should come as no surprise, therefore, why harder normative cases like this one are not amenable to Russellian-like, top-down normative assessment in which general principles such as the internal and external principles are called on to resolve ground-level, communally anchored disagreements over the relevant institutional facts. For the fate of any disagreement predicated on institutional facts, unlike disagreements about natural facts, is that they are strictly intramural rather than extramural matters, matters that are resolvable only within communities of discourse that count as such just because they agree on the relevant institutional facts.

In drawing this distinction between the institutional properties of sport and natural properties such as throwing and striking, it is important to note that I am not denying that social institutions like sport are causally independent of the athletic communities that confer the nonmoral and moral properties they possess at different times and places or that institutional facts of this kind enjoy complete independence from natural facts.

To begin with the first point, that the institutional properties of sport are such only under a description and only under a description affirmed by a particular athletic community accounts for why these facts about sport cannot be derived from or reduced to physical actions like throwing and striking. But the irreducibility of such institutional properties does not entail or suggest that social institutions like sport are mere intersubjective figments of our communal descriptions of them or concurrences regarding their purpose and value. When we attribute particular nonmoral and moral properties to sport based on our descriptions of them and assignments of their purpose, we create a "real" thing "out there" in the world, a social institution, that is causally independent of these descriptions and assignments of purpose. So while pitching, scoring runs, and winning a game are not mere physical things, they are institutional things and, as such, ontological categories in their own right. Though differently constituted, they are as real as mountains and lakes and other natural things in the universe. When we describe social things like sport, as amateurs, professionals, and Russell himself all did, we do so in the same causally independent way as we do mountains and lakes, as things separate from us that we have beliefs about. That is further why social things like sport can, under a prior description and agreement in language game, cause us to change our beliefs (Rorty 1991, 83). For example, suppose an athlete in the amateur community who was recognized and praised all around as a true sportsman was subsequently found to have secretly employed a professional coach—a clear and major violation of the amateur code of sportsmanship. That discovery would then cause his peers to change their beliefs about him and lead them to morally rebuke him for what he had done.

Because we describe social things like sport in this one sense at least in the same causally independent way as we do natural things like mountains, one might wonder why many philosophers like John Searle take pains to warn us against a persistent tendency to mistake institutional facts as "part of the natural order of things" (2010, 107). The answer is that we too often run together "relations of *justification* holding between beliefs . . . , and relations of *causation* holding between these beliefs . . . and other items in the universe" (Rorty 1991, 97). In other words, what nonmoral or moral properties we are justified in holding *about* institutional things like sport is wholly a matter of their coherence with our other beliefs that inform our description of sport and human agreement regarding its salient properties. So understood, justification is strictly a social community matter of squaring beliefs with other beliefs that inform the reigning descriptive and evaluative language game in play and, therefore, not a matter of squaring our beliefs with nonbeliefs, with things "out there" in the world independent of the language game in play. In my example of the rogue amateur who strayed outside the bounds of morally permissible action by violating the code of the amateur community, what caused us to change our beliefs about his moral rectitude happened on the athletic playing field and not in our heads, so to speak. But our justification for morally rebuking his real-world actions is that they ran afoul of that community's beliefs *about* how amateurs, rightly so-called, should act. This latter, what Rorty calls "vegetarian sense of aboutness," does not, therefore, direct our attention to nonbeliefs, but only to the web of beliefs that inform the amateur language game in play (1991, 97).

With regard to my second point that institutional facts are not wholly independent of natural facts, the creation of sports that exceed the natural capacities of human agents to perform them is a nonstarter. Athletic games like baseball simply would not exist were it not for the fact that, among other things, human agents are biologically equipped to throw, strike, and catch spherical objects. In addition to such biological facts, the causal dependence of instituted athletic skills on natural capacities of human beings includes psychological and sociological facts as well, all of which are traceable to human evolutionary history. So our very desire to take up human pursuits like sport, indeed our very "desire to live" itself, as Harry G. Frankfurt avers, "and our readiness to invoke this desire as generating reasons for performing actions that contribute to that end, . . . derive from and express the fact that, presumably as an outcome of natural selection, we love . . . living" (2006, 37). Once again, however, we need to be careful not to run together the causal dependence of such instituted forms of life and actions on natural facts about human beings with the justificatory dependence of athletic institutions on how particular communities describe them, credit specific nondeontic and deontic properties to them, and impute various meanings to what otherwise would be mere physical actions.

I have been arguing at some length that Russell's claim to have discovered the moral essence of sport does not, indeed could not, live up to its metaphysical billing. It is rather, I argue, merely one very general description of sport among many other typically more concrete descriptions of sport. Russell, however, could simply rebut that even if his realist account lacks the metaphysical heft he claimed for it, its descriptive heft remains unchallenged. To bolster his claim for the descriptive force of his account, he might well direct our attention to Suits's own definitionally oriented description of sport. After all, Suits's definition has stood up well to the many objections directed against it. And because Russell merely followed Suits's conceptual lead in developing his normative account of sport, it, presumably, should do just as well in fending off challenges to its descriptive authority.

However, I think the very success of Suits's descriptive project imperils, if not dooms, the success of Russell's normative descriptive project, for descriptions are only as perspicacious and forceful as the purposes they serve. In Suits's case, his aim to define sport dictated he empty out as much of the historical content of the concept of sport as possible to come up with its necessary and sufficient conditions. Had he not done so, his definition would have shipwrecked on the shoals of the different social and historical stages of its long and ever continuing gestation. Only by going abstract in this fashion was he able to uncover the deeper structural features that all (athletic) games share in common that belie their surface similarities and resemblances.

The problem, however, is that this abstract manner of proceeding, which is so nicely suited to definitional purposes, could not be more unsuited to harder normative ones in which the point of sport is in hot dispute. That is because getting these harder cases right requires reinstating the social and historical content and context that Suits made a point of eliminating to get his definitional project off the ground. Russell's mistake, or so I want to argue, therefore, was to follow Suits's abstract lead. By doing so, his internal and external perfectionist principles turned out to be as abstract as the formal features of sport Suits unearthed. It is little wonder, therefore, why rival accounts of sport like the dispute between the amateur and professional athletic communities have no trouble passing the only test Russell's principles actually pose for them—namely, whether they treat sport as a voluntary perfectionist practice rooted in standards of excellence. That is the one central thing both of these athletic parties, indeed most such parties, rival or not, can agree on.[9] However, their mutual agreement on and commitment to this abstract perfectionist precept conceals much more than it reveals. What it conceals is owed to the fact that normative principles of this highly general character are constitutionally unfit to detect, let alone resolve, the contextually sensitive differences that pitted these two communities against one another, and that are the signature feature of what I have been calling harder normative athletic cases.

When it comes to these harder normative cases, the devil is in the details. In lieu of such social and historical details, it is hard to see how Russell's normative principles can do the critical work he asks them to do—that is, when he puts them to use, as noted, to criticize the amateur community for exaggerating the morally deleterious consequences of trying too hard to win and to criticize the professional community for not fully appreciating the moral dangers of doing so. There just is not enough determinative content in either one of his principles to generate particular criticisms of this kind, let alone to make them stick. Beyond telling us whether community-backed descriptions of the point and purpose of sport meet the perfectionist and voluntarist requirements his principles mandate, which the rival amateur and professional camps do and, I have surmised, other similar harder normative cases do as well, I do not think they have anything more to say to us about how sport should be done.[10] To do anything more of a critical nature, we would have to backfill the social and historical content that Russell, after Suits, emptied out to generate his two principles.

If I am right about this, then the only way he was able make the specific criticisms of both athletic camps was to smuggle the substantive content he needed into his normative principles. I can only speculate what that content was, but the best clue he gives us is his split judgments regarding the moral permissibility of certain strategies and tactics in sport. I am referring, on the one hand, to his moral blessing of strategic fouls in sport and, on the other hand, to his moral censure of managerial tactics of the sort Billy Martin used in the Brett pine tar bat episode. His dueling moral pronouncements in this regard suggest to me that he is relying on an updated, contemporary version of the best tradition of the professional paradigm, which does countenance most instances of strategic fouling but finds fault with Martin-like managerial tactics. Identifying just what historical context Russell was invoking here is crucial, given what I have argued is the limited normative shelf life of normative standards of appraisal. These normative standards can do their critical work only if they are congruent with the descriptive and evaluative vocabularies in play in the athletic community in question. In the harder case of the amateur and professional athletic communities, if Russell has indeed smuggled the reigning language game of the contemporary professional community into his account, it is the wrong content to make good on his criticisms of either side, pro or con. After all, neither the amateur nor the professional community put any normative stock in this updated description of sport; nor could they, given the historical contexts in which they did their bidding. That is why both communities would dismiss central institutional moral facts that inform this contemporary iteration of the professional perspective as facts at all. All of which brings us right back, once again, to the normative standoff we began in the examination of this harder case.

Russell, however, has one more card in his moral realist deck he can play to shore up whatever normative problems I have claimed to find in his account. That card is the aforementioned coherentism that, he argues, provides further evidence for his moral realist theory; evidence that is straightforwardly of the historical sort, I argue, he has not given its rightful normative due.

Russell treats coherentism as a "truth-tracking methodology" in its own right, and thus as another way to acquire the evidence needed to divine realist normative principles of sport; it also guides the application of such already discovered normative principles. By coherentism, Russell meant something roughly akin to Rawls's notion of reflective equilibrium, in which theoretical principles and considered judgments are played against one another to ground our moral judgments of sport. Because the evidence to be gained by a coherentist methodology is exclusively of the historical kind that can only be gleaned from a careful scrutiny of the social and historical contexts in which sport takes place, Russell recognizes it is an "alternative to foundational approaches to justification and knowledge" of the sort he employed, following Suits, in his philosophical analysis of the nature of sport (2004, 155). What Russell leaves unsaid, however, and what sets up a basic contradiction or, at the very least, a fundamental tension in his realist methodological commitments, is that coherentism so understood is not only an alternative to foundational epistemological approaches but a rival approach that aims to replace rather than complement them.

Russell's attempt, in effect, to have it both ways, to enlist both a foundationalist conceptual analysis of the nature of sport and a coherentist historical analysis of sport to underwrite his moral realist project, therefore, seems misguided. Especially because when Rawls introduced his notion of reflective equilibrium, he took pains to point out that his intent in doing so was to put moral theory on a new, nonfoundational footing. Whereas, then, most moral theorizing before Rawls's magnum opus, *A Theory of Justice*, was published sought nothing less than the moral truth—that is, principles of justice that "represent, or . . . [are] true of, an already given moral order" (Rawls 1999, 347)—Rawls sought nothing more than principles of justice that are most reasonable to us, to members of "the public culture of a democratic society," and to a conception of justice "implicit in that culture" (355). That is why he argued that principles of justice cannot be derived "from the recognition of a prior and independent moral order, but from everyone's affirmation of the same authoritative social perspective" (356)—namely, the conception of a person, of social cooperation, and of fairness congenial to a liberal democratic society. It should come as no surprise, therefore, that Rawls disavowed any "appeal to the analysis of concepts" like the "right" in moral inquiry (1971, 130).

However, before I further probe this apparent contradiction, or at very least fundamental tension, in Russell's use of these two quite different methodologies, it might be useful to consider one way he does manage to combine them to good effect, but only up to a point. I am referring here to his theory of adjudication for the regulation of athletic conduct by game officials that does rely on both a conceptual and historical analysis of sport. In fact, what Russell christens as the internal principle of sport was in its first incarnation called by him "the first principle of games adjudication" and put to use for that very purpose (1999, 35; 2011, 265). In that adjudicative context then, just as Dworkin insists that judges should base their judgments on "backward-and-forward-looking elements" to ensure their decisions are the most comprehensive and coherent interpretation of past judicial decisions, Russell insists that game officials should do the same to ensure their decisions are the most comprehensive and coherent interpretations of past game decisions. In both cases, the historical backward looking served as a check on the soft discretion judges and game officials exercise when trying to clarify ambiguous rules, or to ignore or overturn rules, to make sure their rulings do not stray too far from what past judges and game officials said and did.

When it comes to game officials' decision making, therefore, Russell's combining these two methodological approaches seems very much in point and effective.[11] But only up to a point. What point? The point at which Russell recasts reflective equilibrium, the tacking back and forth between theoretical principles and considered judgments, as "an attempt for particular sports to genuinely work themselves pure—toward a better realization of sporting games" (2011, 267). What he has in mind here can be readily seen in his previous example of the Brett pine tar hard case, in which a game official's decision that home runs should not be disallowed because of technicalities like a foreign substance being applied too high on a bat, made baseball, as a consequence, a better game. Better not in the sense that it coheres better with a particular game community's best interpretation of baseball, but better because it is truer to the basic nature of the game itself. The phrase "sports working themselves pure" is thus a normatively loaded one, in which the authoritative social perspective of an athletic community is overridden by, rather than played off against, an authoritative philosophical perspective that supposedly puts us in closer contact with the basic reality of sport, with its essential features rather than its historically contingent ones. There is obviously no real, substantive back-and-forth going on between Russell's internal and external principles and the considered judgments of a relevant athletic community, and so no actual reflective equilibrium being attempted, when game adjudication is understood as a way to make the game purer.

We can be confident this scanting of history in favor of philosophical analysis that is the not so subtle message signaled by this idea of "sport working itself pure" is what Russell has in mind because he borrows the phrase directly from Dworkin, who also talks about the "law work[ing] itself pure" and understands the phrase as signaling a shift in perspective from the community's best interpretation of the law to a philosophical analysis of the law unloosed from any such community or institutional standpoint (1986, 400). In Dworkin's view, "present law contains another law, which marks out its ambition for itself" (406). Realizing this ambition requires passing the normative baton not only from the legislature, which makes the law but often does not fully recognize what justice entails, but from judges as well, who are constrained both by the law made by the legislature and the present community's best understanding and interpretation of the law, and handing it instead "to philosophers, to work out law's ambition for itself, the purer form of law" (406). For both Dworkin and Russell then, the notion of law and sport working themselves pure is a way to bypass the community's best interpretation of the aim of such social practices at a particular time and place in favor of a philosophical analysis that purports to tell us what is, in fact, the true aim of law and sport, to uncover approximately true facts about what these social practices are, at bottom, really all about. Of course, the philosophic working out of sport's ambition for itself upends any notion that even in game adjudication conceptually generated normative principles can meaningfully work in a complementary fashion with, rather than in opposition to, historically mediated efforts to square such principles with our community-based intuitions regarding how sport should be done.

So much then for the idea that we can coax, under the guise of reflective equilibrium, philosophically derived normative principles of sport to work with the considered judgments of particular athletic communities to adjudicate our way to better, in the sense of purer, sports. Any claim we can make that these two methodologies work more seamlessly outside the framework of game adjudication is also not in the normative cards. Nevertheless, when Russell drops his adjudicative pose and concentrates his focus on the internal principle strictly as a general normative principle of sport, he betrays no hint that pulling off such a two-tiered analysis poses any kind of methodological conflict. He thus positively asserts that his philosophically derived realist normative principles "explicitly take account of historical context," put no limits on "potential sources of . . . evidence" for these principles, acknowledge that the philosophical analysis of the nature of sport, like the philosophical analysis of the nature of anything, is "limited by . . . historically given epistemological starting points," and show that his "perfectionist and voluntarist arguments about the nature of sport" are not contravened but justified by "using examples from the history of sport" (2011, 6, 8, 9). In sum, he continues to insist that his moral realist theory of sport takes the best that conceptual and historical analysis have to offer and seamlessly combines them to churn out historically mediated, approximately true facts about sport from which we can confidently take our normative bearings.

The main evidence Russell furnishes for his confidence that philosophically derived normative principles of sport can accommodate the kind of historically grounded disagreements that are characteristic of the harder normative cases I have featured is the claim he makes for having successfully done just that in sorting out the particular historical disagreements over the purpose of sport that divided the amateur and professional athletic communities. His criticism of the former community for exaggerating the moral dangers of placing too high a premium on winning, on the one hand, and his criticism of the latter community for not taking those moral dangers seriously enough, on the other hand, are regarded by Russell as perfectly "reasonable criticisms of each historical position," and, therefore, as proof "that they can be fruitfully defended and critically assessed from a realist internalist perspective" (2012, 13). That is, he argues that his realist critical take on these rival historical standpoints is "evidence in favor of internalist realism that it is able to make sense of the debate between such competing conceptions, provide evidence for resolving those disagreements, and lay the ground for further debate and progress on these and related issues" (13).

I think, however, we have good reasons to doubt Russell can cash out this bold claim. To begin with, I am already on record as having disputed that Russell has successively resolved the historical disagreements between these two athletic communities on the grounds that his normative principles are much too formalistic, much too abstract, to arbitrate harder normative cases like this one. Indeed, I argue that neither the internal principle nor the external principle is equipped to get at the historical issues in dispute here, because what divides athletic camps in this and other representative kinds of harder cases is not whether sport is a perfectionist pursuit, about which there is unanimity all around, but rather what such pursuit of athletic perfection entails in the way of skills, commitment, regard for opponents, and related matters. In all these so-called harder normative cases, history matters above all else.

My second reason for doubting Russell can make good on his claim that realist normative principles of sport are well suited to account for and critically evaluate such historical differences in point of view is a corollary of the first. His moral realist position can do what he says it can do with regard to the history of sport practices only under one crucial assumption—namely, "that our ideas about the underlying values, or principles, of sport were relevantly and approximate true" (2012, 9). The problem, of course, is that arriving at such "approximately true" normative principles of sport is strictly a matter of philosophical, not historical, analysis, of discovering the alleged nonmoral and moral essence of sport. It could not be otherwise on Russell's realist account because philosophical analysis, or more to the point, conceptual analysis, is the only kind of analysis with the requisite epistemological power to turn up such supposedly approximately true facts about sport, to get us to the facts of the matter that define athletic conduct no matter the historical setting. By contrast, the evidentiary value of the historical considerations that go into the attempt to achieve reflective equilibrium pales by comparison, because the best it can do, on this realist story, is tell us what historically contingent features of sport practices are at stake in conflicts like the amateur and professional one. That means that when it comes to generating or even modifying normative, approximately true principles of athletic conduct, history can in principle play no role whatsoever and, in fact, did not play any apparent role in Russell's formulation of his internal or external principles. That makes it very difficult indeed to see how historical analysis in general, and the historical vetting that is an integral part of the method of reflective equilibrium, could ever lead, as Russell claims, to amending or discarding approximately true normative principles of sport (2012, 8).

The third and last reason to doubt that Russell can employ a two-track methodology that does justice both to the conceptual and historical facts about sport can be seen if we consider just what a coherentist account of sport entails. Central to such an account is a rather simple rule of thumb that kicks in whenever an athletic community has reason to question and reflect on its core moral beliefs. Such reflective probing is often elicited when an athletic community encounters another athletic community whose stock moral beliefs and standards of evaluating sport differ significantly from its own moral beliefs and standards of evaluating sport. Encounters like these are, of course, a signature feature of the harder normative cases I have been discussing, and in particular of the contentious encounter between the amateur and nascent professional athletic communities. The rule of thumb in all of these harder normative cases is to ask whether the new beliefs of the, to stick to my main example, professional community can be woven together with the beliefs already held by the amateur community. The test of whether they can be made to cohere in this sense is not a matter of determining whether they can be shown to more closely approximate the truth of the moral facts represented by Russell's internal and external principles, principles deemed true prior to and independently from the core moral beliefs of any athletic community, let alone the amateur community. Rather, it is a matter of seeing whether these unfamiliar moral beliefs about how sport should be done from the professional community's perspective—for example, how seriously winning should be taken or whether strategic tactics have any legitimate place in athletic contests—can be taken on board by the amateur community without capsizing its moral beliefs and, therefore, its distinctive moral outlook on sport.

Rightly understood then, coherentism is strictly a social, intracommunal matter, rather than an epistemological, extracommunal one, of trying to bring our familiar moral beliefs into reflective equilibrium with, in this and other harder normative cases, the unfamiliar moral beliefs of another athletic community. This suggests that the most a normative analysis of sport can hope to accomplish or aspire to in these harder cases is to serve up generalizations of the core moral beliefs of the relevant athletic communities in question that are not "supposed to ground" the culturally rooted intuitions of its members but "to summarize them," and to summarize them in a way that speaks to and resonates with their distinctive moral identities (Rorty 1991, 171). This puts paid, I believe, to the idea that coherentism is a truth-tracking methodology, in which the moral beliefs of athletic communities are tested by determining how they measure up to normative principles that are the most rational because they bring us into closer contact with the basic reality of sport, with what sport really is all about. On the contrary, coherentism is best understood as a justificatory device, in which the moral beliefs of athletic communities are reflectively assessed by how they measure up to normative standards (generalizations) that are the most rational for them given their particular conceptions of sport. After all, this is what it means for athletic communities to reflectively work out what they should believe about sport by their own lights, by starting with their own moral beliefs and the moral stories in which they are embedded, and by honing in on, rather than distancing themselves from, the historical context that gives these beliefs and narratives whatever intelligibility and moral gravitas they possess.

When properly posed then, the answer to the question of whether the amateur community can accommodate the moral beliefs and evaluative vocabulary of the professional community about how sport should be done is, and can only be, a resounding no. The answer, of course, does not change if we ask the same question of the professional community regarding the moral beliefs and vocabulary of the amateur community. There is just not enough overlap in their moral beliefs and vocabularies to bring them into reflective equilibrium with one another, to commensurate their disparate moral outlooks on sport, not without betraying what each morally stands for in all matters athletic.

If I am right about this, then Russell's affirmative answer to the contrary regarding this harder case, and presumably others, cannot be defended, not at least on coherentist grounds. For what Russell counts as "reasonable criticisms of each [amateur and professional] historical position," in this particular instance on the relative importance of winning (2012, 13), would not, indeed could not, count as such by either one of these communities. What counts as a "reasonable" criticism of a historical position for Russell is not what counts as such for a coherentist, in which criticism is warranted if and only if a community's context-dependent moral beliefs are revealed to be out of synch with its context-dependent normative standards. Rather, what is a reasonable criticism to Russell's realist way of thinking looks very much like a correspondence rather than a coherence theory of truth, in which a community's contextually dependent moral beliefs and standards are evaluated by how well they match up with avowedly decontextualized, de-historized normative principles of sport. To a coherentist like Rawls, evaluating moral beliefs in terms of how they correspond to alleged essential nonmoral and moral properties of sport arrived at by an analysis of the concept of sport is a nonstarter because the very gesture betrays a rejection of coherentism root and branch.

In a later essay, Russell (2011) comes close to conceding this very point: that his metaphysically based criticisms of historical conceptions of sport such as amateurism and professionalism may not, after all, be taken as evidence in favor of his robust moral realist version of interpretivism. In this same essay, he explicitly disavows his earlier claim that Dworkin's interpretive theory of law is a realist theory at all. What makes this a significant concession, of course, is that he modeled his own self-proclaimed realist moral theory of sport on Dworkin's interpretivist theory of law. What prompted his retraction of Dworkin's realist bona fides is nothing other than his belated recognition that his indebtedness to Suits's conceptual analysis of the essential nonmoral features of sport, which was the same conceptual path Russell followed to arrive at the essential moral features of sport, put him at odds with Dworkin's community-friendly interpretation of the law. It could not but do so because the internal and external principles he identified by means of Suits's essentialist account are not evident in, or derivable from, the best interpretation of the gaming community. That is because the normative principles of an athletic community are not the essential moral principles of sport, the principles that most closely approximate the true moral facts about sport, but only the principles that inform its best interpretation of the morality of sport (267). This was the very problem that plagued Dworkin's theory, as Russell now saw it, because the legal principles of a community are also not necessarily the most just, but only the principles that inform its best interpretation of the point of law. He thus came to the conclusion that Dworkin "is not a genuine moral realist or a realist about essential moral features of legal systems" (267).

What we are to make of Russell's above declaration that Dworkin is not a realist after all is, I think, crystal clear. If we are committed as Russell is, given his fondness for Suits's essentialist take on sport, to coming up with normative principles of sport that bring us into closer contact with the true moral essence of sport, then we have no other recourse but to work up a philosophical (conceptual) analysis of the moral nature of sport. In other words, we have no other alternative but to be a realist from top to bottom in our moral inquiry into social practices such as sport or law, and leave the coherentist work of trying to bring the gaming community's normative standards into reflective equilibrium with its moral beliefs to more metaphysically timid souls.

Finally, that Russell's professed moral essentialism/realism cannot be reconciled with his professed historicism does not mean history does not play any role in his theory—only that it cannot play such a role in generating his normative principles given his metaphysical, realist commitments. However, he does appear to sneak some historical content in the back door, so to speak, when assessing the amateur and professional conceptions of sport. I have already indicated that the specific historical details that are hidden in plain sight in his split moral judgments regarding the moral views of both athletic camps look an awful lot like our best contemporary professional interpretation of sport. But a particularly telling example of that contemporary outlook involves Russell's favorable assessment of the professional Harold Abrahams, and his athletic sprinting tactics and his hiring of a professional coach, both of which were featured in the book and film *Chariots of Fire*, which were roundly condemned by his mostly amateur peers. Russell, by contrast, viewed Abrahams's professional gestures in a positive light because they chimed with "game related obligations in *our* time" (2004, 156; emphasis added). I think he is right about this, and that is why I think many of Russell's normative assessments of this harder case are perspicacious to contemporary admirers of sport like us. The problem, however, is that our present moral intuitions about sport reflect our distinctively contemporary moral outlook regarding how sport should be done. This is concerning because it is the wrong historical vantage point by which to evaluate the moral outlooks of our predecessors on either side of the amateur and professional divide. What this should tell us is that whether history is slipped into our moral investigations of sport through the back door, as a committed, full-throated moral realist like Russell must do if his moral pronouncements are to have any determinative force at all, rather than being simply written off as empty platitudes, or through the front door, as the conventionalist theory I offer in Chapter 6 proposes to do, it must be the right history, the right social context, and the right audience to fulfill the normative work it is charged to do.

I now want to turn my critical attention in Chapter 4 to the second realist version of broad internalism (interpretivism) championed by Simon and Dixon, which dispenses with metaphysical arguments about the moral nature of sport in favor of a discourse approach in which all comers are welcomed to the table to hash out how sport should be done. What such discourse has to offer us, as they see it, is an opportunity for all parties to this open deliberation to venture their best moral takes on sport, in which only the view that survives critical scrutiny from all sides, that has the strongest reasons and arguments to support it, is considered warranted to serve as our moral guide for how sport should be conducted and evaluated.

4

Broad Internalism, Moral Realism, and Sport

The Discourse Version

I turn now to the discourse version of broad internalism/interpretivism championed by Robert Simon and Nick Dixon. As noted, unlike John Russell's metaphysical version, Simon and Dixon aim to generate moral principles of sport not by scouring for independent moral facts about sport that taken together make up its moral essence but rather by divining such moral principles through a rational dialogical process open to all. They think this dialogical route has two main things going for it. First, since no restrictions are placed on who gets to say what concerning how sport should be done, there will be as many moral principles of sport considered as there are discoursers to offer them. This ensures possible candidates for such principles will not be denied, wittingly or unwittingly, a hearing. Second, by requiring all proposed moral takes on sport be thoroughly reflectively vetted, we can be assured that whatever moral principles manage to survive such rational back-and-forth scrutiny will possess the requisite justificatory force. As Simon and Dixon see it then, there is no need to go metaphysical in search of what part of the "world" our moral judgments correspond to, so long as we can marshal moral reasons that ground the moral principles we settle on. What is more, we need not give up on moral realism in taking this rational dialogical route, since the reasons and arguments that count here "have justificatory force independent of particular historical and social contexts," and, therefore, are "independent of cultural, linguistic, or pragmatic considerations" (Simon 2004, 127, 125). Indeed, moral principles of sport secured in this dialectical manner might even better serve the cause of moral realism than Russell's theory because they have none of the metaphysical baggage his version does.

Basic Tenets of a Discourse Realist Moral Theory of Sport

Several features distinguish Simon and Dixon's discourse ethics of sport. The first concerns what they regard to be the appropriate starting point of rational dialogue itself, which eschews a transcendental philosophical perspective in favor of a down-to-earth social and historical one. Simon and Dixon want to begin the dialogical interchange here, in the social and historical context in which the discoursers presently find themselves, because their aim, ultimately and ideally, is to arrive at universal moral principles at the end of inquiry rather than claiming, presumptively, that such universal principles can be somehow had at the beginning of inquiry. That is why they are chary of any Kantian-like effort to put discourse on a higher, supposedly more sure footing, by appealing at the outset to a general conception of rationality or by tapping into some alleged neutral, asocial, ahistorical vantage point, what Thomas Nagel famously called the "view from nowhere," to evaluate different moral takes on sport (Simon 2004, 127). For the same reason, they oppose placing any hypothetical, idealized constraints on the reasons traded back and forth in the actual dialogue itself, the kind of constraints Jürgen Habermas proposed in his conception of the "ideal speech situation" (1993, 56).

The second feature of Simon's and Dixon's discourse ethics of sport is that it must be open to all comers. To their mind, this is a practical requirement that issues from the notion of rational dialogue itself. After all, placing constraints on who can engage in such exchange seems at odds with the whole point of dialogue. In particular, Simon argues that the idea of an open dialogue speaks against a claim I have previously made that such a give-and-take of reasons concerning how sport should be conducted is best restricted to particular practice communities who are of one mind as to the purpose of sport (Morgan 2004). Simon thinks there are two major problems with restricting discourse in this way. The first is a lack of clarity about the membership of such practice communities—that is, about just "who is to do the discoursing" (Simon 2004, 128). Is it, he asks, "critical media types, or perhaps philosophic theorists or social critics of sport, or maybe members of a particular practice community of, say, golf, who think sport in general would be better off if all practice communities followed their ethical lead?" (128). The second and perhaps more acute problem with moving discourse to the interior of practice communities is that it wrongly puts the accent on "*who* said what," rather than on where it rightly belongs—namely, the rational cogency of what was said. The remedy for these two defects, as Simon sees it, is simply to free discourse from the grip of particular practice communities altogether, which means dropping the very notion of such communities, and instead invite all interested parties to the table to express their views on how sport should be morally considered and governed.

The importance of inviting everyone to weigh in on how sport should be done becomes even more apparent when we consider Simon and Dixon's third requirement of discourse ethics: that all moral views on sport are to be subjected to rigorous critical scrutiny based on independent standards of reflective appraisal. This is, of course, the central feature of discourse ethics and this second version of broad internalism/interpretivism, and its claim to be a viable form of moral realism, if not the go to moral realist theory of sport. There are several aspects of this idea of rational scrutiny that Simon lumps under what he calls the "inquiry" and "respect" views of dialogical inquiry, which I take up in that order.

The first important feature of this "inquiry" view of rational dialogue is the accent placed squarely and exclusively on the intellectual cogency of the reasons advanced to support moral principles of sport. Whatever gets said in this trading back and forth of reasons for moral principles regarding the nature and purpose of sport, therefore, is to be evaluated solely on the strength of the arguments provided. In fact, Dixon claims this emphasis on the intellectual quality of arguments is "constitutive" of the discourse brand of broad internalism he and Simon go in for and of the moral realism they are peddling (2003, 111). As Dixon makes crystal clear, "Moral realists believe in moral truths that lay claim to our assent by virtue of the reasons that support them, not by virtue of their being an expression of our personal feelings (subjectivism) or those of any particular group (relativism)" (110).

The other features of the inquiry view of rational dialogue concern the conditions that it must obtain if its aim of generating intellectually cogent moral principles of sport is to be successful. Foremost in this regard is the necessity that the rational standards of reflective appraisal used to judge the intellectual strength of the reasons given for candidate moral principles be truly independent of the historical and social context and background in which they emanate, and, more generally, of cultural, linguistic, and pragmatic considerations that might initially have informed them (Simon 2004, 125). So although the actual giving and asking for reasons is a wholly social and historical matter, since it must begin and unfold in the particular social and historical settings in which the discoursers find themselves, the standards by which the justificatory force of what they have to say is evaluated are, by contrast, a wholly asocial, ahistorical, context-independent matter. For rational cogency, rightly understood, is not a local, partisan notion. That means both the arguments put forward in dialogue and the standards that inform them are both fair game for criticism (2004, 128). For that to be possible, the standards by which we judge the rational cogency of arguments for moral principles to guide athletic conduct must be truly independent ones that do not help themselves to the prevailing standards of some particular community or other.

Further, if these context-independent standards of reflective appraisal are to do the rational work that Simon and Dixon ask them to do in this moral regard, they must be impartially applied across the board by discoursers themselves. Discoursers are thus obliged to set aside their own personal evaluative preferences as well as their historically situated evaluative perspectives (if they differ from their personal views) so arguments advanced for moral principles of sport are judged on their intellectual merits alone (Simon 2004, 130). Otherwise, the independent standards for evaluating reasons put forth in dialogue will be compromised by the personal and/or local prejudices of the discoursers. Failure to honor these standards, therefore, is a basic violation of rational discourse itself.

Finally in this "inquiry sense," the point of putting in play independent standards of rational dialogue and requiring discoursers to impartially follow them is to ensure that whatever moral principles of sport that survive critical scrutiny from all quarters are the most rationally defensible moral principles. There is no reason in this regard, Simon and Dixon argue, to shoot for anything less than moral principles that command universal assent by all relevant parties. That is, while insisting on universal validity on the front end, before rational dialogue even gets off the ground, is at best a philosophical conceit, aiming for universal validity on the back end, at the end of inquiry, is anything but. Indeed, Simon and Dixon regard it as a quite reasonable aim of rational dialogue, even if it is not always realizable. After all, if we avail ourselves of independent standards of rational evaluation and plausibly expect discoursers to shed their personal and social preferences to comply with them—thereby letting the dialogue run its natural reflective course—it is not unreasonable to suppose that we will end up with moral principles that are universally valid. Typically, the best explanation of why deliberative parties have converged on a particular moral view of sport after having considered and met all objections raised against it is that it is the most intellectually cogent moral view of sport in the offing, and thus warrants our universal support (Simon 2004, 135).

Still, Simon and Dixon, like Russell, are committed fallibilists and, therefore, are under no illusion that when dialogical parties converge on a common moral view of sport, its universal validity can simply be presumed, not at least with complete surety. For one, there can be no assurance that in future dialogue, when new voices and new points of view are added to the conversational mix, whatever common conclusion reached about how sport should be done in the past may not survive further critical scrutiny. For another, it cannot even be assured that deliberative parties will be able to converge on a single, considered moral view of sport, one that meets the rational concurrence of all concerned. Indeed, more often than we might care to admit, compelling arguments are often presented on moral matters like this one from several different and conflicting perspectives, none of which can win the day. In such all too common instances, what we get instead of the hoped-for rational consensus is a rational deadlock, a rational impasse that prevents us from moving the rational needle forward. Simon and Dixon, however, remain steadfast in their commitment to the universal promise of rational dialogue and are persuaded that "stability, long-term immunity to refutation, coherence, and cogency" are not only reasonable expectations of such discourse but reliable evidence that when convergence on a common moral view of sport is attainable, such outcomes cannot be ruled out a priori as universally valid (Simon 2004, 135). They are also persuaded that when such dialogue does not lead to the sought-after rational consensus, when instead it is rent by competing arguments that lead to conflicting conclusions, that is no reason to wring our hands and give up on rational argument altogether. Quite the contrary, it is reason to keep the dialogue going, to push inquiry further in the "hope that continuing the dialectic of debate at a high level of argumentation will permit emergence of increasingly defensible views, ideally (though in practice rarely) culminating in arguments so cogent that they win almost universal allegiance" (Dixon 2003, 113).

Finally, the "respect" feature of discourse ethics is a natural complement to its key "inquiry" feature. The giving and asking for reasons will not get us where we want to go, rationally speaking, unless the dialogical relations that structure such rational interchange are respectful of persons qua discoursers as the rational and thinking beings they are. So listening and carefully considering what discoursers have to say is how we show them the respect they are owed "as free and equal moral beings" (Simon 2004, 129). And, of course, it is how we keep the path of moral inquiry in sport open for all who choose to traverse it in the pursuit of moral truth.

Critical Assessment of Discourse Ethics Theory of Sport

Before I get to my specific criticisms of Simon's and Dixon's discourse version of a moral realist theory of sport, I first want to acknowledge, as I do with respect to Russell's metaphysical version, the clear advance their theory makes over formalist moral theories of sport. Their success mirrors Russell's success to the extent that they too dispatch moral principles to the rescue when hard cases arise in sport, as is their wont, in which formal elements such as the rules and the lusory attitude prove to be normatively toothless. But where they do Russell one better in this regard is their faith in the dialogical process to generate such principles, and in the case of Russell's own internal principle to provide independent confirmation of its validity, thereby circumventing the metaphysical quandaries that I claimed beset Russell's theory. So when Simon and Dixon vouch for the "internal" principle and put it and other similar general principles to work in their moral inquiries, their confidence that these principles have something more going for them than a mere historical consensus is not attributable, a la Russell, to their alleged command of the moral facts of the matter but, rather, is because of their intellectual cogency (Simon 2004, 138). Unsurprisingly then, Simon's concurrence with Russell in his catcher-interference example that the umpire, Wesley Curry, made the correct decision in calling the runner out who immediately crossed home plate after his teammate tackled the catcher had nothing to do with any claim that that decision was justified by the moral facts of the matter but everything to do with the wide consensus Curry's decision enjoyed and, crucially, that that consensus "is best explained by the relevant features of baseball and the principles (such as Russell's internal principle) that should apply under the best interpretation of the sport" (2004, 136). The moral of the Curry story and similar rule-defying stories in the eyes of Simon and Dixon then, is that the universal validity that can be plausibly attributed to their principles and the normative judgments that are derived from them is owed not to their correspondence to the moral essence of sport but to the intellectual cogency they are owed as a consequence of their dialogical vindication.

That Simon and Dixon spare us from the difficulties that attend ambitious metaphysical investigations of sport that claim privileged access to some neutral, transcendental, decontextual standpoint, or to some special capacity to get at the nonmoral and moral facts of the matter, is no small matter. But that their own discourse approach raises its own difficulties is also no small matter. It is also noteworthy that these difficulties are not entirely dissimilar from Russell's, despite their different interpretive approaches, in at least two crucial respects.

The first respect is that whatever success can be claimed for Simon and Dixon's normative handling of hard cases like the Curry one has mainly to do with the fact that all concerned were on the same page regarding the basic aim and point of sport. In light of this broad agreement, therefore, it is not a stretch to suppose that deliberative parties who even minimally put their minds to such rule-challenging examples will have no trouble converging on the common conclusion that knocking a catcher to the ground in baseball is not a reputable skill of the game and so has no plausible place in it. No such concordance, however, was obtained in one part of the pine tar case discussed in Chapter 3, in which Yankees manager Billy Martin made a tactical gambit to bring it to the umpires' attention that George Brett was using an illegal bat at the most opportune time for his team, and no such concordance can be claimed for the harder cases I cite, which include my main example of the amateur and professional split. Indeed, the signature feature of these harder cases is precisely that the parties in question fundamentally disagree about the nature and purpose of sport. Consequently, it beggars the imagination to think or claim that these rival interpretations of sport can be dialectically resolved to the mutual satisfaction of all parties if they only agree to sit down and talk over their differences.

The second respect in which Simon and Dixon's discourse ethics suffers much the same fate as Russell's metaphysical theory is that they too fail to give their due to the social and historical contexts in which conceptions of sport are germinated. This may seem surprising in Simon's and Dixon's case, since they at least gave lip service to the importance of the historical and social starting points of rational dialogue, resisting any effort to put them on a surer philosophical footing, and made it crystal clear that they reject any appeal to a "totally neutral and abstract point of view" (Simon 2004, 127) from which to issue their moral takes on how sport should be done. The problem, however, is that they quickly turn the tables on these historically situated starting points by insisting as soon as the actual dialogue kicks in gear, and the actual back-and-forth exchange of reasons and arguments commences, that what gets said and proposed is to be evaluated strictly on their intellectual merits.

On its face, that stricture seems perfectly reasonable and uncontroversial. But what it entails, as they take pains to point out, is that both the arguments made and the standards of rational acceptability that inform them are to be judged by objective, context-independent standards of reflective appraisal. Simon and Dixon further insist, as previously noted, deliberative parties must commit themselves to impartially following these objective, impersonal standards, never helping themselves to the local standards that predialogically played such a big part in their moral reasoning about sport.

This creates, I argue, two important problems. The first is where these objective, context-independent standards are supposed to come from, since Simon and Dixon, after having banished local norms from the dialogical scene, make it clear they have no stomach for the kind of foundational, philosophically derived norms that moral realists like Russell go in for. The second and larger problem is that they leave us to wonder what would persuade, let alone motivate, adherents of rival conceptions of the nature and purpose of sport to give up on those conceptions to satisfy the strict objective evaluative standards of rational dialogue as Simon and Dixon conceive it. That this is, in effect, what Simon and Dixon are asking, indeed requiring, adherents of rival conceptions of sport to do to dialogically work out their differences follows from the fact that what put these parties at loggerheads with one another in the first place is the local norms from which they derived the determinate reasons to justify the particular conceptions that they did. To suspend these local norms to gauge their intellectual cogency, as Simon and Dixon insist on, is to gut whatever rational and normative force these conceptions had going for them to begin with that attracted a sizable number of adherents to them. Doing so, of course, gets Simon and Dixon the general consensus on how sport should be done they aimed for. But calling it a rational consensus should be resisted. It is one thing to ask discoursers to respect their interlocutors and to listen to what they have to say; it is another thing entirely to ask discoursers to discount the very norms, reasons, and determinate content of what they have to say so they can converge on a common conclusion about how sport should be done. Doing the former is a basic courtesy all reasonable and decent parties to a dialogue owe to one another; doing the latter is tantamount, or so I argue in what follows, to parties committing normative hara-kiri.

Let us begin with the first problem with discourse ethics I identify above: Where are these objective, context-independent standards of rational evaluation supposed to come from, assuming they just do not fall into our dialogical laps? For if rational dialogue, as Simon and Dixon conceive it, is suppose to begin in a historical key and then quickly switch to an ahistorical evaluative one to assess the intellectual cogency of reasons ventured, and end, ideally, with universal moral principles that betray no trace of their historical lineage, then it seems theorists of discourse ethics owe us some explanation of how this is to be impartially pulled off.

One possibility that Simon mentions is John Rawls's theory of justice, which relies heavily on a notion of impartiality in the form of what he called "the veil of ignorance" to arrive at a philosophical account of justice that is acceptable to all concerned deliberative parties. Rawls's basic idea is that by requiring people to deliberate behind a veil of ignorance that conceals, among other things, their social class position or social status and their fortune in the distribution of natural assets, they will not be able to tailor principles of justice to their particular advantage. In other words, they will have "to evaluate principles [of justice] solely on the basis of general considerations" (Simon 2004, 137). By "general considerations," of course, Rawls means impartial ones. What this philosophical view of discourse has going for it that is congenial to Simon's and Dixon's take on discourse is that it forces parties to generate moral principles from a perspective shared by others, "rather than a vanishing point separate from any perspective whatsoever" (133). That is, it demonstrates how it is possible to achieve a universal consensus on such principles based strictly on their intellectual merits without appealing to some Archimedean, perspective-free vantage point of the philosophical, foundational sort that Simon pointedly eschewed. What is more, it also shows how "a view that arises in a particular historical situation" can come to be regarded by all parties to the discourse as a universally valid one (133). In short, it demystifies how we can begin on a historical, contextual, partisan note and end on a universal, context-independent, nonpartisan one.

However, Simon does not directly follow up on Rawls's philosophical approach to discourse in his own attempt to spin out moral principles of sport. Part of the reason, no doubt, is owed to his general wariness of philosophical discourse, despite the fact that Rawls's version largely makes do without the customary metaphysical and epistemological trappings of other kindred philosophical efforts.[1] But I think it is more likely that the main reason he does not follow in Rawls's footsteps has to do with a view he shares not only with his fellow discourse theorist Dixon but as well with his fellow broad internalist Russell. That view is that it is easier to pin down the nature and purpose of sport than it is most other social practices because of its relatively clear, carefully demarcated features so ably limned by Bernard Suits. For as Suits's account showed, which all broad internalists endorsed, the central aim of sport is "to develop and exhibit excellence at overcoming the sport specific obstacles created by the rules" (Simon 2007, 44).[2] Because sport is nothing if not a paradigmatic perfectionist practice, the objective, context-independent standards needed to assess the conceptions of sport and the moral principles divined in its name by deliberative parties has been staring us in the face all this time. After all, if excellence is, literally, the name of the game, then the standards of excellence of sport itself provide the impartial standards we need to test the intellectual cogency of candidate moral principles advanced in dialogue. Hence, there is no need to go through Rawlsian hoops or any other philosophical hoops to put discourse on the right objective and, ideally, universal track. We, thus, should not have been surprised in the least that Simon and Dixon so quickly and effortlessly signed on to Russell's internal principle in spite of their insistence on going their own dialectical way.

The answer to the first problem concerning where these objective standards for reflectively evaluating the various moral principles advanced in dialogue regarding how sport should be done are to be found is the notion of athletic excellence itself. Of course, if Simon and Dixon are to derive their objective evaluative standards from this notion of athletic excellence, then they will have to abstract from the particular, historically rooted understandings of athletic excellence that each party brings with it to the dialogical table. Otherwise, they can be justifiably accused of their own partisan bias.

Now that we have a clear answer to the first problem of determining what impartial standards Simon and Dixon had in mind to guide the dialogical process, we can turn to the second and more important problem I previously mentioned concerning whether these abstract standards of evaluation culled from the perfectionist purpose of sport can do the moral work they ask them to do. My negative answer here should not be surprising, given that their answer to the first problem brought us back to familiar abstract normative territory. After all, we have been down this abstract path before when we considered Russell's moral principles of sport, which were found wanting in Chapter 3 because they proved far too abstract to handle harder cases like the amateur and professional divide. Because Simon and Dixon's own favored moral principles, especially their retention of Russell's internal principle, are every bit as abstract and detached from the social and historical milieu in which the amateur and professional athletic communities midwifed their particular conceptions of the purpose of sport as Russell's, I think they are vulnerable to the same criticism, notwithstanding the different route they took to divine them. However, because Simon has responded to similar criticisms of his and his fellow broad internalists' work along this abstract line that I have made in previous essays, my critical response takes its point of departure from his pointed and thoughtful objections.[3]

First, however, I need to briefly rehearse my main argument that Simon's and Dixon's moral principles, like Russell's, are too abstract for their own good. My argument in a nutshell is that asking objective, impartial standards of rational evaluation drawn from a general notion of athletic excellence to resolve conflicts over the nature and purpose of sport of the sort posed by the amateur and professional dispute is asking them to do something they are constitutionally unfit to do. For what each party is disputing in this and other kindred normative cases is not whether sport involves the pursuit of excellence—on that general point they all concur—but rather what conception of athletic excellence and the mix of skills, attitudes, resolve, and the like that follow in its wake best capture its perfectionist character. On this very specific point, each party to the dispute is convinced its account is the correct one and the other's mistaken. Resolving harder, knottier normative conflicts like this one, which confidently, and I think presumptively, suggests one party has to be right and the other wrong, is not in the cards if an ahistorical and asocial conception of athletic excellence is our standard bearer.

Simon's and Dixon's efforts to install just such a context-independent notion of athletic excellence to determine who is in the right and who in the wrong here is thus bound to disappoint, if not fated to fail.

Although I am persuaded that Simon's appeal to a general, objective conception of athletic excellence to derive moral principles of sport does manage to avoid one horn of the normative dilemma he sketches of "too uncritical immersion" in our "actual situation," I am not convinced that it is successful in avoiding the other horn of this dilemma, what he labels "excessive abstraction from our actual situation" (2004, 126). It is precisely its excessive abstraction that I regard as its major drawback.

Simon begs to differ, however. His first line of attack is simple and direct, which is to reprise an argument made famous by Donald Davidson to the effect that the differences that pit these two athletic communities against one another cannot be as radical as I claim; if they were, neither of the contending parties would be able to recognize the other's account of sport as a conception of sport at all (2015, 30). This clearly was not the case in the amateur and professional conflict, and I suspect Simon thinks in most conflicts over the nature and purpose of sport, it is true as well that each side understood what the other was saying. In this particular conflict, however, there can be no doubt that members of the amateur and professional communities recognized and understood the other community was committed to an intelligible conception of sport, even if a conception at odds with its own. This is relevant to Simon's point because it means amateurs understood the particular points and arguments professionals were trying to make and vice versa. More important, it also means there was enough overlap in their respective beliefs about the nature and purpose of sport to work out the differences that remain between them. But only, Simon hastens to add, if the standards of reflective appraisal each abides by in their rational interchange with one another draws from this common fund of beliefs rather than from beliefs they disagree about, which, if referenced, would lead to a partisan outcome favoring one side over the other.

On this view, then, everything hangs on just what beliefs about sport each rival party shares. Simon's ready reply: "Both sides view sport as a rule-governed activity creating obstacles that exist to challenge the competitors and both sides presumably view the attempt to meet these challenges as valuable" (2015, 31). Simon thinks this is commonality enough to iron out the differences between the amateur and professional communities, to come up with a hybrid conception of sport agreeable to both camps, despite their starkly different starting points (31).

I think Simon's Davidsonian, antiradical incommensurability argument, however, misses the mark; it mistakenly presumes that the overlap in beliefs that explains why each side of the amateur and professional divide can *understand* the arguments made by the other side is sufficient to make *rational argument* between them fruitful as well. It is this inference that I dispute. But to do so I must first address the former point and make plain that, contrary to Simon's assertion, I have never claimed that amateurs and professionals shared no beliefs regarding the nature of sport; if this were true, as Simon, following Dixon, aver, it would render each side clueless as to what the other side was trying to argue. Quite the contrary, I concur with Simon that both amateurs and professionals alike did share the general view that sport is a rule-governed activity, the point of which is to determine who is the most excellent in overcoming the obstacles and challenges the rules create. I also agree with him that this shared view of the aim of sport meant that amateurs understood perfectly well the particular points professionals were trying to make and vice versa. Indeed, with this very point in mind, I criticized Simon's and Dixon's moral theory of sport as normatively unworkable when dealing with harder moral cases like the amateur and professional conflict. For if the impartial standards for rationally assessing the intellectual cogency of a proffered view of sport are drawn from such a general and thin conception of athletic excellence as Simon and Dixon require, then not only would both the amateur and professional perfectionist views of sport pass that test, but they would do so with flying colors. This is not, of course, a compliment to the abstract level at which their theory is pitched, but rather a criticism of it as much too abstract, bereft of determinative content, to offer a useful rational way forward to resolve the substantive differences between them, let alone to recognize and address these differences.

So my beef with Simon's and Dixon's discourse ethics is not that it fails to explain how each side of this dispute could understand what the other was up to—on that account they clearly succeeded—but rather its failure to show how each side might rationally resolve the differences between them to the mutual satisfaction of both. This is the normative crux of the matter, and this is where I think discourse ethics fails to deliver. To rationally resolve such conflicts would require a much greater overlap in their beliefs about the proper aim of sport, a meeting of the minds that is conspicuously absent in these harder normative cases. What stands in the way of any such happy rational, dialectical resolution is none other than the disparate historical starting points from which rational dialogue is supposed to take its point of departure, starting points that Simon and Dixon consistently and steadfastly maintained are to be honored and not replaced in favor of some other more secure, philosophical starting point. But giving these historically situated starting points their dialogical due is tantamount to blocking any rationally inferential path that might lead from an amateur to a professional or from a professional to an amateur way of seeing sport. If we start with the amateur premise that sport is a leisurely avocation, or from the professional premise that sport is a deadly serious vocation, there does not seem to be any rationally satisfactory way to settle the dispute over which is the correct conception of sport, short of taking leave of rational argument altogether and making a leap of faith in either direction.

This is why I am not persuaded by Simon's conjecture that even if someone in a historical context put forward the modest proposition that competitors should not cheat to win, "it not only might win the assent of all reasonable parties," but the ensuing discussion "might also provide strong (although not infallible) grounds for thinking that such a conclusion would be found warranted by any reasonable person who considered the issue on the merits" (Simon 2004, 134). My skepticism here is not because I have doubts that reasonable deliberative parties would have any trouble signing on to the general proposition that cheating to win in sport is morally wrong but because I have serious doubts that members of either the amateur or professional community, or of any other communities who do not see eye to eye on what is the purpose of sport, would be able to agree on just what constitutes cheating in the local sense at issue in these harder, conflicting normative cases. What goes for cheating in this regard goes doubly so for Simon's bolder claim that interlocutors who hold conflicting accounts of the purpose of sport, especially those of the amateur and professional persuasions, might mutually arrive at the rational conclusion that strategic fouls are best regarded as "a price for exercising a strategic option" rather than "a punishment for misbehavior" (2007, 46).

I have a lot more to say regarding the limits of rational argument in harder normative cases like this one, but for now I want to move on to Simon's second objection to my criticism that discourse ethics is guilty of excess abstraction. His objection in this instance is that I have wrongly, and perhaps conveniently for my critical purposes, "divided" the amateur and professional conceptions of sport into "isolated paradigms," thereby immunizing them against external scrutiny (Morgan 2015, 45).[4] This criticism differs from his first criticism because it does not just try to show that these two athletic camps share a common perfectionist view of sport but offers a possible explanation as to why such an overlap in their beliefs regarding the purpose of sport is highly likely, even inevitable. His explanation is that I have, in effect, stacked the deck against any possible rational commensuration of the amateur and professional conceptions of sport by trying to pass them off as ideal types whose borders are so tightly sealed that they allow no possible cross-contamination, so to speak, of their core features. But nothing could be further from the truth, Simon argues, because both the amateur and professional views of sport are not pure, ideal types, but decidedly mixed and messy social constructions put together, and this is the important bit, in part by incorporating elements of their predecessors' social constructions of sport. When we disabuse ourselves of this bad idea of isolated paradigms of sport, Simon argues, we will have reopened the door to their possible rational commensuration, to putting dialogue back on track in the effort to reach a universal consensus on the nature and purpose of sport that warrants the assent of all rational parties.

However, I do not think I am guilty, as Simon alleges, of trying to pass off amateur and professional notions of sport as ideal types. Rather, I readily agree with Simon that they are indeed messy social constructions that liberally borrow features from other equally messy social notions of sport. But I have first to own up to the fact that in some of my earlier essays I carelessly portrayed these two rival conceptions in ways that gave the impression they were indeed "isolated paradigms," and in doing so misled Simon. However, in a subsequent essay I do try to clarify that I do not, in fact, regard the amateur and professional takes on sport as ideal types (2015). That clarification bears repeating here, which means reiterating that both of these conceptions did indeed purloin some of their core features of sport from past conceptions of sport. In the particular case of amateur sport, its heralding of the gentleman approach to sport partly borrowed from a medieval conception of social hierarchy and partly from the Renaissance ideal of the courtier who was adept at many things "but supreme (by dint of hard practice) at none of them" (Guttmann 1978, 31–32). In the particular case of professional sport, at least in the incipient phase that I choose to focus on, its heralding of sport as what Michael Walzer calls a "career open to talent" (1987, 23) toned down but did not wholly repudiate the amateur-rooted wariness of doing sport mainly for financial remuneration. So Simon is entirely right that both conceptions of sport are not pure, unadulterated, ideal types. However, I think Simon is wrong to claim that their mixed historical pedigrees make them eligible or credible candidates for rational commensuration. That is because the amalgam of features that define their respective cores, some of which are genuinely novel creations and others of which have been cribbed from their predecessors, paint a conflicting picture of the nature and purpose of sport. That is why for all their innovating, mixing, and matching, they cannot agree on how sport should be done.

I also do not think, and have not claimed, that these different conceptions of sport are immune to external reflective scrutiny as Simon insinuates. I see no reason why, therefore, adherents of amateurism cannot have a critical go at its professional counterparts or adherents of professionalism returning the favor to its amateur counterparts. It is true, however, that my position on the limits of moral argument suggests such external criticism seldom bears fruit, that most of the time it amounts to little more than hurling invective at one's opponents. Indeed, much of the critical parrying back and forth that took place between amateurs and professionals of the day, at least that part reported in the press, did not lead to any rational breakthroughs, since each side insisted on attacking the other by its own lights, by appealing to its local norms, rather than by the lights, the local norms, of the other. There is, however, a long and distinguished line of external criticism in philosophy itself, which consists of exposing how alternative normative systems of belief fail by their own lights, by their own norms and on their own terms.[5] The aim of such criticism is to show that a particular normative system commits an important self-referential inconsistency. Perhaps one of the better-known examples of such criticism in the recent history of analytic philosophy concerned the positivist trichotomous classification of linguistic expressions as either tautologies or empirical hypotheses or cognitively meaningless assertions. Critics of positivism retorted: Which linguistic category does this positivist claim fall under?[6] Had either side of the present dispute tried this immanent critical route, it might have been able to do some real damage to the other, presuming, of course, that either one of these rival conceptions of sport were guilty of such a self-referential inconsistency.

Simon's remaining important criticisms zeroed in on what he took to be the negative fallout of my rejection of his and Dixon's own dialogical moral theory of sport, in particular, of giving up on its universalistic aspirations and settling for a local, historically situated moral view of sport. It was in this vein that he criticized me for opting for an ill-defined local community version of discourse rather than a universal community of discourse, for effectively abandoning all pretense of impartiality in moral inquiry, and, perhaps the most egregious related offense in their eyes, for swapping out intellectually cogent rational arguments that justify a conception of sport to all reasonable parties for what particular communities find agreeable as a conception of sport based on their collective particular preferences.

According to the first criticism then, Simon objected to my relegating rational dialogue to the confines of particular practice communities on two grounds: (1) It is not clear "who is to do the discoursing" in such a community—is it critical media types or philosophical theorists or social critics or spectators or athletes themselves?—and (2) it inappropriately shifts the focus from the intellectual cogency of what gets said to "who said what" (2004, 128). I do not think it does either of these two things. My short answer to the first question—who gets to do the discoursing?—is simply whoever shares enough beliefs, ideas, and discursive standards to make rational argument possible and productive. My short answer to the second question, with this first point in mind, is whoever has the strongest reasons to defend the view of sport under consideration. My longer answers to both questions, in the order presented, follow.

The idea that belonging to a community means, among other things, trafficking in a shared evaluative vocabulary that binds members of that community to a common fund of beliefs, reasons, and norms that guide and shape how they practically and morally think about a social practice like sport is nothing new and certainly not an especially outlandish, radical idea. In fact, this view is held by a number of philosophers, though expressed in a variety of ways. For instance, Rawls tells us "a community is . . . an association or society whose unity rests on a comprehensive conception of the good," of what its members regard to be a valuable way to live (1999, 431). Closer to my own notion of an athletic practice community, Wilfrid Sellars thinks morality is a matter of what he calls "we-intentions," the main idea of which is that "people constitute a community, a we, by virtue of thinking of each other as one of us, and by willing the common good not under the species of benevolence—but by willing it as one of us, or from a moral point of view" (1968, 222). To be sure, this is a less intellectualistic picture of a discourse community than Simon's and Dixon's notion, not just in the number of people who qualify as actual or potential members but in the more basic sense that the evaluative beliefs, reasons, and norms shared by members of such a community do not have to be reflectively dredged up every time they interact with one another. Rather, the moral vocabulary members of such a community matter-of-factly converse in is a consequence of their membership in that community, of having been socialized into it and having internalized the common beliefs that define it as the particular moral community that it is. To put the same point differently, to be a member of a moral community, one must to a great extent be, as David Velleman claims, "ordinary" (2013, 55)—that is, to morally think about sport using reasons and rhetoric that one's fellow discoursers can recognize as indeed reasons and rhetoric that have persuasive force, and so, the sort of people (one of us, to be specific) who one can profitably reason with. Not to think in these ordinary moral ways is no small matter because it constitutes grounds for branding a discussant as unreasonable, as ineligible to engage in rational discourse, as someone to be written off as "too weird to [be] bothered with," or, in extreme cases, to be "a humanoid creature . . . of some unrecognizable kind" (Velleman 2013, 54, 55).

My answer to this first criticism also answers the second criticism. The very idea of intellectual cogency, of a convincing reason, is not something that can be determined in a vacuum. In a word, there is no such thing as an intrinsically good reason, a reason whose intellectual force is wholly independent of the context in which it is asserted. So there is a good reason why asserting the divine right of kings in an argument, say, about political justice is no longer considered a good reason, let alone a reason at all. Just as there is good reason why the intellectual force of the reason English members of the amateur camp gave for criticizing American professionals "boorishly serious" regard for sport, their deficiency in "the gentler feelings" (Crowther 1907, 499) was entirely lost on the Americans, and why the intellectual force of the Americans' counterargument castigating the shocking hedonism of English athletes, their appalling "leisurely dilettantism" (Dyreson 1989, 264) was entirely lost on the English.[7] My argument for moving the giving and asking for reasons to the interior of the evaluative language games of practice communities, therefore, does not take the focus off of the intellectual quality of the reasons given or asked for and put it instead on "who said what," as Simon and Dixon suppose, but, contrarily, furnishes the context for how the notion of intellectual cogency is being used and assessed. And if it is asked how my community-based picture of dialogue and social interaction, which proceeds for the most part quite nicely without the need for reflective scrutiny of what gets said, is even hospitable to reason-giving and asking in the first place, my answer is that it arises quite naturally whenever a member of that community thinks he or she is normatively entitled to make a certain claim about the purpose of sport and is challenged by other members of that community. When that happens, which is by no means a rare or isolated occurrence, what previously had not been a matter of reflective scrutiny between a discourser and his or her fellow members automatically becomes a matter for reflective scrutiny between them. So although my view of rational dialogue is not as intellectualist as Simon's and Dixon's, it is no less friendly to rational argument, rightly contextualized, as theirs.

Simon and Dixon are not likely to be swayed by my first-pass attempt to show that intellectual cogency is not foreign to my local conception of rational dialogue but is one of its central features. For their third criticism to come directly attacks that claim. But their more immediate critical concern, which takes me to their second criticism, is that my local account of rational dialogue is surely guilty, no matter what I may claim about its alleged fealty to intellectual cogency, of violating the other signature feature of a truly rational dialogue, that of impartiality. On this matter, there is no question in their minds not only of the highly partisan character of my take on rational dialogue but that I do not even deign to try to give it an impartial gloss. After all, the kind of intra-community back-and-forth interchange that I countenance and that was on vivid display within and between the amateur and professional camps was nothing if not partisan. For each was championing a homegrown, parochial conception of sport and made no bones about the fact that that was what they were promulgating. Thus, any exhortation that they should bracket their partisan standpoints and consider the matter of how sport should be done from an impartial standpoint would not have sat well with either side. So much then, Simon and Dixon would likely conclude, for impartiality.

The charge that my community-based account of rational dialogue requires giving up on impartiality is true in one important sense. My account does, in fact, rule out the idea of impartiality between and among the evaluative vocabularies of different athletic practice communities. But so does, I hasten to add, Simon's and Dixon's account of discourse ethics. As should be all too clear by now, they, too, insist rational dialogue must give credence to, not breach, the historical starting points in which discoursers find themselves; this is why Simon rejects the idea that an "impartial perspective" is synonymous with "a view from nowhere but rather . . . a view from a morally appropriate perspective" (2004, 139). Appealing, then, to some normative super vocabulary to evaluate local normative vocabularies is out of the question for them and me. But where I differ from Simon and company is what I take to be "a view from a morally appropriate perspective." For me, a view from a morally appropriate perspective is a view from a community perspective, not a view, as they would have us believe, from some yet to be determined extra-community perspective. This is crucial to my rebuttal of their charge that I put no credence in impartial moral inquiry, because my view that a community perspective is the morally appropriate perspective, the view from this particular "here" rather than "the view from nowhere," serves notice that I endorse rather than reject impartiality when it is suitably qualified in this contextual sense. That is, I fully subscribe to the notion that a rational dialogue requires that it be open to all comers, no matter who they might be, as long as they share enough beliefs, ideas, and normative standards regarding the nature and purpose of sport to make fruitful rational interchange between and among them possible. Impartiality of this intra-community kind is, therefore, indispensable to, not a victim of, my local notion of rational dialogue.

This brings me to Simon's and Dixon's third and final criticism, that my local, community-grounded account of rational dialogue and what makes for intellectually cogent argument is a sham, a thinly disguised attack on rational dialogue and practical rationality itself. Although both criticize me on this score, their arguments differ somewhat with Dixon offering the more full-throated rebuttal; however, Simon's counterargument is no less potentially damaging. I begin with Dixon.

As Dixon sees it, accounts of rational dialogue and argument like mine do not have a critical leg to stand on because they crudely substitute what a community simply agrees is the right or wrong thing to do for defensible rational arguments as to what is the right thing or wrong thing to do in and outside of sport. The effect of this substitution of community assent for rational justification is that it indemnifies whatever happens to be the prevailing view on how sport should be done within such a community from rational scrutiny and criticism. Which is just another way of saying that "what makes the status quo right is just that it is the status quo, not that it is supported by defensible reasons" (Dixon 2003, 108). As an illustration of what he is getting at, he asks us to consider the hypothetical example of "a skating community" who had come to view secret "quid pro quo arrangements among judges as an accepted practice . . . hop[ing] that true talent will still rise to the top in spite of these backroom machinations" (106).[8] Given Dixon's complaint that views like mine run together rational acceptability with community assent, he claims there is no way we can "account for the possibility that the dominant view of an athletic community," in his hypothetical, the skating community's acceptance of such a quid pro quo arrangement, "might be mistaken" (110).

Simon, too, criticizes me for holding that "the actual consensus of some community of practitioners" is all that is required to meet the test of rational acceptability, countering that "we agree to [a view of sport] because of the intellectual considerations in their favor rather than find them intellectually favored because we agree" (2007, 48). Unlike Dixon, however, Simon grants that my communitarian account of intellectual cogency does not amount to endorsement of the status quo just because it is the status quo, because the reigning views of an actual community may be found intellectually indefensible if they violate its own normative standards. For instance, the amateur community's gentleman-based conception of sport and the professional community's vocational conception of sport would both find Dixon's example of the skating community's secret acceptance of quid quo pro arrangements among judges as intellectually indefensible, given their respective conceptions of the nature and purpose of sport (2004, 125). So Simon thinks my position has some critical heft, but not enough, he hastens to point out, to pass muster. Why? Because in my view, intellectual cogency is solely determined by the reflective standards and norms of a community, such that if any view runs afoul of these local standards and norms, its intellectual merit is either not recognized or dismissed (128). This is a problem, indeed a fatal one, as Simon sees it, because in a rational dialogue worthy of the name everything should be up for grabs, both the particular arguments proposed and the standards that inform them. Intellectual cogency rightly understood requires thinking outside the community's normative box—that is, "a willingness to strive for supporting reasons that have force apart from our interests in the matter"

(133). In Simon's view then, "there is no reason for discoursers to regard the intellectual second-order standards of the community as sacrosanct" (128).

These are serious criticisms, and they need to be disarmed if my account of practical reason and moral inquiry as it relates to sport is to stand. I begin by responding to what I regard to be Dixon's mistaken account of what theorists like me understand by a community's agreement or consent. I next respond to Simon's criticism that intellectual cogency rightly understood is and must be an extra-community rather than an intra-community normative matter and argue that when we are dealing with thick conceptions of the good qua sport that characterize both the hard cases Simon and Dixon feature and the harder cases I feature, seeking extra-community justificatory support is unnecessary in the hard cases and not a rational option in the harder cases.[9]

My claim that rational agreement or consensus within a community of inquiry or practice is what determines the intellectual cogency or quality of rational argument and dialogue piggybacks off of Ludwig Wittgenstein's claim that "the *speaking* of a language is part of an activity, or of a form of life" (1958, 23; emphasis in original). I think what Wittgenstein is driving at here is that agreement on what moral language to speak with regard to sport, on what evaluative vocabulary to draw our rational judgments and normative standards from to assess how sport should be done, is an agreement first and foremost on the point and purpose of athletic forms of life. If we cannot agree on the point of sport, which is no small matter, since local agreements regarding the purpose of sport are always historically dense and contextually thick conceptions of athletic purpose, then we will be at a loss, I take Wittgenstein to be saying, as to how to think and justify moral claims regarding athletic conduct. This explains why he asks himself, "So you are saying human agreement decides what is true and what is false?" and why he responds to the contrary in his following answer: "It is what human beings *say* that is true and false; and what they agree on in the *language* they use. That is not agreement in opinions but in form of life" (241; emphasis in original). So agreement on an athletic form of life is not agreement on whatever happen to be the nonmoral or moral opinions the members of a community might have at any one time; this would reduce rational justification, as Dixon claims, more or less to crudely tallying or polling their opinions to see which ones dominate sans actual rational deliberation. Rather, to reiterate, the crucial agreement here is on the purpose of sport. Why this point is so important is that such agreement does not preempt rational deliberation on the right thing to do in sport but, contrarily, puts in place the relevant norms and creates a logical space of reasons in which moral deliberation can do its critical bidding. Community agreement rightly understood is what makes it possible to criticize the status quo, to attack prevailing views of sport, such as the secret machinations of Dixon's hypothetical skating community that run afoul of local standards of rational acceptability.

That community agreement on a form of life is normative agreement enough to get rational dialogue off on the right footing and to keep it on the right footing should not be all that surprising. After all, when we inquire as to whether some action in sport is right or wrong, we are not asking whether it is right or wrong *tout court*, but right or wrong to people like us who hold the specific views we do about athletic forms of life. For moral judgments, reasons, and claims over whether something is right or wrong are, as Velleman tells us, like claims that someone is tall (2013, 49). Questions like these can only be intelligibly posed and answered in context-dependent ways, since, of course, someone may be tall in one community or culture and not in another. Just as it makes no sense to ask if someone is tall *simpliciter*, it makes no sense to ask is some action right or wrong in sport *simpliciter*, unless there is agreement among all rational parties in the past, now, and forevermore as to the aim and purpose of sport. But such general, universal agreements are not in the offing if the history of sport is any indication, save the most basic and morally platitudinous features of sport.

What goes in general for sport goes in particular in the harder cases at issue presently. For the amateur and professional athletic communities, as should be all too clear by now, have quite different views on what sport is and should be all about. So when moral issues arise in and between such rival communities, they are deeply embedded in the cultural understandings and mores of their communities and, indeed, can only arise in these contexts given their particular social views of sport. That means when members of either community ask themselves what is the right thing to do in sport, each is asking what the right thing is to do for "us" (fellow amateurs and professionals) here and now. For amateurs, it means, among other specific things, engaging in sport as an end in itself, seeking a pleasurable experience, treating sport as an occasion for spontaneous activity rather than as part of a plan of action and even less so as a part of one's life plan, checking ambition and hubris at every turn, and exhibiting generosity toward one's opponents. All things we would expect of a gentleman athlete and his peers. For professionals, it means, among other specific things, treating sport as a serious enterprise, making a career out of sport and thus an important part of one's overall life plan, seeking recognition for athletic accomplishment, and trying to best one's opponents in a fair contest. Again, all things we would expect of a professional, vocationally minded athlete and his peers. What is the right thing to do in sport is thus inescapably what is the right thing to do for people who have been socialized in these highly particular ways to value these particular qualities of sport. In both cases, members of these two communities are drawing on a particular point of view, culturally grounded moral ideals, and background social understandings to make sense of their particular athletic lives. That means the moral arguments they trade back and forth in rational dialogue are necessarily local ones that follow from and build on these deep cultural understandings. It also suggests that what these "idiomatic, particularist, and circumstantial" arguments reflect, as Walzer nicely puts it, "is the socially constructed idealism of these people" (1994, 39).

All of which goes to show and underscore that Dixon's criticism of community assent for its alleged normative nonchalance and quietism, for the apparent fact that it cannot help but rubber-stamp every opinion on how sport should be done that shows up on its radar screen, misses the mark. In point of fact, it does just the opposite when rightly understood as agreement on a form of life, which is what gives athletic communities the normative license they need to criticize prevailing views of sport that contravene such community agreement. Whether then owing to coercive economic or political pressures or simple practical or moral expediency, athletic communities that find themselves in situations like Dixon's hypothetical skating community have, in fact, good reason to criticize the behavior Dixon attributed to that community. In the specific cases of the amateur and professional communities, I believe I have said enough about each to confidently claim that both camps, based on their respective agreements on the point and purpose of sport and the norms of rational acceptability and moral ideals they put in play, similarly had good reasons (though not the same reasons) to contest such morally dubious quid pro quo secret arrangements.

But my argument that we should entrust the normative bona fides of athletic communities to carry out the rational work needed to justify how sport should be done at a particular time and place need not confine itself to hypothetical examples like Dixon's when there are plenty of historical examples to choose from. To take just one illustrative and instructive example, as early as the 1912 Stockholm Games, there was grumbling among members of the amateur English community that its mounting losses to American professionals were taking a toll on its collective psyche. In short, they were sick and tired of being defeated time after time by their chief rivals. Two factions subsequently emerged, one of which urged they drop out of the Games altogether, but the other of which contrarily urged it was time to change the English outlook on sport and sink large sums of money into training facilities and the like to reverse their athletic fortunes (Dyreson 1998, 164–165). What the latter faction represents, I think, is a classic case of a community under siege, whose members, under the harsh glare of the press and an increasingly angry and frustrated public, eschew rational deliberation in favor of a quick fix. They are the equivalent, I believe, of Dixon's skating community, since they, too, found themselves searching for an expedient solution to their predicament. But just as in the Dixon example, here too the amateur community is not merely a captive of whatever its members might happen to think and believe how sport should be organized and conducted at any one time, owing to prevailing and pressing dominant social and political forces. For the amateur community has good reason to reject this faction's proposal to, in effect, ape its American rivals because doing so would clearly undermine practically everything it stands for. What is important here is not which faction in the end prevailed, but only that community agreement on a form of life is not the rational dead end and enemy of moral inquiry that Dixon suggests it is. Quite the contrary, it is what makes it possible for any community to rationally deliberate and morally evaluate what it ought to do in such all too common cases. This is why I think that community agreement on a form of life is agreement enough to do the rational and morally obligatory work that falls squarely, as it should in my view, on the shoulders of athletic communities like these.

I can imagine Simon chiming in at this juncture and urging disputants in cases like these to broaden their outlook and outreach and "strive for supporting reasons that have force apart from [their] interests in the matter" (2004, 133). I thus now need to say why I think his objection that intra-community agreement on an athletic form of life is not agreement enough to do the kind of reflective normative work I claim it alone can do fails, and why, therefore, we should resist his suggestion to seek an extra-community perspective to do the job.

To understand Simon's objection here, we need briefly to retrace our steps a bit and try to figure out just what sort of extra-community, impartial perspective he is urging on us. We can safely begin by eliminating Nagel's fabled view from nowhere because Simon has resolutely sworn off any appeal to such an abstract, decontextualized perspective. We can also safely eliminate as a candidate any appeal to a claimed natural order of reasons to put dialogue on a surer footing—that is, the idea that there is a "natural order of reasons . . . which is not determined by any historical or other empirical forces, but which is somehow intrinsic to rationality itself" (Rorty 2000, 1). After all, Simon's disavowal of the view from nowhere and his insistence that the historical starting points of the members of the discourse community be given their just due accords with Susan Hurley's point that "the existence of certain shared practices, any of which might not have existed, is all that our determinate reasons . . . to do anything rests on" (quoted in Rorty 1998, 205).[10]

I am on firm ground in claiming that Simon shares at least this much in common with historicist philosophers like Rorty who argue that "there is nothing beyond vocabularies which serves as a criterion of choice between them" (Rorty 1989, 80). If I am right about this, then that means that the extra-community perspective he is championing is reaching out to other athletic communities and their evaluative norms and vocabularies for "supporting reasons" that go beyond those of our own community. By adding different community perspectives to the mix, Simon thinks we can fortify our homegrown reasons and arguments to justify how we think sport should be done.

But I think such extra-community normative outreach in many cases is unnecessary and in some cases tantamount to committing normative suicide. It is typically not necessary when there is already wide agreement on the purpose of sport of the sort we saw in the hard cases cited by Simon and company. As previously noted, when a base runner crosses home plate and then interferes with the catcher to allow his teammates to score, the loophole in the rules the offending party exploited is easily resolved by appeal to the baseball community's agreement that wrestling a catcher to the ground is not what baseball is all about and, therefore, not how it should be done. In these hard cases, searching for further justificatory support outside of the baseball community is pointless.

However, seeking outside justificatory support in the harder cases is not only pointless but disastrous. In normative conflicts like the amateur and professional one, in which there is deep disagreement as to what sport is and should be, seeking the rational counsel of the other is an invitation to interminable rational conflict and recrimination rather than, as Simon opined, a way to rationally resolve the differences between them. To see why such normative outreach is a rational disaster waiting to happen, we need only to remind ourselves of the very different starting points from which discoursers and the respective athletic communities they belong to launch their normative inquiries into sport. Such communities of inquiry have no choice but to start from where they are, to work by their own lights, as Simon argues, rightly to my mind, which means there are going to be plenty of views about what sport is and should be that they will not be able to take seriously. Which views of sport? Well, any and all views that contain beliefs and values that members of an athletic community are unable to weave into their present web of beliefs and values about sport. In other words, any and all views of sport that fail this basic test of coherence. In the specific case of the amateur and professional communities, that means for the former camp any conception of sport as a serious occupation, and for the latter camp any conception of sport as a leisurely pastime. The normative sticking point in such instances is that neither of the rival parties can take on board the different beliefs and values of sport dear to the other without lapsing into incoherence, let alone without renouncing the core beliefs on which their athletic or cultural identity depends.

What we are thus confronted with in such conflicts is a fundamental incommensurability in their rational views about the purpose of sport and their normative outlooks on what actions are morally permissible and impermissible in sport. What we are *not* confronted with in such conflicts is a deliberate intent by either party to exclude the other, to explicitly and purposely disavow the other's conception of sport and what it considers morally admirable athletic behavior. Rather, what we run up against in such conflicts is not prejudice but nothing other than the limits of moral argument itself. This follows from the fact that we have no other option but to start rational inquiry where we presently are, as Simon, Dixon, and I all mutually concur, with the core beliefs and values we already hold as members of a particular athletic community. The prospect, therefore, of drawing justificatory support from a rival community's normative system, let alone adopting that rival system wholesale, "will not be possible for a reflective person" (Williams 1981, 142). The beliefs, values, and concerns of each community regarding sport do not sufficiently overlap with one another for the rational and normative judgments of either party to have a grip on its rival.

So Simon's admonition to abide the historical starting points of discoursers and the communities to which they belong works against rather than for his notion of extra-community rational dialogue and justification. Simply put, it rules out any noncircular form of rational justification of how we should comport ourselves in sport, because being rational on this working-by-one's-own-lights conception of rational dialogue means "stick[ing] to the logical space given at the beginning of inquiry. . . [and] offer[ing] an argument for the beliefs held at the end of the inquiry by referring back to the beliefs held at its beginning" (Rorty 1991, 95). Hence, seeking outside justificatory support for our rational judgments about how sport should be done is not a real theoretical or practical option when we are dealing with rival normative systems, as we are in cases like the amateur and professional conflict. This is what I think Hilary Putnam is driving at when he claims that "we can only hope to produce a more rational conception of rationality or a better conception of morality if we operate within our tradition" (1981, 216). This also means that it is fruitless to seek a noncircular, nonlocal rational foundation for distinctively social notions like the amateur-gentleman athlete or the career-oriented professional athlete—to, as Rorty put it with regard to liberal society's acute sensitivity to and moral rebuke of cruelty, "look back beyond the processes of socialization which convinced us twentieth-century liberals of the validity of this claim and appeal to something which is more 'real' or less ephemeral than the contingencies which brought those processes into existence" (1989, 198).

It may be objected, however, that I have only shown that seeking to strengthen a particular community's local normative view of sport by enlisting the rational and normative resources of its rival is a nonstarter, given the latter's obvious antithetical normative view of sport. That does not mean, someone of Simon's persuasion might retort, that we cannot try to accomplish much the same thing by letting rivals have at it in a dialogical argumentative encounter to see which side can win the argument one way or the other, to demonstrate that its normative conception of sport is the rationally superior one. The idea then is that if a particular community cannot generate a more rational and better moral account of sport by reaching out to its rival, it can do so by refuting its rival, by showing its account of sport has more going for it rationally speaking than its rival's.

The problem, however, is that we run into the same dialogical roadblock in trying to show the rational superiority of a community's conception of sport over its rival's that we previously did in trying to find support for a community's conception of sport by tapping the normative resources of its rival.[11] If we aspire to show our community's take on sport is the objectively better one, we will have to come up with arguments that are convincing not only to our own members but to those of our rival as well. That would require that we access the standards of reflective appraisal of either our own community or our rival, because, as we have already seen, both Simon and I, *pace* Rorty, hold that there is nothing beyond the evaluative vocabularies of particular communities that can serve as a criterion of choice between them. Naturally enough, we will choose our own rational standards, and our opponents will do the same. That spells trouble precisely because whatever conception of sport is used to start the argument will determine the outcome before the argument can even get off the ground; in other words, it will determine the winner of the argument before opponents have a chance to offer a single argument against it or a single argument in favor of their own position. Hence, instead of rationally deciding the very issue at hand by engaging each side in rational dialogue, we end up begging the question of which conception of sport is rationally superior.

This shows that when, for instance, the amateur community squares off against the professional community to demonstrate rationally that its gentleman take on sport is the normatively superior one, it cannot hope to accomplish its aim by using its own conception of sport and the rational norms and resources by which it justifies that conception. The same is true for the professional community. All of which points once again to the fact that rational dialogue, the giving and asking for reasons, is and can only be in such cases an inside, intramural game. Only if everyone is on the same page regarding the purpose of athletic forms of life can would-be rational discoursers deploy the same evaluative vocabulary and play the same argumentative game according to the same discursive rules.

Simon and Dixon might retort that because my view of the norm-circular, limited scope of moral argument precludes the possibility that either athletic community can rationally demonstrate the normative superiority of its conception of sport *by the lights of its rival*, it should also cast doubt on the rational defensibility of its own conception of sport *by its own lights*. After all, if the amateur community cannot show to the rational satisfaction of the professional community that its gentlemanly take on sport should win the day, or vice versa, then why should either community be confident in the rational defensibility of its own view of sport. All the members of either community can say when confronted with the alien beliefs and reasons of its rival is that it is correct by its own lights. But such self-certification should not, or so the criticism goes, inspire any confidence in the arguments used to rationally justify either community's views in such normative encounters. As Paul Boghossian helpfully puts it, "If we have reason to doubt whether our principles yield genuinely justified beliefs" in terms of persuading others who hold alternative beliefs, "why should we be comforted by the fact that we can construct an argument in their favor that relies on them?" (2006, 79).[12]

But what this criticism misses is that we only have reason to worry about the rational credibility of our own conceptions of sport in conflicting normative encounters like these if we insist on clinging to the already rejected notion that there are objective, context-independent standards of rational acceptability. However, because there is no good reason to suppose there are such supra-community standards of moral argument, there is no good reason to think the rational standoff between the amateur and professional communities will lead either community to second-guess their rival views of sport. They simply do not share enough beliefs about what is sport and how it should be done for either party to think that its inability to rationally get its rival to see sport the way it does should lead it to doubt its own particular way of seeing sport. In other words, *pace* Rorty, our rivals "are the people whose beliefs on certain topics overlap so little with ours that their inability to agree with us raises no doubt in our minds about the correctness of our own beliefs" (1991, 31). This explains why "we cannot imagine going over to the other side without 'self-deception or paranoia'" (31). And so it proved to be the case for these two dueling athletic camps, in which each side remained undaunted in its conviction that reason was firmly on its side.

Whatever the merits of Boghossian's point, however, it does not bear importantly on the central issue in point here: Trying to show one's conception of sport is correct by one's own light stands no chance of convincing one's opponent it is the correct view of sport by its very different lights. Which puts paid to Simon's and Dixon's main claim for discourse ethics that if we invite all disputants to the table to reflectively work out their differences, we can arrive at a rationally defensible view on the aim of sport and how it should be done, acceptable to all parties.

I thus conclude that Simon's and Dixon's discourse version of broad internalism is not up to the normative challenge posed by these harder cases in which there is fundamental disagreement over the purpose of sport. Such disagreements are not amenable to dialogical rational resolution, which is just another way of saying that they block any inferential path that leads, to use my main example, from the amateur to the professional point of view or the professional to the amateur point of view. That is why rational dialogue in these instances is fated to end in a rational stalemate, which can only be broken if Simon and Dixon seek to revive discourse ethics by taking a discredited transcendental route, one that their own arguments helped to discredit, and start asking bad questions based on the bad idea that we can distinguish between what a discourse community thinks the purpose of sport is and what it *really* is.

With my criticisms of the major ethical theories of sport complete, I am now in a position to unveil my own conventionalist alternative. But before I can do that, I have one more matter to take care of, and that is to distinguish the kind of ethical conventions that inform my own conventionalist theory from three other kinds of conventions discussed in the extant philosophical literature. These other conventions include what David Lewis famously called coordinating conventions and what Andrei Marmor called deep and surface (constitutive) conventions. I tackle the explication of these latter three kinds of conventions in Chapter 5 and then present my own theory in Chapter 6, which features what I call, after G.W.F. Hegel (1977b), ethical conventions.

5

What a Conventionalist Ethical Theory of Sport Does Not Look Like

The Case against Coordinating, Deep, and Constitutive (Surface) Conventions

As I note at the end of Chapter 4, the background understandings that inform our different conceptions of the point and purpose of sport, and that mark the divide between the rival amateur and professional views of sport I have given pride of place, are what I call ethical conventions. In Chapter 6, I argue that these conventions ground our changing ethical judgments about how we should comport ourselves in sport at particular times and places. However, I want to distinguish this kind of ethical convention from three other kinds of conventions canvassed in the relevant philosophical literature: what David Lewis (2002) calls coordinating conventions and Andrei Marmor (2009) calls deep and surface conventions. I argue that while these conventions figure in sport as they do in the rest of our social lives, they do not figure in any important sense in the ethical life of sport or the other social practices that are characteristic of modern societies like our own. My principal aim here, therefore, is to show why a conventional ethical theory of sport worthy of the name cannot follow the same path that Lewis and Marmor went down to derive their three respective notions of conventions and the disparate roles they play in our lives.

The Ubiquity of Conventions and Their General Features

I first need to say two things about conventions in general, in all of their varieties, including the ethical variety I showcase in Chapter 6, first, how widely they figure in our lives and, second, what general features they all share.

On the first point, it is hard to imagine human life without the conventions that underlie our daily intercourse with one another and make our lives go as smoothly as they do when they do. In fact, just about everything we do as human agents, from the most mundane to the most sublime, depends in one way or another on such conventions. I have in mind, among other things, the conventions of language, etiquette, and basic courtesy, without which we could scarcely conduct our affairs with our peers (Marmor 2009, 55). The same goes, of course, for sport, art, music, and the like, which, unlike most everyday fare, only come to play a part in our lives if we so choose but, once engaged, are no less dependent on the conventions that sustain them.

That conventions are implicated in so much of what we do as human agents explains why they vary according to the particular role they play in our various activities and social practices. That said, however, there are at least three features that are common to all conventions:

1. A community or comparable social unit (C) typically follows a norm (N) in a particular social practice (S).
2. There is a reason or reasons (R) for members of C to follow N in S.
3. There is at least one alternative norm (N1) that if members of C had actually followed in S, then R would have been a sufficient reason for members of C to follow N1 instead of N in S.[1]

The first feature underscores that conventions are quintessentially social norms. That is, a convention is something that is followed by most members of a community. In fact, its very existence depends on it being followed by nearly every member of the community. A norm observed by only a few members of a community is not a convention. Numbers matter here because in the case of a small number of people, a norm can be created, modified, or eliminated by simple agreement (Marmor 2009, 4). As Lewis noted, conventions typically emerge as an alternative to agreements precisely because agreements among large numbers of people are very difficult, if not impossible, to secure. How many members of a community must abide a norm to qualify as a convention cannot be specified more precisely than quantifying words such as "most," "almost all," the "great majority," a "large number." But that we cannot be more definite than this should not give us pause, because, as H.L.A. Hart observes, this question is no more worrisome "than the question as to the number of hairs a man may have and still be bald" (1997, 56). In other words, we do not need greater precision than words like "most" provide to settle the question of whether a sufficient number of people follow a norm to count as a convention.

Conventions are quintessentially social norms in the further sense that they are responses to social purposes and needs. If we hope to realize our social purposes and be responsive to the social needs of our community, then we cannot do without norms to regulate our conduct accordingly. Conventions fill the bill nicely because, like the social goals they serve, they, too, are "up to us" to establish when mere agreement is beyond our reach. The social character of conventions also means, as David Hume long ago pointed out, that they do not require "the interposition of a promise" on the part of the members of the community, "since the actions of each [member] . . . have a reference to those of the other[s], and are performed upon the supposition that something is to be performed on the other[s'] part" (quoted in Lewis 2002, 4).

The "common interest" that Hume tells us conventions express and that induce people to regulate their actions to accommodate that interest should not, however, be confused with mere regularities in people's behavior, with what people typically do in their lives. More succinctly, conventions should not be conflated with statistical norms that tell us how people normally act in the course of their lives (Brennan et al. 2013, 2). For example, in a particular society people generally go out for dinner to a restaurant or entertain friends at their homes on the weekend. That some people choose not to act in these habitual ways, perhaps instead using their free time to catch up on work or sleep, is not rightly regarded as somehow a failure on their part, something for which criticism of their atypical behavior is warranted. In other words, statistical norms simply describe what people typically do rather than prescribe what they should do. They are thus not binding in the sense in which conventions are. For conventions are prescriptive in the relevant normative sense. They are norms that obligate us to act in particular ways and warrant criticism of those who violate them.

At the same time, the normative authority of conventions is not that of so-called objectively valid norms, the kind of validity moral norms are often supposedly said to possess, norms that bind us no matter if they are not routinely observed, or even completely ignored, by members of some community. Objective norms are practice-independent, whereas conventional norms are wholly practice-dependent. The moment most people no longer follow conventions, but only honor them in the breach, not only do they lose whatever authority or point they may have had, but they literally cease to exist. As Geoffrey Brennan and company (2013) nicely put it, conventions bootstrap their own normative authority rather than derive it from some external, objectively binding normative principle (6). Their authoritative status, therefore, directly derives from the social practices in which they operate, specifically from their acceptance by the members of the relevant practice community as binding norms on the actions that take place there. As Henry Aiken observes, "Inter-subjective [conventional] norms are not agreed to by members of a society because they are objective, but, in effect, become objective because they are jointly accepted" (quoted in Manley 1981, 32). Just what joint acceptance means and entails in this normative sense varies, as we shall soon see, according to the type of convention in question.

The second feature characteristic of all conventions is that they give people a reason for following them, for acting in light of the norms they prescribe. This is what distinguishes *following* conventional norms from merely *acting in accord* with them (Marmor 2007, 587). One is doing the latter rather than the former whenever the relevant governing conventional norm is not the *reason* one complies with it. For example, one may comply with a convention because of circumstances that force one's compliance, as, say, when one is threatened with personal harm by someone for not complying. One may comply with a convention because one is *motivated* to do so by considerations that having nothing important to do with the convention itself, as, say, when one follows the convention of shaking the hand of a stranger one has been introduced to at a fancy party in order not to offend one's socially conscious spouse. By contrast, to follow a conventional norm means I have a reason that counts in favor of my doing so, that following the norm is a good, valuable, and justifiable thing to do in the relevant context because it serves some valuable end (Marmor 2007, 588). This is just another way of saying that conventions give us specifically normative reasons for following them as opposed to causal or motivating ones.[2] But these normative reasons are *pro tanto* ones, reasons in favor of acting on the norms they prescribe, rather than all-things-considered reasons. That is why a convention is still a convention if other independent reasons override following it (Letsas 2014, 556; Marmor 2009, 7).

The third common feature of conventions, no matter their kind, is their arbitrary character, which also has something important to do with what Marmor calls compliance dependence (2009, 8). To say conventions are arbitrary can mean different things. It can mean, for example, an absence of any plausible or good reason for acting in some way. Clearly, conventions are not arbitrary in this sense, since there are good reasons for following them. To claim conventions are arbitrary can also mean they can be changed at will. Conventions in this sense are also not arbitrary not only because, *pace* Lewis, they typically emerge as alternatives to social agreements, given the large number of people whose behavior they regulate, but, more important, because they are normatively binding. That is, they are not the sort of norms one can violate without being criticized by one's peers for not following them.

Rightly understood, conventions are arbitrary in two related and important senses. First, they are human inventions, better, social concoctions, which might not have ever seen the light of day were it not for the utterly contingent historical circumstances that led to their creation. Their historically contingent character is further borne out by the fact that they are context-relative norms, which vary according to time and place, given the ever-changing historical circumstances in which we find ourselves and in which we respond accordingly by crafting new conventions to suit the altered historical circumstances. Conventions are arbitrary in a second related sense because they admit of at least one alternative that, ceteris paribus, if it had been followed instead would have resulted in no "significant loss in the purpose. . . or values" served by the original conventions (Marmor 2009, 78). However, Marmor is quick to point out that the alternative convention in question must be a "conceivable" alternative, one that could actually be followed by the relevant community (9).[3]

Like Lewis, Marmor is also quick to point out that the fact that a conventional norm has at least one alternative does not mean or require that members of a community are indifferent as to the choice between the two (8). They may have a reason for opting for one over the other as long as their reason for favoring that one is not stronger than their reason for following the convention that is eventually settled on. This attests to the aforementioned ineliminable social character of conventions, the fact that most people follow the conventions of the community to which they belong. Marmor provides a helpful example here. Suppose, he proposes, there are two ways of greeting people in a culture: either by shaking their hand or nodding their head. Presumably, some people in that culture would have initially favored the former greeting over the latter, and others the latter over the former. In other words, they would have been partial rather than indifferent to one of the options. However, as long as the reason to act in concert with one another is stronger than the reason to act on one of the alternatives, the convention that emerges as the "common practice" will end up being followed (Marmor 2009, 9), thereby confirming its arbitrary status.

That people need not be indifferent to the two or more alternative conventions available to them suggests that the arbitrariness of conventions comes in degrees (Marmor 2009, 9). For example, a convention would be wholly arbitrary if people were wholly indifferent to which option is followed. By parity of reason, therefore, it follows that a convention is less arbitrary if people are more invested in the one that is followed than its alternatives. That means the reason to follow the convention that is actually followed only needs to be "slightly stronger" than the reason to follow its alternatives, without, that is, compromising the central arbitrary status of conventional norms (9).

The final thing to be said about the arbitrariness of conventions concerns their previously mentioned compliance dependence. General compliance with a convention is a necessary feature of a convention. Indeed, without such compliance there can be no convention at all. That means that part of the reason for following a convention is that others are following it too.[4] Or as George Letsas pithily puts it, "a convention is something we do around here partly *because* that is what is done around here" (2014, 536; emphasis in original). This compliance-dependent aspect is an important part of the arbitrary character of conventions because the reason for following one of its alternatives is because most people are actually following it rather than them. The same would hold, of course, if one of its alternatives were the one that was actually followed by most people. So, for example, the fact that nearly everyone drives on the left side of the road in England, rather than the right-side alternative, is why the former rather than the latter is the reigning convention; that nearly everyone in the United States drives on the right side of the road, rather than the left-side alternative, is why the former rather than the latter is the reigning convention. Of course, if the situation were reversed, people in England would drive on the right side, and people in the United States would drive on the left. So the compliance-dependent character of reasons for following a convention figures crucially in which of its alternatives emerges as the go-to convention that guides people's actual conduct.

Having canvassed the general features characteristic of all conventions, it is time to examine the three types of conventions Lewis and Marmor have so deftly analyzed, and that I, to reiterate, want to distinguish from what I have been calling ethical conventions that underpin the conventional ethical theory of sport I set out to develop and defend in Chapter 6.

Coordinating Conventions

Most philosophers who are interested in the topic of conventions think of them almost exclusively as what Lewis, in his path-breaking and widely heralded book, *Convention* (2002), calls "coordinating" conventions. One of the main reasons why the multiform character of conventions, the fact that they come in importantly different varieties, is so unacknowledged and underappreciated in philosophical circles is because of the major influence of his book. Nonetheless, my interest in Lewis here concerns his acute analysis of coordinating conventions, which makeup an undeniably large and important part of our social commerce with one another.

What mainly distinguishes the different conventions that figure in our social lives is the particular purposes they serve. As its name suggests, the chief purpose that coordinating conventions serve is to solve large-scale recurrent coordination problems (Lewis 2002, 8; Marmor 2009, 19). Prominent examples include: what to wear to a wedding or funeral, what to bring to a dinner party, what side of the road to drive on, who should return a cut-off phone call, how to greet one another in social settings, and the like. All of these problems, of course, are independent of and antecedent to the conventions that emerge to solve them, which accounts for their instrumental character. That they count as large-scale problems has to do with the significant number of people they involve, which precludes a simple agreement among them as to how to proceed. What makes them recurrent problems is that they constantly arise in our social commerce with one another. What makes such problems coordinating ones is that they require us to act in concert with one another. And what makes such coordination challenging is because there are several ways in which they might be solved.

Coordinating conventions are by definition, therefore, inescapably social artifacts in which each member of the relevant social unit or group has a stronger preference to act in concert with one another rather than alone. That is because to solve a coordination problem, they must behave in a regular, uniform manner. If they choose instead to follow their individual preferences, chaos would likely and quickly ensue. In short, the roads would not be fit to drive on, interrupted telephone calls would not likely be returned because neither party would know whether to call back or wait for a call (if they opt for the former, they will only get a busy signal; if they opt for the latter, they will only get silence), and so on. In other words, unless they can coordinate their behavior in the requisite manner, they will be unable to achieve their desired outcome. So the success of their interactions depends on their concerted action. And in game-theoretic terms, which are the terms Lewis premises his account of coordinating conventions on, success means that some combination of the agents' actions among the several alternatives open to them achieves an "equilibrium," such that "each agent has as done as well as he can given the actions of the other agents" (2002, 8). The achievement of said equilibrium thus rules out the possibility that any of the relevant agents, either yourself or someone else, would have been better off if she had acted differently than everyone else.

Coordinating conventions, like all other kinds of conventions, give us reasons to act in light of them. Unlike other conventions, however, coordinating ones traffic exclusively in desired-based reasons or preferences. The charge of practical reason in these instances is not to *evaluate* the qualitative worth of our occurrent desires or preferences, but to *weigh* which of these desires will get us the outcome we are seeking (Taylor 1985, 18). So we reject desires not because they are somehow base or unworthy, but because they are not instrumentally efficacious. Desires double as reasons, therefore, when they get us a solution to the coordination problem we are after. This explains why the reasons to solve a coordination problem are not especially "strong or compelling reasons," because what is at stake in these situations is not, again, the worth of our desires but only their instrumental fitness in achieving outcomes that are largely matters of convenience and rarely matters of great importance (Marmor 2009, 134).

The actual mechanics of the practical reasoning that figures in coordinating conventions is not complex, but that does not mean it is easy to pull off. Basically, what each member of the relevant group is trying to do is figure out what the other members of the group prefer to do. This requires real reflection because we must resist the impress of our immediate desires, which typically prompt us to act on our own strongest desires. The task then is to replicate each other's practical reasoning, to try, as Lewis puts it, "to figure out what you will do by replicating your reasoning, [just as] you . . . [are] trying to figure out what I will do by replicating my reasoning" (2002, 27). Again, this is no easy matter, but its instrumental payoff is significant because it allows us to dispense with many of our first-order reasons for action, of having to deliberate about what we should do every time we encounter a coordination problem.

Because the reason for having coordinating conventions is one and the same for complying with them (Marmor 2009, 134), we have in part answered the question why we should comply with them. But just how much force does the "should" of these conventions really have? After all, we have already seen that the reasons for having coordinating conventions are weak rather than strong or compelling. That would suggest the reasons for complying with them are similarly weak rather than strong. Further, as Lewis reminds us, what partly makes them weak reasons is that they give us a presumptive, rather than *pro tanto,* reason for following them, a reason, in other words, that presumes, ceteris paribus, everyone else will think and do as we think and do. This would explain why Lewis does not include normative terms such as "ought," "should," or "good" in his definition of a coordinating convention (2002, 97). Further, because these conventions do not involve any promise on anybody's part to abide by them, they cannot be said to obligate us in the way promises do. Indeed, it might be wondered whether they have any normative oomph at all, since they seem to have more in common with what Marmor calls "generally recognized" reasons that explain why we regularly do the things that we do—his example, eating breakfast—but do not obligate us to do any of these things (2009, 13). Perhaps the most that can be said of the reason for complying with coordinating conventions is that it would be irrational, in the relevant instrumental sense, not to, that it would be imprudent to skip breakfast but not a normative failure to do so. All of which suggests that the "should" or "ought" of coordinating conventions is decidedly not a normative one and, a fortiori, not a moral one.

But claiming such would be wrong. For even though Lewis made no bones about the fact that his definition of a coordinating convention purposely excluded any normative terms, he argued, nonetheless, that conventions are "a species of norms: regularities to which we believe one ought to conform" (2002, 97). He reasoned such because conventions that synchronize our various social interactions create bona fide normative expectations that the members of the relevant social unit justifiably count on, and if violated, elicit their critical displeasure if not sanction. So if the convention is to bring a bottle of wine or a suitable equivalent to a dinner party, your host would have good reason to be miffed at you if you show up empty handed. Similarly, driving on the right side of the road in England and refusing to bow when meeting people where that is the convention will similarly result not just in ruffled feelings but in critical rebuke, if not more.

Still, while these examples show people have normative reasons to comply with coordinating conventions, they do not rise to the level of a moral "ought" or "should." Or do they? The reason for complying with some subset of these conventions does seem to give people a *pro tanto* moral obligation to do so. In the case of the driving and social greeting conventions examples above, people have not only a reason to conform to these conventions because they make it easier to negotiate the roads or interact with strangers but also a reason to comply to these conventions because in the driving case, failure to do so can lead to great harm (collisions that not uncommonly are fatal), and in the social greeting case, failure to do so can plausibly be taken to be a sign of disrespect. And it is no exaggeration to say that we have a moral obligation not to harm or disrespect others.

However, two further things need to be kept in mind here. First, most conventions of this kind do not entail any *pro tanto* moral obligation to follow them. Second, even those that do like the driving example do not necessarily create a moral obligation to comply with them. It is quite enough, in other words, that our obligation to drive on whatever side of the road the convention requires is limited to the coordination problem it was crafted to solve. Whether the moral obligation not to unnecessarily harm others is part of the equation in such circumstances is not internal to the convention itself but rather an external consideration that people may or may not entertain.[5]

Finally, it is clear that coordinating conventions are arbitrary in the relevant sense. That is, they are historically contingent responses to historically contingent coordination problems. Further, they admit of at least one alternative that if it had been followed instead would not have resulted in the loss of the purpose served by the convention already in place. So Americans could well have ended up driving on the left rather than the right side of the road, and Oxford dons passing the port to the right rather than the left would not have suffered any loss in purpose or efficiency in meeting their coordination challenges. And, of course, the reason one of these alternatives emerged as the preferred solution is that most members of the relevant social unit happened to comply with it.

Coordinating conventions, unsurprisingly, play a role in sport as they do in almost all social affairs, but that role appears to be at most a marginal one. For instance, if one attends an organized football game in the United States, one can expect it to begin with the playing of the national anthem; if one is a spectator at Wimbledon, one can expect all the players to be dressed in white. The reason, of course, is that these are well-settled conventions that regulate how one is expected to behave in both venues. So if players or spectators fail to stand during the playing of the national anthem, they can count on being the target of criticism or even worse, as the recent NFL players kneeling in protest to condemn the mistreatment of people of color by the police readily attests;[6] the same goes for tennis players at Wimbledon who defy the all-white dress convention. These are not unimportant conventions of sport, but they are hardly crucial to the sports themselves, to the actual action and behavior that takes place on the playing fields. Most of that behavior of the coordinating variety on the field is based on explicit social agreements and extensive planning, not arbitrary conventions. And most important for my purposes, the ethical conventions that I am arguing do the lion's share of the normative work in sport, and without which I maintain we would be ethically clueless in and outside of sport, are decidedly, as we shall see, not of the coordinating kind.

Deep and Constitutive (Surface) Conventions

The main purpose served by deep conventions is that they are normative responses to basic social and psychological needs that underpin cultures like ours and from which the social practices (art, music, theater, games and sport, and the like) that define them emerge (Marmor 2009, 58). Accordingly, the deep conventions of games and sport are normative responses in their own right to our social needs to play them, which partly constitute our concept of the "general human activity [of] playing a competitive game" (Marmor 2006, 364). They can play this generative conceptual and practical role by providing a deeper layer of shared understandings about what is a competitive game and what is its essential point and purpose.

Because deep conventions are responsive to our fundamental social needs to play and observe games and sport, they cannot be glossed over as solutions to coordination problems. That is because the social needs they answer are not problems in the relevant sense, and the normative responses they elicit are too abstract and indeterminate to qualify as solutions to coordination problems (Marmor 2007, 593). Further, what makes these conventions deep is they are not, like recurrent coordination problems, simply things that we just happen to do. Although it may be easy to imagine a culture in which people do not play sports that are commonplace in our own culture, it is well-nigh impossible to imagine a culture whose inhabitants do not play any sports at all. If there were such a sport-less culture, its people would be so different from us sociologically, psychologically, and historically speaking that we would be unable to understand what they are about, let alone interact with them in any meaningful way. All of which suggests that playing games has a profoundly deep hold on us and on the culture we have created in our own self-image; the deep conventions that give rise to them are more enduring and less amenable to change than the coordination problems that are inescapable features of our daily social interactions with one another (Marmor 2007, 604).

Marmor singles out three crucial deep conventions of games that inform our general concept of them, which, he makes clear, are not to be regarded as exhaustive or to be taken as a definition (2009, 60). The first is that playing a game is essentially a rule-governed activity. Rules figure in games, he observes, in three important respects. To begin with, playing a game entails following some basic rules; the rules establish, among other things, what counts as a game and what is its central purpose as well as what values can be derived from engaging in it; and, a feature he included in his later book on the topic, the rules of games purposefully create challenges by making it more rather than less difficult to accomplish their goals in order to require players to demonstrate certain skills in trying to achieve them.[7] The second deep convention of games and sport is what, for Marmor, establishes their distinctive artificial character: that engagement in such activities requires participants bracket the concerns that occupy them in their ordinary, everyday lives. This second deep convention marks off games and sport from the rest of our lives, and that is essential to understanding what they are all about. Just how essential is nicely conveyed by Marmor's example of his undergraduate history professor's quip, surely made in jest, "that when his king is threatened by checkmate he would simply declare a republic" (2006, 367). The third and last deep convention of games and sport he mentions has to do with the "fairly sharp demarcation" it draws between participants and nonparticipants, whether they be spectators or other interested parties (2009, 60).

What further needs to be said about deep conventions concerns what Marmor calls their "elusive" nature, the fact that they cannot be easily isolated and their main features readily articulated. For the deep conventions on which the very intelligibility of games and sport depends can only be observed and grasped in the corresponding surface conventions they engender and that constitute particular sports like soccer. What we see and observe when playing or watching a soccer game, therefore, are the various actions that take place on the pitch that are governed by its particular constitutive rules. These rules mandate, among many other things, that when the ball is in play, it may not be advanced by using one's hands—with the exception of the goalie. Marmor calls these "surface" conventions because they are located at the surface of sport practices like soccer, which is why their constitutive function is obvious for all to see. Conversely, deep conventions are more opaque because they do their normative work in the background rather than the foreground (surface) of sport practices, rendering intelligible why we have sports like soccer and why we find it compelling to play games like these that challenge us in these distinctively physical ways. So when we follow the surface rule of soccer that forbids us to use our hands in propelling the ball forward, we are following as well, if indirectly, the underlying norm of the deep conventions of sport that makes such physical artifice understandable, meaningful, and valuable, something worthy of our effort and commitment.

As is characteristic of all conventions, the deep conventions of games and sport give us reasons for following them and executing the actions they require. What is different about deep conventions, however, is that they provide would-be participants with especially strong *pro tanto* reasons for acting on them. That is because the reasons for playing games and sport derive from the reasons for having such social practices in the first place, which is, to reiterate, to challenge ourselves by creating artificial obstacles that require us to demonstrate certain intellectual and/or physical skills. The reasons these deep conventions evoke are required and not optional—presuming, that is, that games and sport are our passion. This means deep conventions are less arbitrary than not only coordinating conventions but surface conventions as well (Marmor 2009, 73). Said otherwise, deep conventions are more bound up with reasons than either of these other conventions, which is why their binding force is such that scarcely any participant who engages in social practices like games and sport could plausibly allege to be unaware of their binding force (73).[8]

If the reasons evoked by deep conventions are as strong as Marmor contends, then it might reasonably be asked in what sense are they arbitrary and, so, conventions at all. Marmor's answer is that there are two basic ways in which reasons can constitute norms: They can either wholly determine their content or partially determine their content (2007, 605). On the first count, norms that are completely determined by reasons are not conventions because they are most assuredly not arbitrary. He gives as an example the moral norm against torture. The reasons for having and complying with that norm are, as he sees it, solely based on reasons, which means it has no alternative that could be followed instead and still comply with the reasons that forbid torture. On the second count, reasons that partly determine the content of a norm are conventions because they do admit of an alternative that could be followed instead and still comply with the reasons for that norm.

According to Marmor, deep conventions in general, and the deep conventions of games and sport in particular, fall into this second class. So even though deep conventions are normative responses to basic social needs and the reasons that give rise to them, they are, as Marmor claimed, underdetermined (or only partly determined) by these social needs and reasons. It is not hard to see, therefore, how alternative practices of games and sport might have emerged in different cultures without any loss in the purpose served by our present crop of games and sports. As Marmor muses, "Perhaps we could have some rituals that are not games but would serve similar functions; or we could have 'games' that are not winnable; or we could have 'games' that are not detached from real-life concerns, such as the Roman gladiators 'game' for their life" (2006, 365–366). Adding to Marmor's list of alternative sport practices is not difficult to do because they are so plentiful. To mention only two prominent historical examples: The German *Turnen* (calisthenics) movement of the early nineteenth century renounced modern athletic games and answered our apparent social need to challenge ourselves physically by encouraging systematic noncompetitive collective gymnastic exercises; and going back even further, the medieval folk games and sports chronicled by the late Henning Eichberg (2016) that were much more about giving people an opportunity to enjoy themselves, to have and poke fun at one another, often in ribald and violent ways, rather than to demonstrate the kind of athletic perfection we moderns go in for, and that, again unlike we moderns, made no sharp distinction between participants and spectators.

Marmor thinks there should be no doubt, therefore, that the strong *pro tanto* reasons that deep conventions elicit somehow undercut their conventional stature, that the reasons we follow them are partially owed to the fact that most people followed them rather than their possible alternatives. There should also be no doubt, Marmor further maintains, that deep conventions are resistant, as most conventions and things are certainly not, to institutionalization, that the norms they put in place are impervious to what he calls "legislative codification," in which only one way of playing games and sport is allowed and any alternative ways of playing them are outlawed.[9] This apparent resistance of deep conventions to institutionalization, a point whose significance will become clear in the ensuing discussion, is attributable to the former's constitutive relation to the latter. As Marmor pithily puts it, "Institutions have no role to play in determining the deep conventions we follow partly because it is the deep conventions that we follow that constitute the institutions we have" (2007, 608). That deep conventions are normative responses to social needs that are deeply engrained in our culture matters here because that gives them the upper hand constitutively speaking and makes them recalcitrant to institutional encroachment. But again, the undeniable constitutive normative role they play in our athletic lives does not tell against their arbitrary conventional standing, that for all their normative prowess, the norms they midwife are essentially contingent. Hence, "we could have lived in a world that is, all things considered, equal to the one we live in, yet followed a different [deep conventional] norm . . . without any significant loss in the purposes, functions, or values that the [current] norm serves for us" (Marmor 2009, 78).

Constitutive (Surface) Conventions

The deep conventions of games and sport give rise to constitutive (surface) conventions that determine the specific local games and sports played in particular communities and cultures; in so doing, they provide the general normative background for our understanding and evaluation of these particular local athletic practices. Given the dependent relation of constitutive conventions on deep ones, it is accurate to say that part of the purpose and values of the constitutive conventions of local sports derives from entrenched social needs to play such competitive games that are independent of and antecedent to them. This is just another way of saying that the constitutive conventions that reside at the surface of athletic practices instantiate the deep conventions that they owe their own emergence to. However, deep conventions only partly determine the general point of constitutive conventions because the latter are "radically underdetermined" by the former (Marmor 1996, 367). That accounts for why local communities and cultures have the great variety of games and sports that they do; these various games and sports express different and particular ways in which they can be played and valued.

When it comes to these local games and sport practices, however, constitutive conventions do not play, as it were, second fiddle to deep conventions or any other considerations for that matter. After these conventional practices are established, everything that goes on within them is dictated by their corresponding constitutive conventions and not anything external to them. That includes their central purposes and values, because some of the most important normative work these conventions do is to set the internal point and purpose of these local games and sport practices and establish their internal goods and values. They thus add to and refine our general concept and understanding of playing games by constituting local ludic practices that are not directly held hostage by social needs that are antecedent to or independent of the conventional aims and ends they ordain. It could not be otherwise because it would be absurd to suppose that before, say, soccer was constituted by its relevant conventions, before it became the athletic practice that it is, we could independently determine what its point and purpose is and how it should be evaluated (Marmor 1996, 367). And, of course, that purpose and its corresponding values can only be realized by engaging in it and only appreciated by observing it.

It is with these self-constituting features in mind that Marmor assigns conventional games and sports to the class of "autonomous" practices whose signature normative feature is that they must be understood and evaluated in their own terms and according to their own intrinsic values. Moreover, he thinks they are more autonomous than most other autonomous conventional practices, like opera, because they operate in a domain more distant and remote "from [the] general, non-conventional concerns they instantiate" (Marmor 1996, 367). Of course, it goes without saying that games and sports, as Anita Silvers and David Wasserman attest, are more conventional than nonautonomous undertakings like work because they "are not dictated by the external objective of making a product or profit" (2007, 455).

The constitutive conventions of games and sports perform two indispensable functions in this regard: They constitute these practices and their central purposes and values, and they prescribe norms that regulate the actions that take place within their carefully demarcated boundaries. All told then, constitutive conventions set forth particular conceptions of winning and losing, what actions are permissible and what are impermissible, what specific skills are required and valued, what counts as a good or bad game or an elegant or inelegant move or action, what strategy is brilliant or not, what players should be ranked as superior or inferior based on the quality of their play, and so on (Marmor 2009, 36–38). A very big part of what these constitutive conventions do then is to prescribe an "ought" that concerns how particular games and sports should be played and conducted (Marmor 1996, 367).

There is one controversial feature of Marmor's account of constitutive conventions that I have yet to comment on but which at this point warrants mention if we are to fully understand why he ascribes such a wide range of normative purposes to them. That feature is that all such conventions, he insists, are best understood as rules. Wherever the two words "constitutive conventions" appear in his writings, therefore, we are to understand he means "constitutive rules," whether he is discussing social practices like art or, our present concern, social practices like games and sports. What is controversial about his thesis that constitutive conventions and constitutive rules mean one and the same thing, that they are synonyms, is that it is at odds with most philosophical accounts of conventions like Lewis's classic analysis.

Lewis argues that rules, whether conventional or not, should be distinguished from conventional norms that are not rules. His two-step argument for treating the conflation of the two as a mistake centered, fortuitously and fortunately for our purposes, on a word game he calls "Jotto." Lewis's first step is to specify four rules for playing this game, which he argues are "perfect specimens of rules" because (1) they are easily codified, (2) their violation would be convincing evidence that the violators were unable or unwilling to play Jotto, and (3) their codification provided a handy way to teach people how to play the game (2002, 104). All three features, to his mind, are what we expect rules of any kind to exemplify. And for Lewis these same three features typify conventional rules, as opposed to rules that are strategic maxims or hypothetical imperatives that state how to attain some end. Lewis's second step, however, which sets up the distinction he is trying to draw between (conventional) rules and conventions, is to point out that any group of players of games like Jotto will inevitably "develop understandings—tacit, local, temporary, informal . . . to settle questions left open by the listed rules" (104). We might very well, Lewis acknowledges, call these understandings rules, but only, he quickly adds, if we append qualifiers such as "unwritten" or "informal" rules. But he further ventures, we might be well advised to call them conventions "to emphasize their differences from the listed rules" (105).

Marmor rejects Lewis's distinction between rules and conventions principally because he objects to delimiting the class of rules to only members of the formal, codified kind. The problem with such a delimitation is that it would have us believe that "rules are only those things one would find in rule-books, enlisted and codified systematically" (Marmor 2009, 15). But that is simply not true, he contends, because there are many rules observed in games and sport, if only in a taken-for-granted manner, that govern our actions. That what he has in mind here are the very same "tacit," informal understandings that Lewis talks about is clear from the sole example he offers to support his counterargument for why rules should not be distinguished from conventions, which is that it is a convention of many games that players should make their moves or commence their actions within a reasonable period of time (15). He does not deny these rules are taken for granted and implicit, or that we usually become aware of them only when players fail to follow them, or, for that matter, that they might get codified like any other game rule. What he wants to deny instead is that there is any good reason for calling or treating them as anything other than (conventional) rules. As Marmor writes, "Whether codified or not, . . . such conventions are certainly part of the rules of the game" (15).

Marmor's thesis that constitutive conventions are one-and-all rules is important because it explains the much larger normative portfolio he assigns to what he calls constitutive rules than Bernard Suits (2014) does to what he calls constitutive rules. For Suits, constitutive rules, which he argues prohibit more efficient in favor of less efficient means for achieving the prelusory goals of games, have essentially one main function: to specify what counts as playing a game, which is inclusive, of course, of what qualifies as a move in a game, as winning a game, and so on. That main function narrows the normative scope of constitutive rules to establishing the difference between permissible and impermissible means for playing a game. This narrowing of the normative purpose of constitutive rules is connected to Suits's claim that these rules are part of the formal architecture of games, things that are mostly written down, found in a rulebook, or, whether written down or not, stipulate in explicit terms how the game is to be played. Suits makes no pretense, then, that the constitutive rules or, in fact, any other formal element of his definition tell us anything about what a well-played or good game is or looks like but only what a legitimate game is or looks like. Had he tried to do the former, he would have had to incorporate tacit understandings, informal norms, and taken-for-granted understandings of games into account. Of course, it is precisely because Marmor does incorporate such informal norms and understandings into his rendering of constitutive rules that he claims they tell us not only what are permissible or impermissible ways of playing games but also what are elegant or inelegant or brilliant or stupid ways of playing them.

Marmor's more expansive conception of constitutive rules (conventions) and their attendant normative purposes opens the door for his further claim that they often come in different layers in which some are less shallow and more pivotal than others (2006, 367). For instance, the constitutive rules of chess that govern how the chess pieces are moved are more central to the point of the game than the shape of the chess pieces themselves. Similarly, the constitutive rules of baseball that determine how the game is to be played are more central to the game than the athletic attire players are required to wear. These less shallow, more integral constitutive rules (conventions), of course, do not cut as deep as the deep conventions of chess and baseball without which there would be no such practices to begin with. Nonetheless, in Marmor's intuitively compelling estimation, certain constitutive rules figure more significantly than others in determining the purposes of particular games and sports.

Further, it should be apparent by now that constitutive conventions, like their deep progenitors, are not solutions to coordination problems. Indeed, before chess and baseball were invented, constituted, there were literally no coordination problems to be solved (Marmor 2006, 362). So our very concepts of games like chess and sports like baseball are owed entirely to their corresponding constitutive conventions. By contrast, our concept of a coordination problem like what side of the road to drive on is not dependent on the convention that emerged to solve it. We already know and have a concept of driving on one side of the road or the other before we hit on a convention to sort out just what side of the road we should drive on. This follows, of course, from the fact that the whole purpose of a coordination convention is to solve a preexisting coordination problem.

Marmor also thinks the greater complexity of constitutive conventions distinguishes them from coordinating conventions. Because the purpose of a coordinating convention is simply to solve an antecedent coordination problem, following the relevant rule adopted with that very purpose in mind "is more or less all that there is to it" (2009, 41), whereas constitutive conventions answer to a variety of social purposes and needs that involve more than merely following the relevant rules. For instance, one can follow the constitutive rules of chess or baseball as part of some imagined religious ritual and, as a consequence, fail to play either game at all (40).[10] That is to deny not that the rules of these games constitute them but only that they do not "exhaust" them (40).

But it might be asked how Marmor can make this latter claim, since for him the constitutive conventions of games and all social practices encompass both written and unwritten rules, both formal norms and informal, taken-for-granted ones. It is quite easy to see how someone like Lewis, who distinguishes formal rules from tacit, conventional understandings of games, could plausibly claim there is more to games than rules, that when the rules for whatever reason prove inapplicable or indeterminate, we can rely on tacit understandings to guide us as to how we should go on. But because Marmor lumps both formal and informal norms under the constitutive rules of games and the like, it is not at all clear why the rules could ever be said to fail us, why they could not answer any and all unexpected, novel normative problems that might crop up in our game-playing ventures.

To think Marmor has no plausible retort to this objection and therefore, he cannot back up his claim that constitutive conventions (rules) are more complex than coordinating ones because they require more than following rules is to forget one of his main theses—namely, that constitutive conventions are instantiations of deep conventions. When we bring deep conventions back into the picture, we can see not only how there might be a normative gap left open—even when rules as broadly conceived as Marmor does leave us in the lurch—but how that gap might be closed, to his way of thinking at any rate, by appeal to their corresponding deep conventions rather than the kind of tacit understandings that Lewis invokes. For we have such practices as chess and baseball to begin with in Marmor's view not just because of the constitutive rules that made their practice possible but because of our prior general and deep social needs to play such challenging competitive games. Hence, when the constitutive rules of these games fail us, leave us hanging as to how to make our normative way within their artificial spheres, we can tap what for Marmor is the only normative resource left to us: the deep conventions that underpin them (2006, 359).[11]

It will come as no surprise that the constitutive conventions of games and sports played by particular communities create reasons for action, reasons for acting in light of the norms they establish. But there is one important sense in which these reasons are conditional, why they fall well short of the categorical reasons that are often claimed to be the trademark of moral reasons and norms. Athletic practices create reasons for action only for human agents that have a reason to play and observe them in the first place, that find them normatively compelling human endeavors in their own right (Marmor 2009, 168). What their constitutive conventions cannot do is give people a reason to follow them, a reason that obligates them to take up sports. In short, the reasons for following and obeying game rules cannot be derived from the norms that determine what chess or soccer is, what particular kind of game it is. However, there is no denying that if people do have a reason to engage in these athletic affairs as players or spectators, then they clearly do have a *pro tanto* reason to follow, honor, and respect their relevant constitutive conventions.

That constitutive conventions cannot of their own accord obligate people to play and observe them might suggest that the reasons for action they put in play are not especially strong reasons, reasons that really matter to people. But that would be a mistake. For one, it would elide the historical importance games and sports have had for the great multitudes that play and watch them all over the world. Unlike most social practices, sport practices are not casual affairs of interest only to a few curious enthusiasts. For another, to dismiss or underestimate the normative strength of the reasons the constitutive conventions of soccer, basketball, baseball, and the like put in play is to ignore why the reasons and significance that coordinating conventions create pale by comparison. That such sports matter much more and to far greater numbers of people socially, politically, and morally speaking than what side of the road people should drive on, or what side of the plate they should place their fork on, or who should return an interrupted phone call should tell us something not insignificant about the normative force of the reasons generated by their respective constitutive conventions. That is not to say coordination problems are not important problems that we ignore only at our inconvenience, if not peril, but that in most cases it is not especially important how we solve them so long as the solution is rationally efficient (Marmor 2006, 361–362).

What, then, do the reasons constitutive conventions of games and sports create have going for them normatively speaking that other reasons for action do not? It is clearly not their instrumental efficacy, the rational calling card of coordinating conventions, because the whole point of these athletic conventions is to make the attainment of their ends more rather than less difficult than they need to be in order to make them challenging practices. Rather, those reasons have to do with why we have such sport practices at all, which is to challenge us in the specific ways that each artificially do that call on an array of skills and actions that are intrinsically valuable (Marmor 1996, 367). We invite and relish these athletic challenges, then, not primarily for any external, extra-game ends that we might obtain by virtue of engaging in them, but because we find and regard these challenges as worthy of our devotion and commitment in their own right. Hence, the reasons created by these constitutive conventions are responsive to the values internal to these "autonomous" sport practices, whose status as intrinsic values suggest there is more to human life than the mere struggle for life itself, for overcoming necessary instrumental obstacles that stand in the way of our very existence. So although we may not have any instrumental reasons for having social practices such as basketball and soccer, we clearly do have intrinsic reasons for having these practices that have, as their respective histories bear out, formidable normative force.

Once again, however, we are confronted with the question that if the normative prowess of the reasons we have for engaging the constitutive conventions of particular sports is so impressive, how can they be arbitrary and, therefore, conventions at all? The answer is that each and every sport has conceivable alternative ways they might have been played, which, if they had been followed instead, would have been the way they are currently played. Soccer is a case in point. In the opening decades of the nineteenth century, handling the ball as well as kicking it were both allowed at the elite English public schools in which the game was widely played and fostered. It was not until the middle of the nineteenth century that rules were drawn up at Eton to restrict the use of hands to advance the ball, which became the standard bearer for the other public schools (Dunning 2001, 94–96). Were it not for the fact that Eton's version of handless soccer became the most widely followed way to play it, our reigning contemporary version of the game would have likely looked very different. Soccer, of course, is not an outlier in this respect, but the general rule for the development of most, if not all, of our major sports today.

An important part of the reason why people play and otherwise engage in sports in our time is that these sports exist and are widely followed by the relevant communities (Marmor 2006, 360). Were it not for the constitutive conventions that midwifed them, and for the communities that followed them, there would be no such sport practices. When we factor these two features (conceivable alternatives and compliance-dependent reasons) into the equation, it seems clear that sports are a bona fide species of conventional social practices.

However, Marmor is also of the view that the conventional character of sports, as borne out in part both by their founding constitutive rules and by the different historical trajectories of their emergence, is not the last word with regard to their development. For it is typically the case that the constitutive rules of sport, not to mention most social practices, eventually get institutionally codified. Marmor argues that when sports undergo such institutionalization, when their rules are formulated and enacted by an authoritative ruling body and applied and enforced by legislative officials, they cease to be conventional practices. They no longer count as conventional practices but institutional ones in his view because their rules can no longer be considered as arbitrary, as having conceivable alternatives that if followed instead would have changed how they are played. That most sports played and observed today are of the institutional variety should come as no surprise. But that does not mean, Marmor notes, that conventional sport practices have wholly gone by the wayside but rather that the present sporting scene can be divided into two separate and distinct spheres: a conventional sphere "played by amateurs who care little about official tournaments, and just play the game, roughly, as the conventions determine it," and "an official, institutional sphere" played by participants under the auspices of officials who regulate their actions in "official leagues and tournaments" (2009, 51). Marmor's reference to "amateurs" here is misleading and is better understood as those who play what is euphemistically called "sandlot" or pickup games, or what Europeans calls "park" sports, in which the players themselves organize the games, modify the rules, and self-police their actions.

Of course, understanding the institutional side of Marmor's distinction hangs on just what he thinks the institutionalization of the constitutive rules of sports entails. Fortunately, he is quite clear about what he has in mind here, telling us that it involves two modifications of conventional rules, both of which can be traced, as discussed in Chapter 2, to what Hart calls "secondary" rules, rules about rules that govern institutional practices (2009, 51).[12] The first modification establishes a mechanism for rule changes—that is, rules that determine when new rules can be enacted and old ones modified. Conventional sports and other in-kind practices typically lack such a mechanism; changes in their rules, by contrast, occur gradually over a long period of time instead of being enacted at a particular point in time by a legislative body. The second modification introduces a mechanism for ensuring compliance with institutional rules, which mete out penalties for rule violations as well as determine who is charged to execute them and how they are to be administered. Conventional sport practices ensure compliance with the rules, contrarily, by informal means, usually in the form of social pressure or explicit criticism of those who break the rules (52).

A False Start Corrected

There is much to be said for Marmor's illuminating account of deep and constitutive conventions. Of special note in this regard is the much-needed light it sheds on how conventions play an integral part not just in resolving the inescapable coordination problems that stem from our social commerce with one another, as Lewis shows, but in constituting cherished social practices, like sport, that for many of us make life worth living. That said, the pressing question I need to address now is whether Marmor's account of deep conventions captures the important normative work I claim ethical conventions do, especially when conflicts over the point and value of athletic endeavor erupt like the conflict between the amateur and professional athletic communities. To answer that question, however, it will first be helpful to recap the ethical picture I painted regarding their conflict about how sport should be done.[13]

That picture depicted what were two antithetical conceptions of sport. The source of their discrepant takes on sport, however, was not traceable to the formal, institutional rules themselves. Indeed, the rules were the same for both parties, and each was held equally accountable for observing them. Rather, their differences were centered on the rival ethical conventions each community embraced, which reflected the disparate social and historical understandings, needs, and concerns at work in each athletic community. In short, these conventions provided the normative backdrop for their rival ethical takes on sport as, on the one hand, a gentlemanly endeavor and, on the other hand, a professional one. Their emergence in tandem with that of the formal rules unfolded in much the same way as Lewis earlier suggested, as tacit, local, informal norms to deal with normative issues "left open by the listed rules" (2002, 104). And their tacit, informal, social character and generous scope make them recalcitrant to what Marmor calls legislative codification, to formalization in explicit epigrammatic rules.

Mindful of that picture, I argued in my previously published writings on this topic that Marmor's deep conventions were indeed the ethical conventions I was after. That is, I claimed that the normative background of understandings that informed these two athletic communities, and the evaluative schemes they relied on to form their irreconcilable ethical views on appropriate athletic conduct, were indeed the very same deep conventions of games that Marmor unearthed. When he argued, therefore, that there is more to games than the rules, that the rules constitute but do not exhaust games, and that deep conventions are the additional dimension of games that makes them more than simple rule-governed affairs, I was persuaded that these were the relevant conventions operating within the amateur and professional camps that led to the ethical standoff between them.

I now realize, however, as I briefly noted in the Introduction, that was a mistake, and not an insignificant one at that.[14] My mistake was to run together the deep conventions of games that Marmor argues serve as the common normative backdrop for *all* the particular constitutive conventions (rules) of the sports developed in different cultures with the ethical conventions that serve as the common normative backdrop for the *particular* constitutive conventions of local sports developed in *separate* athletic cultures like those of the amateur and professional communities. What makes this a serious mistake is that what I argued was the main shortcoming of the self-styled Dworkian moral principles employed by Robert Simon, John Russell, and company—their unduly abstract character that reduced them essentially to moral platitudes about how to do sports—is the same abstract deficiency that plagues Marmor's deep conventions. After all, deep conventions tell us only in the most general terms what is a game and how it should be played. So when it comes to abstract moral platitudes about how to do sports that fall woefully short in the contextually sensitive ethical discernment department, deep conventions belong in the same ethically challenged class as the abstract moral principles favored by broad internalists.

Fortunately for my purposes, my normative gaffe in explicating the conflicted ethical picture of the amateur and professional communities has a positive upside; it exposes what has to rank as a major shortcoming not just of Marmor's account of conventional games and sports but of his whole account of conventional social practices. Although Marmor has a lot to say that is insightful about how our general concept of games that derive from their deep conventions gives rise to our particular concepts of games that derive from their constitutive conventions, he has next to nothing to say about how these constitutive conventions of games further give rise to ethical conventions, to a whole host of tacit understandings and informal norms, regarding how we should play specific sports in different social settings. So the deep conventions that for Marmor serve as the general normative backdrop for the constitutive (rules) conventions of a whole array of particular sports are manifestly unsuited to serve as the normative backdrop for these particular sports themselves when their rules fail to deliver, as they inevitably and frequently do, on their normative promise. The reason why points once again to their overly abstract, indeterminate character. As we have seen, when there is no applicable rule to tell us what we should do, as was the case in the turn-of-the-century baseball example of a runner who interfered with a catcher after he had crossed home plate, or when the rules give us the wrong moral counsel, as was the case in the Brett pine tar example, or when the rules cannot be counted on to reconcile conflicting views about what the point of sport is and how it should be done (my pet normative peeve), it is clear that deep conventions cannot make up the normative difference because what goes missing in each of these instances is not our *general concept* of how we should play sports but our quite *specific concept* of how we should play this particular sport at this particular time in this particular context. When it comes to such examples, therefore, there is no normative substitute for the local conventions that develop around sports like baseball, whose stock of tacit understandings and informal norms best equip us to judge what we should do when the rules fail us. What goes for particular sports here goes for sports played by different athletic communities or cultures, like my main amateur and professional example, in which only local, context-dependent ethical conventions, as opposed to general, context-independent deep conventions, can close the normative gap left open by the rules.

However, Marmor might object that he has not failed, as I have alleged, to account for the fact that the constitutive conventions that give rise to different sports played in local cultures also give rise to tacit understandings and informal norms that in concrete, determinate terms tell us how they should be played in certain social and historical contexts, to include when the listed rules prove unhelpful in this regard. He has a plausible case to make in arguing such for two central reasons that, he might further credibly say, I should have been aware of before pressing my criticism. The first reason is that he never intended or pretended that deep conventions can serve as a normative stand-in when the listed rules leave us in a lurch for the very same reason I suggested they are ill-suited for such a task: Their abstract, general status rules out such a possibility. After all, he would likely add at this point, it was my earlier mistake that they could serve in this capacity, not his. The second reason is that he chose to remedy this particular normative shortcoming of listed rules, not as Lewis and I did, by distinguishing between formal, written conventional rules and informal, unwritten conventions that are not rules, but by proposing an expanded conception of conventional rules that is inclusive of both written and unwritten rules. To be sure, this is a controversial account of rules, but it is not a wildly irrational account or one that should have caught me unaware, since I earlier previewed it and made a point of commenting on its controversial character. So the reason Marmor never considered it necessary to appeal to tacit understandings and informal norms to fill the normative vacuum left open at times by the listed rules, as I not only did but found fault for his failing to do so, is that his broad conception of constitutive rules is perfectly capable of handling any normative crises that might come their way. All Marmor needs to do when dealing with normative crises like these is appeal to their complementary co-constitutive unwritten rules to resolve them. That simple move, therefore, should suffice to dispose of the confounding rule-centered dilemmas raised by Simon and Russell, and my own example of the confounding dispute between amateur and professional proponents of sport.

I have two responses to this objection as proposed. The first is that aside from Marmor's initial remarks repudiating any distinction of the sort Lewis made between rules and tacit understandings, and I make between rules and the ethical conventions of different athletic communities or cultures, and aside from the single example he offers of an informal game rule (regarding the acceptable amount of time a player is permitted to make a move in a game or perform an action in sport, which in many games and sports, but not all, are typically legislatively codified), his objection is almost entirely ad hoc. That is, Marmor has written nary a word about how such informal rules are supposed to work in tandem with the written rules, most important, how the former are supposed to come to the aid of the latter in the written-rule-challenged examples posed by broad internalists and the purpose-challenged examples that interest me. Until Marmor tells us considerably more about how the crucial interplay between written and unwritten rules works, about how they, among other things, are able to discharge their respective normative authority as the occasion requires, it is not evident his objection has much going for it.

My second, more important response concerns Marmor's claim that all bets are off regarding the conventionality of social practices like sport when they get institutionalized, as is typically the case in the final stage of their development. Whatever we might think of Marmor's initial claim that the constitutive rules of sports rightly (broadly) conceived are not susceptible to the kinds of normative counterexamples others and I have raised—and I am on record that the jury must remain out on this point until Marmor gives us a much more detailed account of what he has in mind here—his claim that the institutionalization of sports, the formalization of their (written and unwritten) rules, deconventionalizes their practice is unpersuasive on its face. For it would require nothing short of a radical reconceptualization of sports, one that would remove them from the class of conventional practices and remand them to the formulaic, nonarbitrary class of institutional practices.

There are two major problems here, both of which have important implications for the ethical picture I drew of the athletic divide between the amateur and professional proponents of sport; if one thing is indisputably clear regarding that picture, it is that participants from both sides of this divide were engaged in institutional sports in Marmor's sense. The first, less important problem for my purposes is that Marmor's claim that the institutionalization of game rules eliminates their arbitrary character, the possibility of a conceivable alternative that might be followed instead, does not stand up to critical scrutiny. The second, more important problem for my purposes is that Marmor's institutionalization thesis also entails that all, not just some, of the rules of sport practices would be subject to legislative codification (something he left unremarked either because he did not notice this consequence or simply chose to ignore it). This is a strong claim if not a baldly counterintuitive one. It means that for Marmor one of the most normatively telling marks of the transformation of sport from a conventional to an institutional practice is the dislocation of all the informal norms and tacit understandings that, as we have seen, play such vital normative part in the conduct of sports, at least those informal norms that cannot be subsumed under the now wholly codified, written rules of institutional sport. For whatever informal rules or norms prove resistant to such formalization are, in effect, gerrymandered out of Marmor's normative account of institutional sports. That puts, I argue, Marmor in the untenable position of having to deny that uncodifiable, informal, unwritten rules (norms) play any role, normatively or otherwise, in institutional sports. What is untenable about this position is that it opens up Marmor to the very criticism I leveled against him at the beginning of this section: that when the rules prove to be normatively clueless or just mistaken as to how we should act in certain problematic athletic situations, the only normative response he can muster is to tap the deep conventions of games. The rub, of course, is that these abstract, untethered conventions are no more able to remedy such normatively unsettling situations than the institutional rules they were supposed to complement. This suggests that my initial criticism of Marmor in this regard was not wrong but only misplaced, because its target should have been institutional sports rather than conventional sports.

Let us begin then with the first problem raised by Marmor's institutionalization thesis, that institutional rules are not conventions because they are not arbitrary in the required sense. It will be helpful here to see what is problematic about this claim if we refer back to a similar claim made by John Searle that Marmor took exception to. According to Searle, it is the introduction of the constitutive rules of games themselves, not the introduction of Hart's secondary rules, that makes the games in which they figure institutional rather than arbitrary enterprises. As Searle sees it then, "it is a rule of chess that we can win the game by checkmating the king. It is a *convention* of chess that the king is larger than the pawn. 'Convention' implies arbitrariness, but constitutive rules in general are not in that sense arbitrary" (1995, 28; emphasis in original). So after the constitutive rules are in place, argues Searle, these rules cease to be arbitrary and, therefore, conventional. This is why he is so adamant that we not confuse these "institutional" rules with conventions like those that determine the sizes of chess pieces.

Marmor, however, not only does not find Searle persuasive on this score but accuses him of failing even to try to be persuasive, claiming that he offers not a single argument to support his position (2009, 35). While I, too, think Searle fails to make a convincing case that institutional rules are not conventions, I also think it is not hard, contra Marmor, to see the critical point he is driving at. In fact, I think we can see what Searle is up to in this regard by revisiting what might seem the most unlikely sphere of sport to support Searle's claim that it is the constitutive rules of sports that tell against their supposed conventionality—namely, what Marmor calls "amateur" sports and what I say are less misleadingly called and better understood as "sandlot" sports. This is the sphere of sports in which the players themselves rather than bureaucratic surrogates organize, govern, and officiate what occurs on the playing field, and in which Marmor is convinced, for this very player-centric reason, the relevant rules are indeed of the arbitrary, conventional kind. Marmor thinks as much, I think, because when a sport like baseball, for instance, is played in such informal settings, players typically modify the rules to suit the occasion. For example, playing sandlot baseball according to the official rules that mandate nine players on each side is almost impossible to do, given the sheer difficulty of rounding up eighteen players to form two teams. As a consequence, rules like this have to be modified to even get the game off the ground. This might mean that when a side is batting, anything hit to right field by right-handed batters or left field by left-handed batters is ruled an automatic out to compensate for a shortage of outfielders. Similarly, it might mean that when infield grounders are hit to the third baseman, a runner is ruled out if the third baseman throws the ball to the pitcher rather than the (absent) first baseman before the runner reaches first base to make up for a shortage of infielders to man each base. To be sure, many other rule modifications might be required in such sandlot games, and for reasons other than an inability to field complete teams, and of course, all concerned must agree on them at the outset. In all such cases, however, how the rules are interpreted, applied, and called is left largely to the players' discretion.

I take Marmor's disagreement with Searle on the relevant constitutive rules here to be the obvious one that the rules of sandlot sports are arbitrary, that conceivable alternatives are always in play in such sports, and that resorting to them not only does not defeat their purpose but, contrarily, is frequently what makes it possible to realize their purpose. So Marmor seems on sound footing in claiming that sports of the sandlot variety are paradigm cases of conventional sports played by conventional rules. Nonetheless, I think Searle has a different point in mind that gives him at least a plausible, even if not a persuasive, retort to Marmor's contention that sandlot sports are paradigmatically conventional enterprises. That point is that while it is certainly true, to stick with my present example, that players of sandlot baseball have discretion to alter the rules as they see fit to suit their contingent athletic goals, there is one important sense in which their hands are tied regarding the most basic constitutive rules of baseball. For the most basic rules are the ones that determine what counts as pitching, fielding, hitting, base running, and the like. So whether hitting to the opposite field or an infielder throwing to the pitcher rather than a (absent) first baseman ahead of the runner count as putouts is entirely a matter of the players' discretion, it is decidedly verboten to change the rules to allow batters to hit a pitch while wielding a tennis racket or to allow fielders to catch a ball with large nets. In these most fundamental rules, deferring to the players' discretion is no longer an option, even in so-called sandlot baseball. Changing basic rules like these, Searle might argue, is a nonstarter because they change the fundamental skills that a game like baseball is supposed to test. In a word, changing these most pivotal constitutive rules of baseball means one is no longer playing baseball from Searle's perspective.

I think Searle has an argument here, contra Marmor, albeit not an especially good one. For all he is entitled to claim, I argue, is that the constitutive rules of sandlot baseball are more arbitrary than those of organized baseball. In other words, I do not think the determination of whether constitutive rules are arbitrary is a cut-and-dried, either-or matter but rather a matter of the "degrees" of arbitrariness of such rules. Looking at the question as one of the degrees of arbitrariness of constitutive rules is Marmor's preferred way of dealing with this issue (2009, 73). On that account, therefore, I think Marmor wins the day because, to reiterate, I think Searle has shown no more than the rules of sandlot baseball are more arbitrary than those of, say, Little League baseball. This is, of course, to be understood in the same sense in which Marmor argues that the deep conventional rules of games are less arbitrary than those of the constitutive (surface) conventional rules.

However, I think Marmor's insistence that we mostly favor distinctions in degree over distinctions in kind when gauging the arbitrariness of the rules of sports in particular and the rules of social practices in general also tells against his own view that in the separate sphere of institutional sport, when secondary rules of the Hartian kind kick in, the rules of sport can no longer be considered conventional because they no longer can be said to have conceivable alternatives. In this institutional realm, argues Marmor, players no longer have any discretion to tinker with the rules as they did in the sandlot realm. Institutionally speaking then, a baseball team either fields nine players or forfeits the game, either successfully catches outfield flies to left or right field or does not, either throws to a first baseman to put out a runner or does not. No nod to player discretion here; indeed, no tomfoolery with regard to the rules tolerated here whatsoever. That said, however, it is not as if institutional rules are so set in stone that they are impervious to any modification by game agents exercising their arbitrary discretion. True, players rarely if ever are given a say in how institutional rules are interpreted or applied. But the same cannot be said for game officials, who commonly change the way they enforce the rules in certain institutional game situations. Think of the final, climatic moments of a college or professional basketball game in which referees often refrain from calling rule violations they unhesitatingly called in the earlier parts of the contest in order to ensure their outcomes are not determined (wrongly) by them but (rightly) by the players. Further, think of a National Hockey League game in which a team with one player already in the penalty box is commonly less likely to be called for a second penalty, putting them two players down, unless it is a flagrant violation. Yet further, think of the so-called home team advantage that works against visiting teams in many sports that usually results from game officials being cowed by boisterous spectators from making legitimate calls against their local team. Speaking of spectators, the sporting public is also no slouch in the rule-changing department, in which they are sometimes able to agitate successfully for modifying rules or eliminating existing rules or creating new rules that are not in their view in the best interest of the sports.

In all these instances, rules are being modified in various ways at the discretion of game agents that create conceivable alternatives to the official, institutional rules. Here again, therefore, it is more plausible to talk of degrees of arbitrariness rather than a firm distinction in kind between conventional (arbitrary) rules and institutional (nonarbitrary) rules. If there is a distinction to be made between sandlot and institutional sports, it is not a hard-and-fast, in-kind distinction between *conventional* sandlot sports and *institutional* (nonconventional) sports, but merely an in-degree distinction between two varieties of conventional sports, between the more arbitrary conventional sandlot sports and the less arbitrary conventional institutional sports.

When it comes to this first rule-centered part of Marmor's denial of the conventional character of institutional sports, we have good grounds to reject his argument. Institutional rules may be less arbitrary than their sandlot counterparts, but they are arbitrary, historically contingent products all the same, and so conventional in the relevant sense.

However, the second problem with Marmor's account of institutional sports—his claim that the legislative codification of their rules entailed by such institutionalization eliminates or at very least significantly reduces and marginalizes the tacit understandings and informal norms that fill the gap left open by the listed rules in conventional sports—is the more serious and glaring problem. I claim that Marmor is guilty here of either eliminating or reducing and marginalizing informal conventions because it is not clear from what little he has to say in this regard which of these two versions he intends. On the first, more radical version, Marmor seems to suggest that once a sport has been institutionalized—that is, taken on board Hart's secondary rules—the tacit understandings and informal conventions (norms) that heretofore played an important normative role in guiding and regulating athletic conduct no longer play any such role, having been replaced by nonarbitrary formal norms (institutional rules). On the second, less radical version, he seems to suggest that while the institutionalization of a sport does not result in its complete deconventionalization, it does considerably lessen in number and normatively weaken whatever normative role those remaining informal conventions that proved resistant to legislative codification may play. Both versions are problematic because they give a distorted picture of institutional sports that does not square with the actual and indispensable normative work informal conventions do in this athletic realm. However, because the more radical version seems absurd on its face—it beggars the imagination to think once a sport has reached this institutional stage, any and all tacit understandings and informal norms that might have guided athletic conduct in the past or that might yet emerge to play such a normative role in the future simply and suddenly drop out of the picture altogether, never to be seen again—the better, more charitable way to go is to presume Marmor has the less radical version in mind.

What, then, are we to make critically of this latter view? My answer is not much. If the history of institutional sports shows anything, and I presume the same could be said for the history of most, if not all, social practices at this institutional stage, it shows that informal conventions as to how sport should be done at different times and places in different athletic communities is the key to unlocking the otherwise inscrutable normative disputes and conflicts that have been a constant, recurring feature of their history. To suggest otherwise, to hold that institutional sports are by definition, as Marmor would have it, convention-unfriendly affairs, is to willfully ignore that normative history. And with respect to my primary example of the amateur and professional dispute regarding how sport should be done, it would not do justice in the least to the ethically freighted conventions that pitted them against one another, despite their observance of the same batch of secondary rules and, of course, primary rules. Nor is trying to read yet more into his account of institutional sports to make it a more attractive, convention-friendly rendering an option, charitable or otherwise. For it would require, implausibly, crediting Marmor with not only an entirely ad hoc rendering of institutional sport but one in which attributing a stronger, richer normative role to these tacit understandings and informal norms would put him squarely in opposition to his stated, explicit views on this matter.

Conclusion

I argue that neither Lewis's notion of coordinating conventions nor Marmor's notions of deep and constitutive (surface) conventions account for the kind of ethical conventions at work in the normative history of modern sport practices, especially in conflicts like that between the amateur and professional communities, which set the tone for much of that normative history. That is why in Chapter 6 I follow a different path in developing a conventionalist ethical theory of sport, one that takes a page out of G.W.F. Hegel's *Philosophy of Right* (1977b), specifically his notion of *Sittlichkeit* (ethical life). What is distinctive about Hegel's notion of *Sittlichkeit* is that it marked Hegel's attempt to develop an ethical account of the central social practices and institutions of modern Western society (for him, the family, civil society, and the state) by taking as his point of departure the very norms implicit in these social practices and institutions. I aim to do the same for modern sport, by taking as my point of departure the informal ethical conventions implicit in their practice and institution.

6

A Conventionalist Ethical Theory of Sport

I now wish to present my own conventionalist ethical theory of sport. What distinguishes it from formalism and both versions of broad internalism is that it takes its normative marching orders not from rules or Dworkian style moral principles but from what I call, after G.W.F. Hegel's (1977b) notion of *Sittlichkeit*, ethical conventions that govern sport at different times and places. What distinguishes it from other conventionalist ethical theories of sport, or of anything else for that matter, is that the kind of conventions it trades in are not of the coordinating or deep and surface varieties. My first task, then, is to make clear what distinguishes ethical conventions from these other varieties. The difficulty I face in this regard is that many philosophers doubt there are such things as ethical conventions, because they are convinced that coordinating and deep and surface conventions are all the conventions we have available to us and all we need to conduct our social affairs with one another; they also believe that none of them speak directly or substantively to how we should ethically live these lives, whether in or outside of sport. So in trying to carve out a space for ethical conventions, I need to show both that they are indeed conventions and that they do the kind of ethical things I claim they do. After it is clear what ethical conventions are and do, I flesh out what an ethical theory of this conventionalist kind can contribute to our understanding and justification of how we should conduct ourselves in sport at different times and places.

Ethical Conventions of Sport

In claiming that the ethical norms of sport are conventions, I am, of course, claiming that they possess the same three features that warrant lumping them under the general category of conventions. That means that they, too, are social norms, have conceivable alternatives, and give people reasons for acting in light of them. I discuss these three features of ethical conventions in the same order as I do in my discussion of coordinating, deep, and surface conventions.

Like their conventional counterparts, ethical conventions also have to do with the beliefs, values, and norms held by the members of a social unit, in our case what I refer to as sport practice communities.[1] What distinguishes them from other types of conventions is that the beliefs, values, and norms that make them up define the ethical outlook of such practice communities, which colors the social relations among the members of such communities in important normative ways. What is more, what distinguishes the kind of normative work ethical conventions do from the kind of normative work other nonconventional moral norms do also has centrally to do with the social provenance and reach of ethical conventions. So there are several features of the social character of ethical conventions that I need to account for to adequately explain what they are and what important normative functions they perform.

To begin then, the sociality of ethical conventions of sport and the like are owed to their practice-dependent status. Were it not for sport practices and the communities that are their social offshoots and that support them, these conventions would have never seen the light of day. Further, ethical conventions owe their existence not only to sport practices and their corresponding communities but to their normative force as well. Because the norms and standards of rational acceptability they put in play have the grip on the communities of practice that they do, they have binding force on their members. Yet further, the fact that ethical conventions are in-house creations, that they are embedded in and inform the actual ethical life of sport and the other collective practices of society in which they figure, means they give voice to how these communities themselves, not just their individual members, think things like sport should be done. In other words, they provide a distinctive social standpoint by which to evaluate sport at particular times and places, a standpoint not grounded in "subjective opinion or caprice" (Hegel 1977b, §144). Unlike philosophical normative theories such as Immanuel Kant's categorical imperative or utilitarianism, which take as their starting point and ethical data only those beliefs and norms that pass a philosophical test (for instance, Kant's universalizing test) or only beliefs and norms that are the product of a philosophical procedure claiming some special insight (for instance, the utilitarian claim that the basic data of ethics are facts concerning pleasure and pain [Knowles 2002, 230]), a conventionalist ethical theory of sport, at least of the kind I favor, takes as its starting point and ethical data the self-legislated conventional norms that are embedded in and actually inform our sporting lives at particular times and places.

In following this social path, I am taking a page directly out of Hegel's account of the ethical life of modern society worked out in his book the *Philosophy of Right*, in which he introduces the technical term *Sittlichkeit* to describe his unique social take on ethical theory. By the *Sittlichkeit* of a society Hegel means "a way of acting and thinking" in a form of life "in terms of the 'ways things are done'" in that form of life "understood as a background set of norms" (Pinkard 1996, 124). So the *Sittlichkeit* of a society has to do with the shared background understandings and norms that are embedded in and inform the various social practices that gain an institutional foothold in society. These background understandings and norms of social undertakings like sport concern the "way things are done," in which the "way things are done" is understood as a species of conventions.[2] For Hegel then, the ethical life of a society and its characteristic social practices and institutions like sport is mainly a conventional, practical affair in which the point of ethical theory is not to replace the various ways such practices are done with philosophical constructions, to construct, in effect, sport and the like as it ideally ought to be, but to reflectively sort out and articulate what these various conventional ways of doing sport can be said to ethically require of us.[3] In calling such conventional norms ethical, Hegel was claiming that the way things are done in sport and the like includes, and could not help but do so, a specification of how they should be done. Or as Sophie Chappell nicely puts it, when it comes to social practices like sport, "we never find ourselves purely on the 'is' side, cut off from the 'ought' side" (2017, 714).

Hegel provides further insight into the robust sociality of ethical conventions of sport practices and the like by mapping out where they fit in the modern social scheme of things. As he sees it, modern society can be divided into three domains: the family, civil society, and the state (Hegel 1977b, §157).[4] The family for Hegel marks off the private sphere of modern society in which the intimate relations enjoyed by family members is rooted in the love they have for one another. The state oversees the public sphere of political life in modern society, in which individuals understand themselves as citizens bound by their allegiance to a rational state. Sandwiched between them is what Hegel calls civil society, which in the contemporary parlance of liberal modernity is the sphere of voluntary associations. It is in civil society, Hegel argues, that individuals can pursue their diverse self-interests by forming voluntary associations with like-minded individuals. He has in mind here not ethnic associations, or what in contemporary terms we call interest groups formed ostensibly for political purposes, but the kind of associational forms of life that sport and other cultural practices have to offer. By forming such communities of practice, individuals can pursue their personal interests and seek recognition for their efforts to achieve particular goals and goods in the company of kindred others. In doing so, Hegel emphasized, they come to adopt a common ethical outlook internal to the different social practices in which they engage.

Hegel, of course, did not slot sport or any other cultural practices in this sphere of civil society, but they clearly belong here given his general characterization of the social locus of such activities. What is noteworthy about so locating them is the common ethical outlook that Hegel regarded as a signature feature of the associational forms of life that populate civil society, and that I argue is a signature feature of modern sport practices. Before I say more about that common ethical outlook, I should first note that the social space sport occupies as a characteristic form of life of civil society tells us something important about what cannot be morally claimed about sport or any other practice that does its normative work here. And that is that such activities are not things we are morally obligated to take up in the first place. So no one can properly be said to be morally required to do sport or music or literature or anything else of the sort. This is an important moral point that should not be lost sight of in dealing with cultural fare like sport. But it should not obscure the great numbers of people who do, in fact, choose to engage in these cultural activities even though not morally obligated to do so, and who make them an important part of their and their society's ethical life.

Although it is up to individuals to choose whether to take up sport or any other cultural practice, it is not up to said individuals to determine for themselves how they should acquit themselves within their precincts. That is a matter for the socially constructed ethical conventions of these practices and the common ethical outlook they introduce to determine. They are the go-to normative resources in this regard because ethical conventions hold bona fide members of the relevant sport communities accountable to one another in terms of the particular conception of sport—of its particular purpose, values, mix of skills, and the like—they identify with. As Richard Rorty rightly notes, "The choice of what purpose to have is almost always, in practice, a choice among groups of people rather than a choice among abstract formulae, . . . a choice between . . . the sort of people who have one over-riding purpose and the sort of people who have another" (1996, 7). So it is ethically as well, and so it was ethically for adherents of the rival amateur and professional camps. Depending on what ethical group athletes aligned themselves with determined whether they should relate to their athletic peers as pleasure-seeking gentlemen or win-seeking professionals.

The fact that the ethical conventions of sport hold the members of athletic communities normatively accountable to one another is another way of saying that they importantly modify their social relationships with one another. The same is true of any normative social relationship. For example, when considering whether it is normatively justifiable to pay children to perform their household chores, we need to consider what relationship between family members is normatively justifiable. If the answer is that children should be expected to pull their own weight in meeting their family responsibilities without payment, then it is a clear normative violation to pay them to do their household chores. Paying them would be to mistake the relations that should hold between family members by treating them in the way, for instance, employers should treat their employees (Anderson 2000, 191). In sport too, considering whether athletes should be paid for their exploits depends on whether they should be understood as nonchalant gentlemen athletes seeking an enjoyable venture or seriously committed athletes seeking athletic distinction. Paying the former would thus be an ethical mistake as would not paying the latter. When I say ethical mistake, it should be remembered that in each case getting the relevant ethical conventions wrong was not considered an innocent or minor ethical error but, as one contemporaneous observer of the early period of modern sport put it, the "depth of immorality" (Corbin 1901, 6). So being unconventional when it comes to one's actions or judgments on either side of this athletic divide is the same thing as being unethical.

That the purpose of ethical conventions is to hold members of athletic communities ethically accountable to one another is what distinguishes them from the three other kinds of conventions. To begin with coordinating conventions, their purpose is to use the information individuals have gathered about their peers to coordinate their actions with one another. Holding their peers to ethical account is just not what these conventions do and would likely only interfere with people's efforts to coordinate their actions. Further in this same vein, deviating from a coordinating convention may be a regrettable social gaffe, but it hardly ranks as a serious ethical failure in itself. As David Papineau correctly observes, "Somebody who holds their knife in the wrong hand or addresses a duke as 'my lord' rather than 'your grace', may be committing an embarrassing faux pas, but it would be silly" to ethically take them to task for "their social incompetence" (2017, 66). Such people may be appropriately adjudged uncouth but not unethical. The silliness of the ethical charge in such instances goes back to the point that coordinating "conventions . . . govern matters of no intrinsic importance" (64) or, as

Marmor puts it, of matters largely of convenience (2009, 134). Again, that is not to say that coordination problems are not important but only that how we choose to solve them are not, as long as they prove efficacious. Further, to accept the fact that how coordination problems are solved is of no importance, ethical or otherwise, is not to deny that at least some conventions of this type have unmistakable moral consequences that should factor into why they should be complied with. For instance, how a society comes up with the convention to drive on the right or left side of the road may not be important, again ethically or otherwise, in itself; after all, either alternative will do perfectly fine instrumentally speaking. However, once, say, driving on the right side has emerged as the reigning convention, it would be out-and-out immoral for someone to drive on the left side. Nonetheless, the immorality of doing so is derivative on the settled solution, not on the process leading to it. That is why the way in which a coordination problem is solved is not of moral import. Whereas violating an ethical convention of, say, Major League Baseball by playing aggressively with a big lead late in the game, which entails "the cessation of stolen-bases, sending runners in search of extra bases, swinging at 3-0 pitches" (Turbow and Duca 2011, 18), is nonderivatively an ethical transgression of baseball as it is currently played.

Holding our peers ethically accountable also distinguishes ethical conventions from deep conventions of sport as Marmor conceives them. To be sure, deep conventions, unlike coordinating ones, are normative ones, but normative only in the sense that they inform our general concept of sport and our general normative requirements in playing games of this type. As such, they have nothing determinative or substantive to say about how sport should be done at a particular time and place. So whether an athlete should eschew strategy in doing sport so as not to offend against the ethical sensibilities and valued social relationships prized by one's athletic peers, which captures the ethical intuitions of the amateur but not the professional athlete, cannot be answered by appealing to human nature, to our general need to play competitive games. Hence, the very feature that makes deep conventions in Marmor's view conventions, the fact that their normative responses underdetermine the basic psychological and social needs that give rise to them—in short, their arbitrariness—is what marks them off from the determinative, context-sensitive character of ethical conventions. That is further why we should resist giving a Kantian gloss to the appeal to human nature that is emblematic of deep conventions, be it of sport or anything else, because the appeal to human nature, to our general need to do sport, underdetermines the many different ways sport has been done and likely will be done in the future.[5]

We can further distinguish the normative accountability that is the function of ethical conventions from the local constitutive and normative functions that surface conventions perform. Surface conventions, it will be remembered, are the constitutive and normative force behind the wide array of sport practices that have emerged over their long history. However, on Marmor's account the normative part that surface conventions shoulder is short lived, since once the inevitable institutionalization of these various sports kicks in, surface conventions are nowhere to be found, having been replaced completely, or at least substantively, by legislatively codified rules. From that point on, Marmor would have us believe that nothing about sport, ethically speaking or otherwise, can accurately be claimed to be conventional. But he is clearly mistaken because ethical conventions, as I argue, are normatively crucial to almost everything that goes on in institutional sports, whether we are talking about the amateur or professional athletic community. It is ethical conventions, then, that take up the normative slack once sports are institutionalized, and in so doing can be distinguished from the former, pre-institutional normative role that surface conventions once played.

Two further things about the social makeup of ethical conventions need to be discussed before we move on to its other main features. The first is that in holding us ethically accountable to our athletic peers, they do so not as individuals qua individuals but as individuals qua members of a particular practice community. This is especially important because becoming a member of a practice community and committing to its internal norms and goods creates what Margaret Gilbert (1989, 377) calls a collective subject.[6] We can speak of a collective subject, a "we," because by taking on board the ethical conventions and the goods they serve of a sport practice, each of its members acquires a new collective practical identity, a new way of seeing themselves and their actions, which they share with their fellow members. I am using the notion of a practical identity here as a term of art in Christine Koorsgaard's sense, as that "description under which you find your life worth living, and your actions to be worth undertaking" (1996, 101). So what made the members of the amateur community a collective, normatively like-minded subject, was that they regarded their athletic lives as worth pursuing and the actions they undertook on the playing field as worth undertaking only as gentlemen athletes. That is why they were of one mind that the proper end of athletic endeavor is to wring as much pleasure as they could muster out of the competitive challenges it poses, which mandated they do so exclusively in a spirit of moderation and generosity. That is why they were of one normatively contemptuous mind that to pursue sport as seriously and wholeheartedly as members of the professional community deign to do is ethically untoward in the extreme. As they saw it, it would be better not to do sport at all than to stoop so low as to make a mockery of the gentlemanly manner that typifies sport at its best. Of course, the professional community was equally of one normative mind that sport is a vocation, a career open to talent, that warrants each member's most strenuous efforts and that to give less than one's all is an ethical abomination in its own right that no self-respecting professional athlete would ever entertain, let alone do.

The normative point not to be missed here is that we are not dealing with the narcissism of minor differences but with the substantive normative differences that go to the very core of the different practical identities adopted by amateur and professional athletes. That means, among other things, that what distinguishes the athletes from these two rival camps were not, as John Russell suggests (2018), their disparate psychological outlooks; Russell opines that gentlemen athletes forswore a more serious approach to athletic competition because they were pessimistic that sport could be taken that seriously without leading to ruinous consequences and that professional athletes welcomed a more serious approach to athletic competition because they were optimistic that it would not lead to such ruinous consequences. Rather, what better explains the gentlemen athletes' refusal to take sport too seriously is that doing so militated against everything they stood for and valued about sport, and what better explains professional athletes' refusal to give anything less than their all to sport is that it militated against everything they stood for and valued about sport. In short, what was at stake in the dispute between them about how sport should be done is the normative self-image each had of themselves that defined their valued athletic identities.

The upshot then is that committing to the overriding purpose, ethical norms, and internal goods of a sport practice is a self-transformative process, a process by which, to parrot Hegel, an "I" becomes a "we" (1977b, §177), a tightly knit, normatively like-minded practice community. This process involves members of a sport practice community internalizing the ethical conventions of the practice and its attendant goods and incorporating the practical identity that corresponds to them into their own subjectivity. In the case of the amateur community, for example, by making the ethical norms of gentlemanly conduct (self-restraint, moderation, gallantry) their own, they were able to integrate the practical identity of the gentleman athlete into their own subjectivity. Once this transition has been effected, the self-conception of the members of that community and their freely chosen end to take up sport are made continuous with their newly acquired common identity as gentlemen athletes and the shared ends and norms characteristic of amateur sport. That explains why in making the ethical conventions of amateur sport and the practical identity of the gentleman athlete my own, "I am not," as Charles Taylor pithily puts it, "in any way pulled outside of myself" (1992, 48). That also explains why in abiding these ethical conventions and in acting in the self-disciplined and generous manner required of a gentleman athlete,

I am not constrained but enabled to act on my free self-determination to live my athletic life in this ethical manner. Rightly understood then, ethical conventions are not external impositions that limit my athletic agency but enabling conditions that further it. They "can appear as a restriction," Hegel tells us, "only on an indeterminate subjectivity or abstract freedom" (1977b, §149).

This self-transformative process by which an "I" becomes a "we" is also one in which, to quote Hegel again, a "we" is also an "I" (1977a, §177). This latter "I" is, of course, a new, socially constituted "I." In athletic terms, it is the "I" of a gentleman athlete or a professional athlete and the like, and in nonathletic terms, the "I" of a father, a professor, a politician, and other such practical identities that individuals can acquire by engaging in different social practices and internalizing the social roles and ethical norms that compose them. Further, one's normative entitlement to claim the mantle of a gentleman athlete or a father requires being recognized as such by one's peers. That means becoming a gentleman athlete, self-recognized as such, counts as a social achievement, as showing that one does things according "to the way things are and should be done" in the practice as recognized by the amateur community.

This practice- and recognition-dependent notion of the self is, in Hegel's view, a central feature of the ethical life of civil society in general and of social practices like sport in particular, and provides a contrast to what he dubs the standpoint of morality in which it is "the worth of the subject in himself that is in question" (1977a, §151) Moral theories that feature the standpoint of morality, such as Kantianism and utilitarianism, are able to assume this standpoint only by extricating individuals from their social milieu. That philosophical feat requires nothing less than "abstracting [subjects] from existing traditions, customary practices, and present motives, in short, from the established ethical life of a society" (Habermas 1993, 160). By cutting the self loose from its social attachments in this abstract way, Kant and company were free to train all their reflective efforts on singling out and valorizing some generic feature possessed by all human beings. For Kant that feature was our rational capacity; for utilitarians, our capacity to feel pleasure or pain; for contemporary moral philosophers like Stephen Darwell, our irreducible normative human dignity (2006, 21). The basic idea behind each of these claims is that individuals deserve to be recognized and treated "as . . . person[s] equal to others" by virtue of their possession of the relevant generic feature (rationality, pleasure and pain, dignity). Because the select generic feature that normatively entitles individuals to be recognized and treated with respect is something they all already possess by virtue of being the human agents they are, the recognition they are owed antedates, and is thus independent of, their social relations to one another (Brownlee 2015, 396). This is why Hegel claims that "moral consciousness does not possess this moment of recognition by others" (1977a, §384). Koorsgaard provides a paradigmatic Kantian version of this moral standpoint when she argues that "the value of values comes from valuers, and not the reverse" and "makes us [human agents] worthy of moral consideration. Humanity, not the standards implicit in social practices, is the ultimate source of value" (2003, 85). From the vantage point of morality, therefore, simply being a human agent, someone who possesses the requisite feature that marks one as such, entitles one to "immediate recognition" (Hegel 1977a, §488)—what Brownlee aptly labels the "automatic" model of recognition (2015, 377).

However, from Hegel's ethical standpoint, it is not some inalienable feature or other that human beings already possess that makes them a self that is worthy of our recognition, but rather the self that "has made itself what it is and for that reason is actual" (1977a, §489). For Hegel then, it is not the feature(s) that makes everyone the same that makes someone a self worthy of recognition, but the feature(s) that distinguishes individuals from one another, what he calls their "actuality" or "particularity," that makes someone a candidate for recognition. Selfhood and the recognition that goes with it in this ethical sense is entirely a social affair, something achievable only in a normatively structured world of social practices and institutions. Only by virtue of being a participant in a norm-governed social practice can an individual make oneself what he or she is (an athlete, parent, mayor, and the like), become a determinate self, and so be recognized as such by one's peers. That was the case for would-be amateurs and professionals and their corresponding practice communities. To be accounted as a gentleman athlete or a professional one is not something that can be conferred by simply proclaiming oneself to be either but something that can be achieved only by one's actions, by doing things "the way they are and should be done" in a particular practice community. In other words, no one simply is an amateur or professional; rather, one can only become such by proving through one's actions one is worthy of being called and recognized as such. Selfhood and recognition so understood are both social achievements, both wholly dependent on one's social interactions and relations with one another. And because these are social achievements, they can fail, for it is always possible that one's peers will challenge that one has acted according to the relevant normative standards that govern amateur or professional athletic life and deny one the recognition one seeks. This is significant because to fail to prove one's amateur or professional mettle with one's peers is the worst thing that can befall one, because, after all, one cannot win recognition from everyone as is possible in the moral realm. By contrast, in ethical life our common humanity just does not count for anything because it is too abstract, too indeterminate, to have any normative significance. Rather, the only others that matter when someone seeks recognition for its particularity as an athlete of a certain kind are those like-minded others who have the requisite normative standing and authority to confer such recognition. In my account, of course, that means only local practice communities such as the amateur or professional community.

The second, and final, remaining thing to be said about the indelible social character of the ethical conventions of sport is the mutual dependence between and among practitioners that is for Hegel a crucial feature of their normative authority. As noted, to be an amateur or professional athlete is to be recognized as such by one's peers. However, one can only be so recognized by the "right" sort of people, by the people who share our normative beliefs, standards, and values and, as a consequence, are in the social position necessary to hold us, and we them, mutually accountable for our particular talents, skills, and actions. But having one's normative status recognized by the right sort of people (one's peers) is for naught, in Hegel's view, if the recognition is not freely given. If it is not freely given by relevant others, if, rather, it is coerced or given under duress or issues from threats or other sanctions, then the recognition does not normatively count for anything. This is why Hegel argued the mutual recognition that underwrites the normative authority of the ethical conventions of sport and the like cannot be achieved by the brute exercise of power. This was the central lesson of Hegel's famous master and slave dialectic, which, as Taylor points out, upends what "sends people after recognition in the first place" (1992, 50). This is not just because the one who loses the struggle (the slave) is not recognized but because the one who wins the struggle (the master) is recognized by someone (the slave) who does not give it freely and thus lacks the requisite normative standing and authority required.

Ethical conventions are further defined by their arbitrary character, a feature they share with all other conventions. Fortunately, we can account for the arbitrariness of ethical conventions with more concision than we did their complicated and extensive social character because it mainly concerns two features that we have met up with in our previous discussion. These two features are, first, that they always have at least one conceivable alternative, and second, that they are compliance dependent. Both of these features derive from the historically contingent status of the ethical conventions that frame our historically contingent athletic lives. For had the social and historical circumstances that gave rise to them been different, the ethical conventions that came to define amateur and professional sport, not to mention all the other conceptions and practices of sport that have emerged over its long history, would have been different as well.

The ethical conventions of amateur and professional sport are arbitrary in this first sense because they each admit of at least one plausible alternative way they might have conducted their athletic affairs that would have remained true to, rather than betrayed, their characteristic ethical outlooks. A moment's speculation bears this point out. For instance, in the amateur case, the pleasure its adherents sought in pursuing sport might well have taken a normative page out of the hedonistic playbook of pre-modern folk games and sports, which favored festive physical challenges over disciplined efforts to achieve recordable athletic feats of excellence (Eichberg 2016, 196–200). Similarly, professional athletes might well have followed the lead of their fellow budding professionals in law and medicine in forming associations (the American Bar Association and the American Medical Association, respectively), in which they set their own standards of practice and excellence rather than having them set for them by independent agencies (professional team owners and their emissaries). Of course, had either camp thought of and opted to go in these alternative directions, they still would have been able to pursue and realize their different normative agendas. As previously noted, however, to say either athletic community had at least one conceivable alternative to their current ethical way of doing sport does not entail they actually envisaged or even were aware of such an alternative. Quite the contrary, all that is required is that each community had at least one plausible alternative to the current ethical way it was doing sport, and had either community envisaged and/or been made aware of such an alternative, it might well have followed that alternative instead.[7]

The ethical conventions of sport are arbitrary in the further sense that they are compliance dependent. It is in part because the ethical conventions that governed the athletic affairs of these two communities were followed rather than their conceivable alternative that they ended up being the reigning ethical conventions of each in the first place. So, once again, an important reason why amateurs and professionals followed the ethical conventions they did is because their relevant peers followed them as well.

However, the fact that the ethical conventions of amateur and professional sport are arbitrary in these two senses should not be construed as a sign of their normative impotency. On the contrary, conventions of this sort are not things that can be violated, ignored, or changed at will or on a whim, not, that is, without being subject to stiff ethical criticism and rebuke. That is because although ethical conventions always have conceivable alternatives, that does not mean the choice between them is indifferent to the members of the athletic communities in question. Further, while it is also the case that the ethical conventions different athletic communities follow is owed in part because their fellow members follow them too, that is not the only reason they comply with them. Regarding the first point, Andrei Marmor makes it clear that "arbitrariness should not be confused with indifference" (2009, 8), with the mistaken idea that the conventions people end up following mean no more to them than the alternative ones they might have followed instead. Regarding the second point, it should be remembered that compliance dependence is never the whole story when it comes to why athletic communities follow the ethical norms they do; they also follow the ethical conventions they do because of the good-making features and values they instantiate. In other words, doing sport as these ethical conventions prescribe is itself considered a good and valuable thing by the members of such communities. This bears as well on Marmor's (2009, 73) earlier point that the arbitrariness of conventions is a matter of degrees, which is why he argues that deep conventions are not as arbitrary as surface conventions and why I argue that ethical conventions are not as arbitrary as surface conventions and, of course, coordinating ones.

This leads to the third feature ethical conventions share with the other members of this class: They give us reasons to act in light of them. The reasons these conventions put on offer are, like their deep and constitutive conventional counterparts, *pro tanto* reasons. Whereas deep conventions give us *pro tanto* reasons to play any sort of competitive game and sport in ways that are directly responsive to our deep-seated social and psychological needs to be challenged in the special way in which they only can, and constitutive (surface) conventions give us *pro tanto* reasons to play particular sports in ways that are directly responsive to our particular social and psychological needs to be challenged in the distinctive way in which they only can, ethical conventions give us *pro tanto* reasons to play particular sports in ways that are directly responsive to the normatively charged social and historical contexts in which they occur. That is not to say, however, that ethical conventions have a normative monopoly on how sports are practiced, since both deep and constitutive conventions not only constitute sports but regulate them as well. For instance, if it is asked why participants are not allowed to hand carry the ball into a hole in a game of golf, or why players are not allowed to scoop the ball into their arms and advance it in a game of soccer, the simple and decisive reason is there are rules against such actions, which, of course, implicate their corresponding deep conventions. But the function of ethical conventions is first and foremost a normative one, which requires we take into account the practical reasoning at work in our normative deliberations regarding how sport should be done at different times and places. It is only by doing so that we can account for why it is that a particular athletic community, for example, thinks (reasons) that a game in which no rules are broken or untoward violence occurs but the participants relied heavily on science and technology in their efforts to win is, nonetheless, unmistakably an unethical game; or why a different athletic community thinks (reasons) that a game in which strategic rule bending and vigorous challenging of referees' calls against one's side were a constant occurrence is, nonetheless, unmistakably a perfectly good, ethical game. Seeking normative refuge in abstract philosophical principles or decision procedures, which pride themselves on their bracketing of such on-the-ground ethical conventions, only serves to render us clueless regarding what to make of such disparate ethical judgments.

What distinguishes the conventionalist ethical theory of sport I favor from its rivals, therefore, is its strong historicist and contextualist commitments. These commitments entail that we treat, in Robert Brandom's pithy words, "as fundamental norms *implicit* in *practices* rather than norms *explicit* in *principles*" (1994, 23; emphasis in original) and, I hasten to add, norms *explicit* in *rules*. That means that the practical reasoning that informs our ethical considerations and deliberations about how sport should be done are grounded in our deep cultural understandings regarding what is the point and value of athletic endeavor. This goes for the starting points of ethical inquiry into sport as it does for the whole structure of rational argumentation that takes place in different, historically situated athletic communities.

To begin with these starting points then, on my account they consist of the conventional, historically contingent beliefs, understandings, concepts, and norms that make up the vocabularies of athletic communities, which they put to use to describe and evaluate their varying conceptions of the purpose and value of athletic endeavor. In the amateur case, to reiterate, they are quite simply the conventional package of beliefs, reasons, and norms that lie behind its notion of gentlemanly sport, and in the professional case, they consist of the conventional package of beliefs, reasons, and norms that lie behind its notion of professional, vocational sport. What such local conventional starting points have going for them is not their conceptual precision. After all, philosophical principles and decision procedures are far more conceptually tidy and uncluttered because they make a point of circumventing the messiness that attends concrete ethical conventions. But it is the reflective altitude necessary to achieve such philosophical precision that counts so decisively against such principles and decision procedures. For it is set much too high to see, let alone fruitfully address, the normative issue before us, which is to crack conceptually the different, apparently irreconcilable ways that amateurs and professionals think and reason about how sport should be conducted.

The problem then with forsaking conventional starting points implicit in the actual practice of sport for philosophically derived ones explicit in principles and the like is that it leaches the determinative content out of the concepts and reasons athletic communities use to make sense of and justify their athletic practices. This, of course, was the principal drawback of the normative principles broad internalists relied on to adjudicate ethical disputes in sport and the principal drawback of the general concepts of game playing that Marmor attributes to their deep conventions that do so much of the normative work in his account. For both, the principle that we should always seek to maintain and foster athletic excellence or that we should consult the deep psychological and social needs embedded in our deep conventions of game playing to determine how we should act in sport are just too abstract, too threadbare of substantive content, to be action guiding, let alone motivating, to players trying to come to grips with what is ethically required of them as semi-serious gentleman or as wholly serious professionals. Starting our ethical inquiries into sport with the ethical conventions at work in our actual practices of sport, therefore, is neither an arbitrary move nor a rational cop-out but, on the contrary, a crucial step in getting our practical reasoning about how sport should be conducted on the right evaluative track.

The conventional claim I am pushing here—that our ethical reasoning about sport should take its point of departure not from some abstract notion of the good or some evaluative perspective or objective scale of value for everyone, but from particular conceptions of the good and evaluative perspectives or scales of value specific to athletic communities—is anticipated by Ludwig Wittgenstein's central claim that the language we use is tightly bound up with the activities of life itself, with what he called "forms of life." His key point here, which I quote and briefly discuss in Chapter 4, is that "it is what human beings *say* that is true and false; and they agree in the *language* they use. This is not agreement in opinions but in form of life" (1958, 241; emphasis in original).[8] What I take as the upshot of his claim is that the language we use to describe and evaluate things like sport, or what he referred to as the "language-games" we play in these descriptive and evaluative ways, is the main normative source that different (in our case, athletic) communities draw from in their practical reasoning about social practices like sport. For each athletic community, these concepts in use or language-games or evaluative vocabularies determine what counts as a reason, a good and persuasive reason, and what marks off correct from incorrect reasoning, about how sport should be done. That means that both challenges and responses to whether participants are normatively entitled to act as they did in a sport setting rise or fall on whether the reasons in favor of or against their actions are recognized and accepted by all concerned as bona fide, persuasive reasons. More specifically, that means that whether members of the amateur community or professional community, or any such community, are normatively justified or not in what they do on the playing field depends on whether their actions can be supported by reasons that their fellow members accept or reject as good reasons.

When it comes to these justificatory matters then, the normative language-games in play in the athletic communities in question determine whether the actions of its members pass reflective muster. It is not hard to see why these in-house, in-use evaluative vocabularies have the normative force they do. By starting with, rather than distancing from, the conventions that set, so to speak, the ethical compass of athletic communities, the reasons its members give or ask for in assessing the normative legitimacy of their actions when challenged are fully consonant with their ethical intuitions regarding such matters. That is why ethical injunctions to act as a gentleman athlete or a professional athlete, when aimed at their respective communities, not only flesh out their reasons to so act by giving them the determinative content they need to be determinative but also give them the intuitive plausibility and force they need to be action guiding and motivating. And that is why ethical injunctions based on reasons that are external to, and independent of, these evaluative vocabularies—to wit, the Kantian who insists it is the demands of rationality itself or the utilitarian who insists it is what is conducive to the greatest good of the greatest number or, more specifically, the broad internalist who insists it is what maintains and fosters athletic excellence that should serve as the normative guide and motive for our actions—more often than not fall on deaf ears because they do not chime with the ethical intuitions of the members of these athletic communities. That is further why it is counterintuitive to try to justify our ethical judgments about how we should act in sport by ignoring the internal conventional normative standards that govern its practice at particular times and places in favor of external, timeless, philosophical normative standards that have no, so to speak, normative skin in the practice itself.

The obvious retort to starting our normative inquiries with the ethical conventions actually at work in various athletic communities is that they themselves need first to be reflectively vetted, to be philosophically validated. But the idea that conventional starting points need philosophical backup, need to be justified by philosophical concepts and reasons that swing free of them, fails for the same reason practice- and perspective-independent philosophical concepts and reasons fail as stand-ins for our practical ethical reasoning about sport. For just as we found such philosophical concepts and reasons wanting in terms of their action-guiding and motivational force because of their unconventional, practice-independent grounding, it should come as no surprise that we would find them similarly wanting as philosophical foundations that validate the ethical conventions that guide actual sport practice because of their unconventional, practice-independent grounding.[9]

Hence, going unconventional to put our conventional, practical reasoning about sport on a surer, more stable philosophical footing is a surefire recipe for failure; discounting the normativity of such conventions as a matter of philosophical principle might be an effective way to nullify their normativity, but it is hardly an effective way, or indeed a way at all, to redeem their normativity.

The long and short of it, then, is that there is no perspective outside of the conventional, historically contingent normative language-games played by athletic communities from which to justify these language-games. That is why efforts to philosophically displace or shore them up with practice-independent, philosophically generated concepts and reasons are, normatively speaking, nonstarters. That is further why trying to adjudicate ethical disputes of the kind featured in my amateur and professional example by appeal to some notion of rationality, of practical reasoning, that is neutral between them is also a nonstarter.[10] All of which underscores that our normative inquiries into sport do not and cannot stand, in Charles Sanders Peirce's words, "on the bedrock of fact [or of reason with a capital R]. It is more like walking upon a bog, and can only say, the ground seems to hold for the present. Here I will stay until it begins to give way" (quoted in Blackburn 2018, 48). In my account, of course, we stand not on a bog but on a conventional ground of our own making, but, nonetheless, one no more stable. For the ethical conventions that serve as the starting points of our normative inquiries are only as stable as our shifting views of how we should acquit ourselves in our lives in general and our athletic lives in particular are. It has, alas, ever been so. But though that may seem an especially slender and shaky ground from which to launch our normative investigations into sport, in my conventionalist view, it is all the ground we need to justify our ever-changing social and historical notions of ethical sport.

What goes for the conventional character of the starting points of our practical reasoning about sport goes as well for the conventional character of the whole structure of our practical reasoning about sport. What is crucial to such practical reasoning is not only that it is based in intuitively plausible and compelling premises regarding how sport should be done but that the rational inferences we draw from these premises follow from and are consistent with them. The importance of getting our inferential judgments right in this regard is twofold.

The first reason harkens back to my discussion in Chapter 3 in which I argue that the goal of practical reasoning about how we should comport ourselves in sport, not to mention in the other social practices we engage in in the course of our everyday lives, is the coherence of what we believe and assert rather than their correspondence to mind-independent facts "out there" in the world. Demonstrating such coherence between the premises of our practical reasoning and the inferences we draw from them is especially important in this regard. Indeed, our failure to establish such coherence will not only undermine our efforts to reflectively vindicate what we say about sport at a particular time and place but render what we say about it unintelligible. My previous argument that coherence in this and other aspects of our practical reasoning rather than correspondence is the only viable way to go in our normative inquiries into sport is owed to the fact that, as Rorty tells us, we "cannot find a skyhook which lifts us out of mere coherence . . . to something like 'correspondence with reality as it is in itself'" (1991, 38–39). Lacking such a skyhook, a form of rationality that floats free of the practical reasoning that takes place within communities of inquiry, puts the so-called intrinsic properties that make up the ethical essence of sport into the same epistemically inaccessible category as Kant's famous thing-in-itself. And that, of course, puts them well beyond the reach of our practical reasoning, of just what inferences we are normatively justified in making that follow from, in my example, historical notions of amateur and professional sport.

The second reason why getting our inferential ethical judgments about sport right is that when we claim, for example, sport is a gentlemanly or professional affair, we are committing ourselves not just to the "truth" of this claim but as well to everything that follows from it. Our practical reasoning about sport, therefore, can quickly go off the rails if we err in the inferences we draw from our conventional starting points regarding what we take to be the point and value of sport. For example, amateurs who assert that strategically bending or breaking rules adds to the pleasure to be derived from taking part in competitive sport can justifiably be accused of lapsing into incoherence, of mistakenly thinking that the kind of pleasure to be had by cleverly getting around the rules is the same kind of pleasure gentlemen athletes seek in their athletic pursuits. Similarly, professionals who assert there is nothing ethically untoward about occasionally taking plays off in, say, a football game can justifiably be accused of lapsing into incoherence, of mistakenly thinking one can mix high-minded seriousness with appreciable lassitude in their athletic pursuits. The only way such athletes can learn from their mistakes, then, is if they get better at the inferential ethical judgments they make. More strongly, the only way they and their peers can become more rational is not by changing their criteria, their conventional starting points, but by sharpening their inferential judgments.

To sum up this part of my account, I have argued that our practical reasoning about sport, our giving and asking for reasons regarding our ethical entitlement to act as we do, is, like sport itself, a social practice. Were it not for such sport practices, there would be no values of sport, no conceptions of the good to be had by engaging in it, no reasons to engage in it in light of these values or conceptions of the good. In a word, there would be nothing to ethically deliberate about. This claim tracks what Joseph Raz calls his "social dependence thesis," save in one important respect. Raz's social dependence thesis holds "that some values"—cultural ones, to be exact—"exist only if there are (or were) social practices sustaining them" (2003, 19). I argue the same for the historically and contextually bounded ethical values of sport. Whereas, however, Raz understands his thesis as a metaphysical one, as an account of how certain cultural values come into existence, I understand it primarily as a normative one, as a thesis regarding how we are able to rationally justify the ethical values we impute to sport. That is, I affirm what he denies, "that if the existence of a value depends on a sustaining [social] practice, that practice must be a reason for the value, a reason for why it is a value" (26).[11] Unlike Raz then, I do not think one can hive off the practice-dependent reasons athletic communities deploy to justify their normative entitlements to act in certain ways in sport from the practice-dependent values generated by sport practices.[12] That is why I think rational argument over the ethical values of sport, over whether their status as ethical values can be rationally redeemed, is an intramural matter for communities of inquiry to determine, rather than an extramural matter for an independent philosophical investigation open to all rational interlocutors to determine. When we normatively assess what is ethically required of us in particular sport settings, we do so not as individuals qua individuals according to our own individual, pre-institutional conceptions of what is the right thing to do, but as individuals qua members of a particular athletic community according to what the conventional, evaluative vocabularies at work in that community tell us is the right thing to do.[13] Just then as it is normatively suspect, to say the least, for a father to divine and justify what he owes to his children ethically speaking from a strictly individual perspective that is independent of the social role he occupies as a parent, or for a civil servant, doctor, teacher, and the like to do the same, it is plainly normatively suspect to divine and assess what we owe to our athletic peers in sport from a strictly individual perspective that is independent of the evaluative vocabulary at work in an athletic community. As Anthony Laden argues, "If we insist on always evaluating the claims of others from our individual standpoint, we treat others not as deliberative partners but as complicated parts of our choice environment" (2005, 333–334). All of which underscores once again that practical reasoning about sport is a thorough social enterprise, in which the reasons we deliberate about when our actions are challenged by our peers are quintessentially social ones that could not be in the minds only of the single individuals that make up different athletic communities.

Ethical Conventions and Sport: Some Objections

The forgoing discussion lays out what I regard to be the main features of a conventionalist ethical theory of sport. As I argue throughout, I believe such an ethical theory is better equipped to handle athletic disputes of a normative character that are, as the long history of sport itself attests, a constant feature of its practice, especially when these disputes involve conflicting notions of the purpose and value of athletic endeavor. As noted previously, however, many philosophers in general and philosophers of sport in particular have rejected the very idea that there are such things as ethical conventions and claimed, therefore, that a conventionalist ethical theory of sport or of anything else is a misnomer. In the final section of this chapter, I address these philosophical misgivings as they pertain to sport.

However, before I raise and respond to these objections, some of which come from the hands of critics of conventionalism and some of which come from my own hand, I want to point out that several, but certainly not all, of these criticisms can be traced to a bias in the way moral theory is conceived of and done nowadays. Given the importance of this point to my critical remarks to come, I want to first comment on it before I proceed.

The singling out and criticism of this so-called bias of contemporary moral theory is most commonly attributed to Bernard Williams, in particular, to the forceful and influential last chapter of his important book *Ethics and the Limits of Philosophy*, which he titled "Morality, the Peculiar Institution" (1985). But, in fact, it harkens back to Hegel's distinction between morality, in which leading a *moral* life is all about honoring moral obligations that have nothing to do with the social relationships in which we stand to others at any particular time or place, and what Hegel labels the *ethical* life of society (*Sittlichkeit*), in which leading a moral life is all about pursuing a *good* life that has everything to do with the social relationships in which we stand to relevant others at a certain time and place. With something like this distinction in mind, Williams argues that the disastrous mistake contemporary moral theory made was effectively to cut the ethical sphere and its considerations of the good life out of the moral picture altogether, leaving the moral sphere and our moral obligations to one another as the sole focus and concern of moral theorists. One especially deleterious consequence of this constriction of moral theorizing and morality, I maintain, is that it would have us believe that the norms that govern conventional practices like sport have no "moral" significance or force to speak of. And this constriction is borne out in several of the main criticisms made against the kind of conventionalist ethical theory of sport I champion.

Let me begin then with the objections that betray what I am calling, after Williams, this bias of the moral outlook that informs contemporary moral theory. The first such objection comes from the pen of Marmor, who stoutly insists that "conventional practices" such as the arts and sport have themselves "very little to do with morality" (2009, 136). He argues such because whatever conventional norms hold sway in such cultural activities—and, of course, he is on record as restricting them to deep and constitutive conventions—cannot be moral norms because we have no "moral reasons or duties" to engage in them (136). Marmor does not deny that sport and the like instantiate values, aesthetic and otherwise, but only that they do not instantiate moral values. So although it would be "difficult to imagine a flourishing culture without . . . the various arts, [and] sport," and although not participating in them "may be silly, philistine, perhaps even shameful," he is adamant that "it is not morally wrong" to turn our back on them (136). It is not morally wrong to shirk these sorts of cultural endeavor because it is characteristic that "they can only flourish if the participants . . . willingly engage in them" (136). In short, because we are not morally obligated to pursue a cultural endeavor like sport, it follows for Marmor that it possesses little to no moral significance.

Marmor is entirely right that we are not duty bound to engage in sport, let alone any other conventional social practice. But, I think, he is just wrong to write off sport's moral significance because we are not so obligated. That would only follow if, in fact, there were nothing more to morality than what our moral obligations require of us. But that is clearly question begging because there is surely more to leading a moral life than meeting our moral obligations. That more, of course, is leading an ethically good life, which the bias of the morality system obscures from our view and conceals what is question begging about claiming otherwise. To be sure, sport is not a morality play. But it is, as I note in the Introduction, a moral laboratory, one in which at its best we learn important ethical lessons about fairness, coping with failure, honesty, and other virtues, which can sometimes serve us well outside of our athletic lives. In the case of fairness, to cite just one example, as the legal scholar George Fletcher has argued, one notable advantage that the English and Americans have that their European chums do not in trying to understand the idea of fair play at the core, for example, of the European Convention on Human Rights, as well as John Rawls's classic notion of "Justice as Fairness," is that the former possess and the latter lack an "indigenous concept of fair play" (Fletcher 1997, 331). He is pointing to what he finds to be "a striking feature of English and American culture"—namely, that "we cannot think about human relations without thinking about sports, and the idiom of fair play and foul play" (332). There is, to be sure, much more to be said about the moral salience of sport in this regard. But it is enough, I trust, to rebut Marmor's claim that conventional practices like sport have very little to do with morality rightly (broadly) understood.

A second related common philosophical complaint lodged against ethical conventionalism that also, I argue, reflects the bias of the morality system is given perhaps its clearest expression once again from Marmor. This particular criticism allows that some conventions are, in a sense, moral conventions. But the sense he has in mind here is hardly a consequential one, because it only admits that conventional social practices like sport are appropriate subject matters of moral scrutiny but not themselves moral resources that can be used to conduct such scrutiny. His point is the simple one that because "a very substantial part of our social lives is shaped by conventions . . . a very substantial aspect of morality is to guide our conduct in the social domain" (2009, 144). The real work of moral scrutiny, he contends, is the exclusive province of abstract moral ideals that hover, as it were, above sport and its conventional kin and provide an external moral vantage point from which to assess what takes place within them. The only role that conventions themselves are assigned in this evaluative scheme "is to mediate between abstract moral ideals and their concrete realization in our social interactions" (149). This is a minor role at best. Nonetheless, it is in Marmor's eyes a necessary one because these moral ideals are "too abstract and indeterminate to specify particular norms of behavior" (150). Though conventions are crucial to how we should comply with moral ideals and the moral reasons they beget, he hastens to add that "conventions by themselves, cannot determine whether certain conduct is morally warranted or not" (148).

The moral picture Marmor paints here is familiar enough and one that is not in the least complementary to, or complimentary of, the conventionalist one I have tried to paint. Geoffrey Brennan and his coauthors give an illustrative example of what Marmor is driving at here. They ask us to consider the practice of standing in line, or what our English counterparts call queuing. Queuing is a conventional practice, and the norm it answers to is that people must not cut in line or move to the front of the line but rather wait their turn for whatever led them to stand in line in the first place.[14] Their turn, of course, is determined by their location in that line, and once there is no one in front of them, it is their turn, regardless of how many people might be standing behind them. If someone thinks he or she is entitled to take advantage of the queue and jump the line, criticism will surely and shortly follow. But, the authors contend, we would not have grounds for reproving what that person did by simply citing the queuing practice, by declaiming "that standing orderly in line is 'just what we do'" (2013, 75). Rather, to justify our criticism we would have to appeal to practice-independent moral norms such as "the unfairness of doing so, the diminution in total well-being that would flow from the destruction of the queuing practice, and so on" (75). Just as Marmor claims, then, the conventional queuing practice merely sets the appropriate conditions for applying abstract moral ideals such as fairness and total well-being but does no substantive moral work of its own. In a word, it mediates but does not substantiate why these moral norms ought to be complied with.

The first thing I should say in response is that this criticism is not a new one. In fact, I address it in my accounting earlier in this chapter of what ethical reasoning and argument looks like in a fully fleshed-out conventionalist ethical theory of sport. There I argue that this criticism misfires because it gets morality exactly backwards, in the case of ethical conventions at least. In fact, I take pains to show that abstract moral ideals, such as fairness and well-being that Williams mentions, and abstract moral principles, like the internal principle broad internalists cite, do very little if any of the heavy moral lifting in adjudicating moral disputes that commonly break out in and outside of sport. Conversely, I argue that ethical conventions such as amateurism and professionalism do most if not all of the heavy moral lifting in these instances. This lopsided moral division of labor cannot be avoided precisely because the moral ideals favored by the so-called morality system, as Marmor himself concedes, are too indeterminate, too threadbare of content, too detached from the things like sport they are supposed to dictate to, to be motivating or action guiding. Their being too indeterminate and detached does not mean just that they cannot tell us how they should be applied but, more important, that they cannot tell us anything substantive about how we should act when applied. That is why I opine that they function as little more than moral platitudes when moral conflicts arise about how sport should be conducted. All of which suggests, as I argue accordingly, morality in its fully inclusive, nonideal sense, to borrow Michael Walzer's jargon, is nothing if not thick, because questions of the good are an integral part of our moral lives.[15] The most that can be said for abstract moral ideals and principles in this regard is, therefore, what Rorty said about them—namely, that they are merely summaries, "reminders of, abbreviations for, practices, not justifications for practices" (1989, 59).

The only thing to add to my previous criticisms of this morality system's biased objection to ethical conventions is to underscore just how wide of the mark it misses its target. For the pressing moral questions we face in sport are local, context-sensitive, practice-dependent ones through and through. So, for example, when members of the amateur athletic community grapple with just how seriously they should pursue sport so as not to undermine their ethical obligations to their gentlemen athletic peers, they are not asking a general moral question that can be answered by a general moral principle. On the contrary, they are asking a local, parochial question that requires them to determine just what is ethically required of them as gentlemen amateurs. The same goes for the members of the professional athletic community when they ask what obligations to their fellow peers are entailed by their commitment to professional standards of athletic conduct. This parochial question likewise calls for a parochial answer that requires determining just what their professionalism obligates them to do. Insisting instead that they take up such practice-dependent questions from a practice-independent standpoint, say, by deliberating behind Rawls's veil of ignorance to ensure a fair outcome, or by employing the hedonistic calculus of utilitarianism to ensure the welfare of all concerned, both of which entail members of each athletic community put out of their collective mind the conventional ethical ideals that color their different takes on how sport should be done, will not do because it misses the point of their queries. Besides, what fairness and welfare mean to amateurs will be quite different from what it means to professionals. The same goes for insisting, as broad internalists do, that we address these parochial ethical questions about how we should act in sport from the perspective of the internal principle, which also will not do because it, too, misses the point of their queries. The problem here, as before, lies in insisting we reach for practice-independent moral ideals and principles to answer practice-dependent moral queries. For that enjoins that the relevant athletic parties bracket their own homegrown, battle-tested, socially inflected conventional morality, the very morality that has shaped their practical identity as athletes of a certain sort from the get-go, and from which they have adopted the moral roles they have played throughout their athletic lives.[16]

Two final objections to ethical conventionalism derive from this bias of the morality system. But this time the bias has to do with what Williams refers to as the related aspirational "purity of morality, its insistence on abstracting the moral consciousness from other kinds of emotional reaction or social influence" (1985, 195).[17] This puritan strain of morality is in evidence, I contend, in the jaundiced view its exponents have regarding the arbitrary character of ethical conventions. Their objection in this instance takes issue with the fact that, first, ethical conventions are arbitrary in the sense that they admit of at least one conceivable alternative, and second, that ethical conventions are arbitrary in the sense that they are, in part, compliance dependent. I take up each of these objections in the order presented.

The morality system's criticism of ethical conventions is wanting because they are arbitrary (impure) in the sense of admitting at least one alternative derives directly from its singular focus on and the special significance it accords to moral obligations. Any moral theory worthy of the name, it declares, is one whose moral criteria and procedures (for example, Rawls's previously mentioned "veil of ignorance" or Jürgen Habermas's ideal speech situation) are designed to identify all and only those things we are obliged to do. Given that in its view moral obligations outrank every other moral consideration in sport and other social practices, both the decision criteria and procedures employed by moral theory as well as the moral principles and ideals that they yield must have the requisite rigor to command our compliance with our obligations. They must have, in other words, real veto power so no other moral considerations that stem from what we value about sport are allowed to override our moral obligations to our relevant athletic peers. What this says about moral deliberation and argument itself is that the reasons we give and ask for in determining what our moral obligations in sport are must be equally strong and rigorous ones. How strong? Strong enough to defeat any competing moral reasons and considerations that threaten to trump our moral obligations—as Williams notes, for in the morality system, the only thing that can beat an obligation is another obligation (1985, 180). This suggests that moral reasons must have one or more of the following features: (1) They must be acknowledged and recognized as moral reasons by all interlocutors regardless of their moral outlook; (2) they must make unconditional demands that we are accountable for, regardless of our desires to act in accord with them or whether others are complying with them, and that cannot be overridden by other moral considerations; and (3) they must touch on our "core" human interests that are crucial to our being human agents—for instance, our interest in not being murdered or tortured. The distinction between morality and convention Papineau draws in his account of sport, in which he claims "morality is universal . . . and has to do with genuine welfare, while convention varies across societies, . . . and governs matters of no intrinsic importance" (2017, 64), is a good example of the kind of account one would expect to come from an advocate of the morality system hitting, as it does, on two of the three features such a system claims are true of moral reasons alone.[18]

One thing that moral reasons cannot be on this picture of our moral life is parochial, contingent ones. The concern here is that that would make them vulnerable to competing and potentially overriding moral considerations about how we should comport ourselves in sport. Hence, the necessity of keeping our moral deliberations pristine, free of the social and historical factors that centrally figure in our practical deliberations about what is or is not morally acceptable to do in sport. The morality system's insistence on purity in this regard is meant to safeguard against what Brennan and his coauthors colorfully refer to as a form of "objectionable 'bootstrapping,'" the idea "that reasons may be brought into existence as a result of how we behave and regard the way we behave" (2013, 80). This worry is obviously magnified in the case of ethical conventions, given their arbitrary character and the fact that both they and the social practices they are wed to are arbitrary, wholly socially, and historically contingent normative and rational artifacts, which, were it not for the utter contingency of human life itself, would have never seen the light of day. It is not for nothing, then, that the morality system exhorts us to turn our back on these messy, contingent facets of our practical life in and outside of sport, to step back from this social, moral, conventional morass, so we do not lose sight of what should matter most in our moral lives—namely, our moral obligations.

The problem with the morality's system insistence that we blot out all that is contingent, arbitrary, and so conventional in our moral deliberations regarding how we should live our lives, especially qua participants in social practices like sport, brings us back to its pernicious and debilitating narrowing of our moral purview and all that goes into and constitutes our moral life. One significant consequence of its principled indifference to the arbitrary is what Williams saw as its dangerous skewing of our moral thinking, its failure to see that moral obligations are just one moral consideration among other moral considerations that warrant our reflective scrutiny. But for our purposes, the most worrisome feature of the morality system's vaunted purity is the havoc it wreaks on, *pace* Hegel, the ethical life of society and its roster of social practices in general and sport in particular. By demanding that moral deliberation and argument eschew the inescapably conventional and arbitrary character of our athletic lives in favor of philosophically grounded, unconventional, nonarbitrary decision procedures and criteria, it occludes the background sense of what things are most important and matter most to us morally as engaged participants. Without that normative background that ethical conventions vouchsafe to us, we make ourselves, as Taylor likes to put it, inarticulate regarding what it is good to be and do in sport in order to honor our supposedly higher obligation to consider exclusively what is right to do in sport (1995, 134). We thus render ourselves clueless as a matter of philosophical principle why someone deliberating and arguing from one conventional ethical background would be persuaded and moved not to exploit an advantage over an opponent whose equipment suddenly fails her, and why someone deliberating from a different conventional ethical background would be persuaded and moved to do the opposite in the same circumstances. And it goes without saying, I think, that adherents of the morality system would be similarly clueless and mystified why Kant's categorical imperative or utilitarian's hedonistic calculus were not given deliberative priority in these cases, why such carefully worked-out philosophic decision procedures not only did not and would not carry the day in such practical circumstances but were most likely not a part of anyone's moral thinking about such matters.

Going the pure, nonarbitrary, unconventional route the morality system compels, therefore, confirms one of Williams's worst fears about this system—namely, that it gives us "a false image of how reflection is related to practice" (1985, 198). This is no small matter when it comes to sport and kindred social practices in which there is precious little that is morally obligatory about such practices, to include our very engagement in them. Most of what is morally important regarding athletic conduct is morally important despite the fact we are under no moral obligation to even give it a parting thought, let alone, according to the morality system, our moral attention and critical scrutiny. So even though our conventional moral reasons for engaging in sport in certain ways as opposed to others (which we use to guide our conduct and to respond to challenges regarding their moral propriety) are not categorical or universal in scope, or bound up with our so-called core human interests, and even though they are arbitrary, contingent, and not matters of life and death, they are, nonetheless, persuasive, perspicacious, moving, and deeply important to our athletic lives.

Because the main concepts and conventional reasons that make up the moral vocabularies of athletic practice communities are wholly social ones based on social meanings that vary, just as Papineau asserts, according to time and place, aiming to distance ourselves from them, as the morality system mandates, is a recipe not for sharpening but for blunting our moral criticism of sport. Moral criticism worth its salt does not demand, as Walzer nicely puts it, "to step back from society as a whole but only to step away from certain sorts of power relationships within society. It is not connection but authority and domination from which we must distance ourselves" (1987, 60). We should not worry then, as the morality system would have us believe, that "without its very special obligation there is only inclination, . . . without its ultimately pure justice, there is no justice" (Williams 1985, 196). Nor should we worry that without the morality system's assurance, only its heralded "pure" moral reasons have the obligatory, binding force necessary to keep us on the straight and narrow in and outside of sport. That is because, as Rorty remarks, "a belief [or reason] can still regulate action, can still be thought of [as especially important and binding], among people who are quite aware that this belief [or reason] is caused by nothing deeper than contingent historical circumstance" (1989, 189).

The second attack emanating from the puritan strain of the morality system on the arbitrariness of ethical conventions is directed at their compliance-dependent character. The objection here similarly concerns an "objectionable bootstrapping" of conventional ethical norms and reasons that have nothing more going for them than that they are enshrined in social practices like sport whose very existence and binding force depends on the fact that most people follow them. There are two related worries here about running together moral norms and reasons that are supposedly independent of how we behave and regard how we behave, and conventional ethical norms and reasons that are utterly dependent on how we behave and regard how we behave. The first is that such moral norms and reasons, unlike conventional ethical norms and reasons, are not compliance dependent; the second is that the former, again unlike the latter, makes real demands on how we act in and outside sport that we might well, and not infrequently do, fail to live up to.

The first concern that moral norms are not compliance dependent has to do with the fact that we are duty bound to honor them even if most people, or indeed no one else, pay them no mind. In a word, we comply with moral norms and the moral reasons that underpin them because it is the right thing to do, not because other people might or might not be following suit. Their validity and binding force, therefore, have nothing to do with their practical efficacy, to how many people comply with them. That is why there is no moral safe harbor, no moral immunity, in numbers, in shirking our moral obligations because most everyone else is. By contrast, whatever binding force conventional ethical norms and reasons have on us is decidedly, if only partly, owed to the fact that most people follow them. So I cannot be criticized for failing to follow an ethical convention if most people are not following it. Indeed, if most people are not following an ethical convention, that is a sign not only of its patent impotency but, more important, that it is patently not a convention, ethical or otherwise, at all. Treating conventional ethical norms as genuinely moral norms is thus worrisome for proponents of the morality system because in their considered view it mistakes what is socially acceptable to do in sport with what is morally acceptable to do in sport. To put the same point otherwise, what descriptive force ethical conventions have is no substitute for their obvious lack of prescriptive force.

It might be rejoined, however, that while the validity of moral principles and reasons does not rise or fall, as it does for ethical conventions, on whether people comply with them, it cannot be denied that it does, nonetheless, matter morally speaking whether our moral principles and reasons are generally complied with. For such compliance not only tells us something important about the human agents to whom they are addressed—whether, for instance, they are moral agents at all, or strong or weak willed or possessing or lacking in virtue—but also tells us something important about the moral principles and norms themselves. In this latter sense, moral principles that are not generally followed might be defective, might lack any motivating and action-guiding force that cannot rightly be charged to some shortcoming or other of human agents themselves. Such is the case when the moral principles in question are too demanding, onerous, even alienating, for any mortal being to live by because they are too difficult, if not impossible, to live up to. Here the vaunted independence of moral principles from how people are behaving, from whether it is followed or not that supposedly distinguishes them from the compliance-dependent character of ethical conventions, might plausibly be questioned.

Such an accusation has frequently been aimed at Kant's moral philosophy, whom Williams regarded to be a charter member of the morality system club. What many have found problematic about Kant's moral theory is that it is premised on a strict distinction between reason, which he identified as the seat of our moral obligations, and sensibility, which he identified as the seat of our sensible desires and inclinations. To be a moral agent for Kant entails that human agents subject their desires and inclinations to the dictates of pure reason. As he views it, we act morally when we successfully constrain our desires and inclinations and do what we ought to do; we act immorally when our desires and inclinations get the better of the rational part of us and we try to satisfy them instead of our obligations. It is this separation of reason, of a rational faculty that sets what moral ends and obligations we ought to observe, from sensibility, of that sensible part of us that determines what desires we have to live our lives in certain ways, that has led many to argue that the demands his system of morality makes on human agents—for example, to treat everyone as an end in itself (one version of his famous "categorical imperative")—are far too rigorous and detached from people's lives to have any relevance to, let alone meaningful affect, on their behavior.

Theorists of the morality system persuasion, however, have a ready answer to this objection. It is that "ought implies can" no more. The basic idea is that no moral system can ask, indeed demand, human agents to abide by moral principles and standards they are constitutionally unable to abide. That means that if Kant's notion of morality does ask and demand too much of human agents, that is good reason to reject it. But claiming "ought implies can" is a long way from claiming moral principles, like conventional ethical norms, are or should be compliance dependent. As Southwood and Erikson neatly put it, "Perhaps 'ought' implies 'can,' but it does not imply 'does'" (2011, 205). The upshot, then, is that while it is good if moral principles are generally complied with, it is not necessary that they be generally complied with, notwithstanding the fact that it necessary that human agents are at least capable of complying with them. This is sufficient reason, according to the morality system, not to conflate them with conventional ethical norms and reasons.

The second concern or worry over an "objectionable bootstrapping" of conventional ethical norms and reasons is that moral norms and reasons make real and tangible demands on how people behave in and outside of sport. That is, a in-built feature of moral norms and reasons is that human agents can fail to live up to them, can fail to act as these norms and reasons require we ought to act.[19] Their capacity to make such demands on our behavior would not be possible if moral norms were themselves behavior and practice dependent, if their very status and existence as norms would vaporize into thin air the very moment people failed to act on them. By contrast, conventional ethical norms and reasons, it is argued, can make no such demands on us, cannot tell us how we ought to live, precisely because they are behavior and practice dependent. In other words, conventional ethical norms, not to mention conventional norms in general, are not the sort of things we can fail to live *up* to because they would not be what they are were we not already living *by* them. Nor are conventional ethical reasons the sort of things we can appeal to in order to criticize currently acceptable ways of acting, to take to task existing social practices like sport, since how we are presently behaving and comporting ourselves in and outside sport is informed by these same reasons. The long and short of it, then, is that conventional ethical norms and reasons cannot help but lock us into the status quo, to how things are presently done in some society or community. And this is why, according to the morality system again, we should resist any "objectionable bootstrapping" of these ethical conventions that would make them into something that their compliance-dependent character tells against—namely, that they are bona fide moral norms and reasons that obligate us to act in certain desire-independent ways.

These are forceful objections but not, I think, persuasive ones. Let us begin with the first worry engendered by the puritan outlook of the morality system that the compliance-dependent (arbitrary) character of conventional ethical norms and reasons is their Achilles' heel and ultimate undoing. The first thing to be said in response is that moral principles themselves are in an important sense compliance dependent as well. If this is right, then moral norms, like conventional ethical ones, not only imply "can" but imply as well a certain level of general compliance. The case of doping in sport is illustrative in this regard. The prohibition against doping is commonly viewed as an offense against such moral principles as harm to others, fairness, and the like. The latter count as moral principles or norms because, among other things, they are considered binding no matter if they do not comport with athletes' actual preferences or meet with their uniform compliance. But it is a well-known fact that in a sport like professional cycling, a significant number of cyclists do dope, and it can be further plausibly assumed, I believe, that many more would do so were it not for ever stricter doping controls. What we have here, then, is an example of a moral norm and rule that is routinely not complied with by the athletes in question, so much so that the expectation among them is that, save for a minority of riders, the norm will be violated. Notice, however, that this is not an extreme case of total noncompliance because some justification would be needed, as David Holley argues with another example in mind, "for not acting in accordance with a rule would ordinarily presuppose that the rule is sometimes obeyed" (1997, 167). Furthermore, because moral blame, along with stiff legal sanctions, is still meted out for such noncompliance, we can further assume that some cyclists are still acting in accordance with the moral antidoping norm.

The important question I intended to raise by this example is whether the general noncompliance with the moral norm and rule against doping in a sport like cycling counts against the norm itself rather than the "offending" riders. The morality system, of course, would unequivocally respond that it does not tell against the norm because it cannot if our moral obligations are to count for anything. But might a plausible case be made that accounting for the cyclists' general nonconforming behavior in this instance is determinative of whether the antidoping moral norm is an actual, operative part of the riders' moral code? That is, might such widespread noncompliance count as a justification for violating the antidoping norm and rule on the grounds that it is not, in fact, a moral norm of the cycling community and, therefore, that it would be morally pointless to follow such a behavior- and practice-independent external norm?[20] At very least, would such general noncompliance not give us at least a prima facie reason for doubting that the antidoping norm is part of the cyclists' moral outlook?

I think it does give us such a prima facie reason to cast doubt on the validity of this norm but not, to be sure, a *pro tanto* or all-considered reason. This cracks open the door for my main argument why the compliance-dependent feature of conventional ethical norms and reasons counts as a positive mark in their favor rather than a knock against their validity.

I view it as a testament to the ethical prowess and relevance of conventional ethical norms and reasons because in an important sense "ought" implies "does" and not just "can." How so? Well, it is next to impossible to live a moral life if the moral ideals, norms, and reasons that it embodies are not embedded in social practices that make possible their realization in the normal course of things. Lacking such an institutional anchor closes would-be moral agents off from the social world in which they matriculate as well as the people who populate that world. Not a happy prospect because it would make moral life a rarity, reserved only for the heroic among us who are somehow able to slough off their own socialization into athletic and other communities of practice and set their moral compass according to coordinates nowhere to be found on any existing social map. That is why the practice-, behavior-, and compliance-dependent features of conventional ethical norms and reasons are so important; they make it possible to live a moral life in concert with our peers according to standards mutually acceptable to all members of athletic communities we belong to. Indeed, it is only because we have social practices like sport that allow us to behave in certain ways that are viewed in a positive light by certain athletic communities that it and the behavior it licenses has the value it does. That value gives members of athletic communities reasons for acting in particular ethical ways that would be for naught if we were unable to act on them.

Sport and kindred social practices, then, are good examples of how the ways in which we behave and regard how we behave in certain social and historical contexts constitute what we value about them morally and otherwise, and furnish us with the moral ideals, norms, and reasons we need to justify our actions within them. There is no denying that a kind of "bootstrapping" of these ethical conventions is at work here and explains their binding force. But I do not think there is anything objectionable about it as the morality system stoutly insists. For moral life rightly understood is nothing if not a historically contingent affair of our own collective making, which is subject to many different twists and turns as we change our minds regarding what things we value and how we value them at particular times and places. Such historically contingent bootstrapping is, I think, the point of Hegel's famous claim: "What is rational is actual, and what is actual is rational" (1977b, 10). His basic idea seems to be that "since rationality . . . enters upon external existence, simultaneously with its actualization, it emerges with an infinite wealth of forms [and] shapes" (10). In other words, it is only when social forms of life are created that the reasons and values that animate them and the normative ideals in whose image they are fashioned can gain a foothold in our actual lives and so become things that we can engage with, argue over, and try to live by along with the other like-minded members of the communities that spring up in their wake. And so it is with the bootstrapping of the ethical conventions of sport, which similarly unfolds as we change our collective minds as to what is the point and value of sport. This is what accounts for the infinite wealth of forms and shapes that sport has so far donned and will surely don in the future. Such conventional bootstrapping, therefore, would not be what it is morally speaking (action guiding and practically realizable) were it not for its compliance-dependent character. Which is, as far as I can see, all to the good morally and otherwise for sport and other cultural practices of its ilk.

But this brings us to the second criticism leveled against ethical conventions by proponents of the vaunted purity of morality—namely, that the reason why most people comply with them is that they morally demand so little of us. For all they ask of us, or so the argument goes, is that we follow the existing morality we have already been socialized into and typically take for granted as certifiably authoritative. Ethical conventions are thus found to be as agreeable and undemanding as they are because they are so wed to the status quo that nary a second thought is, or needs to be, given by the human agents that follow them as to whether the existing morality is itself moral. What the human agents under the sway of these ethical conventions fail to grasp, let alone recognize or appreciate, is that the ease with which they are able to comply with them is the product of the decided lack of moral rigor possessed by such conventions.

What this criticism of ethical conventions misses, however, is that the norms and reasons they put in play are themselves desire independent. That is, ethical conventions obligate us to act in certain ways that often go against what we might actually desire and prefer to do on the playing field. For instance, we might be averse to acting like a gentleman in athletic situations in which we feel we have been disrespected. Our reactive desires in such situations are understandable and even justified under the conventions of amateurism, but they can easily get the better of us and cause us to act in ungentlemanly ways. But those same conventions obligate us not to act on such desires. The same goes, of course, for the conventions of professionalism, in which our commitment to athletic excellence might well succumb to our desire to win by whatever it takes, especially in the heat of competition. Once again, however, the conventions of professionalism obligate us not to act on such desires. In cases like these, which are common in sport, ethical conventions turn out to be quite demanding indeed, and anything but hospitable to our occurrent feelings and desires.

Athletic ethical conventions prove to be desire independent not just with regard to individual desires to defect from them but further with regard to larger social forces emanating from other, nonathletic sectors of society that engender desires and preferences hostile to these conventions. A prime example in capitalist societies like our own is the financial incentives the market unleashes that not infrequently overstep their boundaries and intrude on the internal affairs of sport and other cultural practices. The ethical problem this creates is that such mercenary motives are too often disruptive of, rather than responsive to, gentleman-amateur conventional norms of athletic decorum and professional conventional norms of athletic excellence. Rather than giving us additional reasons to act in light of these ethical conventions, they tend to give us reasons to violate them in the name of the almighty dollar. The dominant win-at-all-costs mentality of elite sports today is arguably owed to these very market incentives. These are, to say the least, powerful incentives, and the ethical conventions of amateur and professional sport are an important bulwark against their wholesale cooptation of sport. Once again then, the ethical conventions of sport ask quite of lot of us as moral agents, obligating us to resist the siren song of the market run amok.

The objection, then, that the reason ethical conventions are widely complied with is that they are morally toothless, that they make no real moral demands on us that we could somehow fail to realize, is mistaken. However, what can rightly be said about the wide compliance ethical conventions of sport normally enjoy, which speaks for, rather than against, their moral force and salience, is that, unlike the morality system, it betokens no strict separation of "is" and "ought," of what "does" in the normal course of our life occur from what "ought" to occur. Such reconciliation of what typically "is" the case with what "ought" to be the case in sport attests to the fact that when moral norms are conventionalized, our desires typically come to reflect and instantiate our moral commitments and convictions. This conventionalization of ethical norms is what for Hegel accounts for their actuality (*wirklichkeit*), the process by which they become second nature such that the way we characteristically engage in sport is congruent with the way we ought to engage in it. This is what explains the motivational force and action-guiding prowess of ethical conventions. As we have just seen, however, their impressive prowess in this regard does not mean they are indefeasible, that they indemnify us against moral failure to act in light of them. That is why Hegel is careful to distinguish the actuality (*wirklichkeit*) of ethical conventions from the existence (*Dasein*) of social norms that betray them, between when they are at work in our athletic lives and when they are not as a consequence of having been overridden by alien desires and inclinations.[21] So their actuality is never a fait accompli, but always a work in progress. That is why the dominant moment in sport, which in our contemporary era is largely a tale of how the market has managed to insinuate itself into just about everything we human beings undertake, is a formidable foe that stands in the way of living a truly ethical life, whether it be in or outside of sport. Nevertheless, that is not to deny or take away from what has already been claimed on behalf of the critical force of ethical conventions, in which, in accord with the kind of internal criticism they uniquely afford, what counts as criticism is, as Raymond Geuss writes, "only what could in principle be part of the self-criticism of the agents to whom it is addressed" (1981, 65).

The final three objections I consider against the very idea of ethical conventions are not tied to the morality system, not directly at least. The first of these contends that conventions are not the sort of things that can be rationally justified or vindicated. For when someone asks why we are obligated to follow conventional norms, the only answer that can be given is simply that is the "done thing around here." This stands to reason because what human agents in a particular social setting normally do—for example, drive on the right side of the road, form a queue to get into a movie theater, or, in the case of Oxford dons, pass the port to the left—is clearly "irrelevant to what [they] ought to do" (Southwood and Erikson 2011, 788). By contrast, when someone questions why one ought not murder someone or why soldiers ought not rape their captives, the only answer that will do is a rational argument, a persuasive and compelling one, that shows why acting in these ways is morally wrong. In such instances, a report of "what is 'done around here' is just the wrong thing to appeal to" (Brennan et al. 2013, 66). According to this line of criticism, then, the contrast between conventional and moral norms could not be clearer. In the former case, upholding the validity of conventional norms involves recounting what we typically do around here; in the latter case, upholding the validity of moral norms involves making a rational case why they should command our assent. It goes without saying, of course, that only the latter defense counts as a true justification.[22]

This criticism can be quickly disarmed because it conflates ethical with coordinating conventions. In point of fact, most of the philosophers who argue that conventions lack such justificatory force are guilty of reducing all conventions, to include what I call ethical conventions and what Marmor calls deep and surface conventions, to the coordinating variety. This is why the examples they seize on are exclusively coordinating ones. And with respect to these particular conventions, they do have a point. For when, say, Oxford dons are asked why they pass the port to the left, all they can say is that is the "done thing around here." If someone were to press them further and ask for a justification for doing so, the dons, no doubt with a puzzled look on their faces, would likely reply, "Didn't you hear what we just said?" Arguments in such cases are obviously not called for. But in the case of ethical conventions, asking members of the amateur community why they take themselves to be obligated not to pursue sport too seriously, or members of the professional community why they take themselves to be obligated to give their all to sport, would not hesitate to give reasons, plenty of reasons, why they believe they ought to act in just these ways. In short, they would not and, as we have seen, did not think they could get away with replying, "This is just the way we do things around here."

Arguments in the case of ethical conventions, unlike coordinating ones, are thus the natural, expected, and called-for response. Nonetheless, there are certain occasions when defenders of ethical conventions do end up saying something that sounds a lot like what Oxford dons say—namely, when the arguments and justifications they put on offer run out. When this happens, as Wittgenstein remarks, "I have reached bedrock. Then I am inclined to say: 'This is simply what I do'" (1958, §217). Hitting bedrock, of course, is the ultimate fate of all rational inquiry, whether it be amateurs and professionals who employ ethical conventions to do their rational bidding or other inquirers who employ different norms to do theirs. However, what distinguishes this declaration of rational inquirers from the declarations of Oxford dons and their kind is that it comes at the end rather than the beginning of inquiry and is, therefore, not intended to forestall such inquiry but only to mark the point at which it is fruitless to inquire further.

The second criticism of my conventionalist ethical theory takes issue with the local, community-based account of moral argument it trades in. The charge here is that such an account of moral argument, in which the ethical conventions at work in a particular community serve as its rational standard-bearers, is at bottom nothing more than a puerile form of relativism that makes a mockery of truth (or as I prefer, rational justification).[23] It is relativistic because it claims that when it comes to truth, one view is as good as any other. And it is puerile because it is a plainly self-refuting and self-contradictory thesis because when it is applied to itself, it necessarily tells against itself. As Hilary Putnam pithily puts it, "If any point of view is as good as any other, then why isn't the view that relativism is false as good as any other" (1981, 119). The objection, then, is that my claim that moral justification is relative to an athletic community (indeed, to any community of inquiry rightly so called), to the shared conventional norms and standards of rational acceptability internal to such a community, commits me to this very same silly and discredited relativism about truth.

But a moment's reflection should dispel any notion that I hold any such unsophisticated, undergraduate notion of relativism. For my community-friendly take on moral argument allows that members of an athletic community not only can err in the inferential judgments they make, can draw the wrong conclusions from the premises they begin with, but further can get better at making such inferential judgments by arriving at conclusions that are rationally superior to ones they may have previously made. There is nothing in my view, then, that moral argument is and should be a local, community affair that suggests that arguments so conducted have nothing going for them rationally speaking, that one argument is as good as any other argument.

However, I do not eschew the relativism moniker completely—only the above self-refuting kind. For I do gladly count myself a relativist in the sense that I hold truth (rational justification) to be relative to the perspective or normative framework of a community of inquiry. I suspect the accusation of relativism leveled against me has really to do with this communitarian-perspectival outlook on truth. My reason for thinking so is because indexing truth to perspectives only appears to be fatuous and self-refuting, to suggest truth is whatever we say it is, when stacked against an absolutist, nonperspectival account of truth. Of course, it is just such a nonperspectival notion of truth that formalism and the two varieties of broad internalism share in common and that lies behind their insistence that truth can be had only if we slough off the particular perspectives we bring to normative inquiry. So the charge of relativism naturally follows from their absolutist conception of truth, as does the charge of puerile relativism, since any version of relativism on their absolute conception is necessarily self-refuting.

However, if my criticisms of formalism and broad internalism and of corresponding moral principles like the internal principle have hit their mark, they should have eroded any confidence in such an absolute, nonperspectival account of truth and, therefore, of any criticisms that are derived from it. Nonetheless, it is one thing to say we should be wary of criticisms, relativistic or not, that emanate from such an absolute conception of truth, and quite another to say that that fact alone indemnifies my version of relativism from the self-refutation objection. The question remains, therefore, how I can defeat this objection? My answer is that my perspectival relativism, though not the puerile form that Putnam shoots down, is congenial to another, different notion of absolute truth, which allows that something can be *true in all perspectives.* My thesis that truth is relative to a (community) perspective is not self-refuting because it can be applied to itself without contradiction; that is, the thesis is itself *true in all perspectives* (but not true independent of perspectives). As long as truth is indexed to perspectives, I can have it both ways; I can assert that absolute and relative truth are not mutually exclusive. What such a relativism has going for it that the puerile form decidedly does not is, as Steven Hales argues, that it "carves out a logical space for absolute truth" and at the same time leaves room within that space for "a robust relativist program" (1997, 39). All of which means, the choice between a nonperspectival absolute conception of truth and a puerile self-contradictory conception of relative truth is a patently false choice.

The final objection to the notion of ethical conventions comes from Graham McFee (2018), who forcefully argues that because of the historically bound character of such conventions, accounts like mine that take their point of departure from them "cannot explain the generation of normativity *as such*" (19; emphasis in original). Rather, all such conventional accounts can accomplish is to tell a causal story of how, for example, the conventions of amateurism and professionalism came to play a major role in the ethical governance of sport at particular historical junctures. What they cannot account for, according to McFee, is how these conventions managed, as it were, to legislate themselves into existence out of an ethical vacuum. That is why he thinks historical accounts like mine can only presuppose that ethical conventions possess the ethical substance and force they do, as opposed to explaining how they acquired such ethical substance and force to begin with. They cannot do the latter because doing so would require in McFee's eyes, quoting Wittgenstein, "try[ing] to go further back than the beginning" (19). And that, of course, is a practical impossibility.

McFee's critical point here, however, is not that my conventionalist account of ethical norms fails because it *presupposes* rather than *explains* their normativity, but rather fails because it commits me to trying to do the latter. Trying to explain the normativity of such conventions counts as a failure in his eyes because it is a pseudo question that cannot in principle be answered. For in his view, "one cannot explain how *normativity* was generated, anymore than one can explain how *language as such* came about" (19; emphasis in original). His basic argument here, which he borrows from Michael Dummett, is that what is required to morally think and argue about things like sport is "precisely [the rationality] required for meaningful language-use" (19). That means roughly the rationality at work in the concepts we use to justify moral judgments about how sport should be conducted cannot be doubted, since any grounds for doubting them must themselves be rational grounds. And it is this "implicit normativity" of rationality, McFee claims, that "is embedded in the very possibility of language," in the concepts of sport we use to discuss and argue about it.

I agree with McFee that trying to go back before the beginning to account for the normativity of the ethical conventions of sport is a very bad idea indeed because it cannot be accomplished. However, I disagree with him that my conventionalist approach requires or otherwise encourages such an effort. On the contrary, it does no such thing because it is premised on the notion that human agents are never in a position to generate, in John McDowell's pithy words, "norms into existence out of a normative void" (2002, 277). That is because we never find ourselves in a "normless" situation that would require us to explain how we transitioned into a normative situation. The idea of such a transition is nothing more than a philosophical conceit, a thought experiment dreamed up by philosophers, the point of which is to imaginatively conjure up a "state of nature," a normless world, to divine a plausible theoretical scenario of how we were able to launch ourselves into a normative world. The antidote to such philosophical flights of fancy is to go historical, which is precisely what my conventionalist theory does, or at least aims to do. Not to try, per impossible, to get back before the beginning, which would put us squarely back into the fictional state of nature. Rather, my going historical by going conventional has a quite different aim, which is to show that "there is no original normless situation, only an on-going, continuous historical process of initiation or socialization into a community's normative practices" (Pippin 2005, 391).

Epilogue

Sport, Moral Progress, and Moral Entrepreneurs

I argue that a conventional ethical theory of sport of the kind I spell out in Chapter 6 is best suited to handle the often vexing moral issues and problems that crop up in sport. In this regard, I claim that it has distinct advantages over rival ethical theories of sport, specifically, formalism and the two versions of broad internalism, most notably with regard to its motivational force and action-guiding prowess. I also try to fend off actual and possible criticisms of my conventionalist ethical approach to sport.

I close by considering an as yet unexamined implication my conventionalist theory has regarding the important topic of moral progress in sport. That implication has to do with the local conception of practical rationality and moral argument that is central to my conventionalist account. In what follows, I briefly reprise that notion of moral argument and show how it does indeed rule out one widely held view of moral progress as it relates to sport. I then make the case that it is conducive to another, more tenable view of moral progress that is ideally suited to a social practice like sport.

Moral Argument and One View of Moral Progress Rejected

My conventional ethical theory of sport is based on an account of moral argument that requires we locate the giving and asking for reasons on how we should comport ourselves in sport to the interior of the moral vocabularies and language games played by athletic communities at a time and place. These conventional moral vocabularies and language games are best thought of as internal "logical spaces constructed for certain purposes" (Rorty 1989, 22). As we have seen, these purposes tend to diverge, sometimes radically, depending on the interests and ethical outlooks of the athletic communities in which they figure. For the amateur community, its view that the purpose of sport is the pursuit of pleasurable athletic encounters led to the opening of a logical space of reasons tailored to its members' interest in and ethical outlook on sport as a gentlemanly enterprise. For the professional community, by contrast, its view that the purpose of sport is the pursuit of athletic excellence led to the opening of a logical space of reasons tailored to its members' interest in and ethical outlook on sport as a serious vocational enterprise. When questions and controversies arose whether particular decisions made and actions taken on the field were morally justifiable, the only answers that were capable of settling the issue had to come from the moral vocabulary at work in each of these communities. Such questions and controversies were, therefore, very much amenable to moral argument and resolution, but only so long as the reasons asked for and given did not stray from the logical space in which they were at home and derived their persuasive force.

What does my conventional rendering of moral rationality and argument tell us about moral progress as it relates to sport? The answer, at this preliminary point, is two important things. First, it suggests that moral progress in sport is an immanent rather than a transcendent matter. That is, we can say we have made moral progress when we get better at the inferential judgments we proffer regarding how we should conduct ourselves in sport that comports with our conception of its point and purpose. Making better inferential judgments in this regard means being able to amend and correct past inferential judgments about how we should act in sport by adducing new inferential judgments that more closely follow on the local conventional starting points of our inquiry. We can justifiably say then that the amateur and professional communities were able to push the moral needle forward as they got better at making moral judgments more conducive to their respective avocational and vocational ethical outlooks on sport.

However, the second thing my conventional take on moral argument tells us is that we cannot speak of moral progress in sport when we are talking about the transition from the evaluative vocabulary of one athletic community to the evaluative vocabulary of another athletic community that follows it. That is, the idea that moral progress in sport is some sort of linear progressive development in which each succeeding athletic community's moral vocabulary and outlook marks an advance on its predecessor by getting us closer to the way sport really is and ought to be pursued, closer to some indelible moral facts of the matter about sport, is at best a romantic pipedream and at worst a deluded rationalization. The reason why is, to reiterate, that on my conventionalist rendering, moral argument is strictly an intramural, intra-community affair rather than an extramural, extra-community affair. So all rational bets are off when it comes to rationally determining whether a wholesale change in moral vocabularies counts as moral progress in this linear sense, as a positive step forward in our moral understanding and appreciation of sport. As Richard Rorty writes, "To accept the claim that there is no standpoint outside the particular historically conditioned and temporary vocabulary we are presently using from which to judge this vocabulary is to give up the idea that . . . intellectual or political [or moral] progress is rational . . . in any sense of 'rational' which is neutral between vocabularies" (1989, 48). The upshot, then, is that we simply lack rational standing to make any claim that one moral vocabulary is better than another. That is why the moral paradigm shift from gentleman-amateur sport to professional vocational sport cannot justifiably be regarded as moral progress. And insisting, nonetheless, that it does amounts to little more than adolescent-like boasting, to baseless declarations that our moral notion of sport is better than yours.

Moral Progress in a Different Vein

However, my conventionalist rendering of moral argument is receptive to a different notion of moral progress in sport that does involve a moral paradigm shift, a change in our moral outlook on sport. In this case, however, the passage from one moral outlook on sport to another is not, rightly understood, as a rational one attributable to an argumentative advance, but an a-rational one attributable to an imaginative redescription of the point and purpose of sport. This sort of moral progress does require that we break the crust of conventions, that we take leave of the ethical conventions that govern sport as we presently know and practice it to divine new future sport practices. And it has the added advantage of ringing truer to the moral history of sport itself, which is one not marked by moral continuities but rather by marked moral discontinuities that lay waste to the idea that we might at some future point converge on some fixed moral end or purpose that is intrinsic to sport itself. What sort of moral paradigm shift in sport I am gesturing at here requires some explanation.

The catalyst for such a change in our view of what is or is not morally acceptable in sport is typically someone's resistance to and protest of one or more of the reigning conventional ethical norms that govern sport. This often involves flouting or even breaking the conventional moral norm or norms in question. The point of such moral "disobedience" is to draw critical attention to the targeted norm or norms as a first step in the effort to change them. The greater the public attention the flouting or violation of the norm or norms garners, the better, since the whole idea is to expose to as many relevant parties as feasible just what the flouters and violators of the norms find problematic about them.

A classic case of just such an act of moral "disobedience" involved the first woman to run the Boston Marathon in 1967, Kathrine Switzer, who managed to circumvent the male-only eligibility provision to secure the official running number she needed to participate in the race. She obtained the number by registering as K. V. Switzer, which the unsuspecting race officials presumed was just another male contestant. In fact, it was not until two miles into the race that she was discovered by a race official, who promptly attempted to forcibly remove her from the course and tear off her race number. Fortunately, the official was prevented from doing so by her boyfriend, who was also a marathon participant and running beside her. And even though she was officially disqualified at the finish line and hounded by journalists nearby who exclaimed that "real women don't run," she successfully cast a much-needed bright and critical light on the male-only requirement of the Boston Marathon (Amer and Dahlgren 2017). Of course, because the requirement was well known at the time, her aim was not to disclose the obvious—that there was such a requirement—but rather to challenge its widespread acceptance. And it is not saying too much, I think, to claim that her act of moral disobedience, as well as of those who followed in her rebellious footsteps, paved the way in eventually getting the norm overturned.

What this example so well illustrates is how acts of moral disobedience of this kind can serve to jumpstart a change in our conceptual and moral outlook on sport, and by doing so alter our notion of sport and, concomitantly, what counts as an athletic body. What is important to notice here is how what I am calling such a moral breach of athletic norms, one intended to change a normatively problematic norm, differs from other instances of norm and rule violations. What Switzer was aiming to accomplish by her violation of the male-only provision was clearly not to secure a calculated strategic advantage over her competitors. That is, she was not weighing whether the benefits of breaking the rule outweighed the costs, as athletes now commonly do in certain competitive circumstances in which a strategic rule violation might give them a competitive edge. She knew full well no such competitive edge was in the offing, since there was no chance she could win the race or garner any athletic accolades or even be considered an official participant once she was found out. Nor was Switzer up to anything like what the so-called enfant terrible is up to when he or she deliberately and openly violates a norm or rule not to change it but merely to get a rise out of those whom the deviant behavior was meant to provoke.[1] In marked contrast to both, Switzer's deviant athletic behavior was, I think, meant to make a moral statement that the present conventional norms of sport needed changing to open up a new conceptual and normative space in which women not only are afforded access to sport but can meaningfully engage in sport. In a word, she was seeking, in however a provisional way, what amounts to a wholesale moral paradigm shift in how we think about and practice sport in which women are accorded a central place and role.

The noble practitioners of this normative craft of moral deviance can instigate a change in the moral vocabularies and language games played by athletic communities, but they cannot on their own effect such a change. That is because their flouting and violation of present ethical norms is still, and cannot help but be, responsive to these very norms. For even though such actions involve defying one or more of them, that defiance itself necessarily depends on these same norms. That means we cannot understand acts of moral disobedience like Switzer's, what she did and why she did it, without referencing the male-only eligibility requirement she was trying to undercut. This odious requirement guided her actions, not some new norm that would make it possible for her to act differently. Furthermore, any act of moral noncompliance of this kind presupposes compliance with most of the other conventional norms at work in sport as it is presently practiced. Just as liars depend on the conventions of truth-telling to be successful (otherwise they could not get anyone to believe their falsehoods), so moral dissidents in sport depend on the reigning conventional norms of sport in order to be successful; otherwise they could not get anyone to take their engagement in sport seriously enough to make their critical case.[2]

To effect moral change itself, we need to enlist what I am calling, after Richard Posner, moral entrepreneurs. They perform a role in bringing about real moral change and progress that nobody else can. As Posner tells us, "'Moral entrepreneurs' . . . have the power to change our moral intuitions," but not, he crucially adds, by "rational arguments" (1999, ix). Rather, they break the crust of existing ethical conventions by imaginatively conjuring up unfamiliar new ways of thinking about and engaging in social practices like sport. Rorty calls this imaginative assault on conventions the poetic art of redescription, the point of which is to throw overboard the concepts, moral norms, and moral intuitions that inform and guide sport as it is presently thought about and practiced, and replace them with metaphorical notions of sport that cast it in a new light. The hope is that the redescription of sport will sway enough people to change the way they think about and practice sport (1991, 124). Moral entrepreneurs are not, then, in the business of formulating moral arguments, but of redescribing the point and purpose of sport and other social practices by either churning out unfamiliar versions of familiar conceptions of such practices or by inventing altogether new conceptions of them. The success of their redescriptive efforts in this regard rises or falls, therefore, on whether they are able to jar our sensibilities sufficiently to get us to see these practices in ways not previously conceived or practiced.

Let me begin for illustrative purposes with a nonsporting example of a successful redescription of marriage. Marriage used to be thought of as a quasi-business affair, the purpose of which was "for uniting property and producing children" (Brennen et al. 2013, 110). So understood, this conception of marriage marked a sharp divide between heterosexual and homosexual relationships, effectively barring homosexual couples from both the concept and practice of marriage. It took a very long time, but eventually marriage was redescribed as a relationship predicated on love. This ushered in a new conception of the purpose of marriage, one centered no longer on property and the procreation of children but on a quasi-sacred, legal declaration of love and fidelity between the lovers themselves. This new conception of marriage erased the previous boundary and barrier between heterosexual and homosexual relationships by extending the concept and practice of marriage to include homosexual relationships (110). This was an important and momentous change and one that most people now rightly regard as genuine moral progress. But it took a redescription of marriage to effect the positive change rather than a battery of arguments, since there is no inferential path that leads from the old notion of marriage to the new one.

Moral progress in sport is similarly keyed to redescriptions of its main point and purpose, which led the way to the advent of new women-friendly and disability-friendly sports. The point of redescribing sport in these new ways was to ensure that women athletes and athletes with disabilities were no longer barred by the purposes and needs of able-bodied male athletes. The feminist philosopher Iris Marion-Young remarks that for most of its history, sport was considered a paradigmatic masculine endeavor in which women were largely excluded "from [the] concept of sport" (1988, 335). The amateur concept and practice of gentlemanly sport was obviously no exception because it was irrevocably bound up with a conception of women as "damsels in distress" whose supposed weakness made them not only unfit for athletic engagement but required the paternalistic protection of men to safeguard their "feminine" honor. The professional concept of serious, vocational sport was no less conceptually or practically unreceptive to the idea of women athletes because it similarly portrayed women as too fragile to play sport, let alone to play it well, which at the time meant in an aggressive manner and with a single-minded emphasis on winning. The same exclusionary view of "disability sports" and "disabled" bodies was also a conceptual and normative signature feature of sport from time immemorial. The prevailing concept of "disability" until recent times, which zeroed in on what the "disabled" could not do, was considered the polar opposite of the prevailing concept of sport until recent times. Disabled bodies were simply written off as athletic bodies, just as women's bodies were. Thus, any effort to include people with physical disabilities in the reigning concept and practice of sport was ridiculed as an attempt, as it were, to dumb down sport, to lower the present standards of athletic accomplishment, so as to open sport to untalented, unskilled participants—the category in which disabled and women would-be athletes were automatically and unceremoniously dumped, supposedly undeserving of admittance into the pantheon of sport.

It took moral entrepreneurs like Jane English, who called for the creation of new sports that privilege female bodies (2018, 360), and other like-minded moral entrepreneurs, who devised new ways of playing traditional male sports that relied more on finesse and less on aggression (think of the contrast between elite men's and women's hockey or elite men's and women's tennis), to pry open a space for women athletes and women's athletic bodies in our concept and practice of sport.[3] It similarly took moral entrepreneurs to pry open a logical and practical space for athletes with disabilities, which zeroed in on what such athletes were capable of rather than what they were incapable of, and which led to the creation of the Paralympics Games that gave these athletes an opportunity to showcase their newly recognized athletic talents, skills, and mettle to an international audience (LaVaque-Manty 2009, chap. 5).

What is important not to lose sight of regarding the shift in moral paradigms of sport such entrepreneurs engineer is that the metaphorical redescriptions they deploy to impel such transitions function as causes, but not as reasons, for changes in our moral beliefs about sport. They cannot be reasons because the new concepts and norms they turn out have no place in existing moral vocabularies and language-games used and played by extant athletic communities. Lacking such a place, they can only poke and prod our moral sensibilities but not provide rational cover for them. So the moral innovations in how we conceive of and practice sport that are the byproduct of these metaphorical redescriptions are best understood as gestalt switches or conversions, rather than as rational inferences drawn from conventional starting points. For there is, to reiterate, no rational inferential path that leads from amateur to professional sport, or to women's or disability sports, or to any moral change in sport worthy of the name. But although there is no rational way forward when it comes to such sweeping changes in our moral outlooks on sport, there is an imaginative way forward that, despite its a-rational bona fides, has proved to be a powerful tool for enlarging our conceptual and moral vision of what is possible in sport and for including more and more diverse people and bodies into its athletic circles.

Moral entrepreneurs are then indispensable when it comes to instigating important paradigm shifts in our moral conceptions and practices of sport. However, while their initial success depends on whether the redescriptions of sport they proffer strike people as sufficiently captivating to cause them to alter their moral sensibilities, their ultimate success depends on whether they are eventually taken up by some community and used by its members in arguments to justify their actions in sport. For this to happen, what was previously just "a noise having a place in a causal network" must acquire "a place in a pattern of justification of belief" (Rorty 1991, 171). This is just another way of saying that what was at first just an unconventional redescriptive stimulus to get us to see sport in a new, unfamiliar light must in due course become a conventional familiar description of sport embraced by a future athletic community. For once the redescription is conventionalized, the concepts and norms it begets can be put to use by such a community to guide and justify how they comport themselves in this new sport setting and to adjudicate any moral disputes that might arise. The conventionalization of such metaphorical redescriptions of sport is, of course, no sure thing. Indeed, a large number of them fall by the wayside and prove to be little more than imaginative flashes in the pan. But those that do happen to resonate, to catch on with the members of some community, gradually see their status change from unwarranted assertions to warranted ones, and eventually to full-fledged moral vocabularies in their own right. In short, they become the concepts and norms used by these members to give and ask for reasons about how they should act in sport and to justify the moral judgments that emerge from their disputations.

Moral change on my conventionalist theory is thus never a purely conventional, consensual matter but also, I hasten to add, never a matter that can ever do without conventions to be successful. But does moral change as presented here count as genuine moral progress? My emphatic answer is yes, but only in immanent rather than transcendent terms. That is, moral innovations such as women's and disability sports qualify in my estimation as real and significant moral progress. But not moral progress in the sense of better than their predecessors or in the sense of bringing us closer to what sport is in and of itself, to some moral facts of the matter intrinsic to sport. In my view again, we simply lack rational standing to make universal claims of this kind. Rather, women's and disability sports count as moral progress according to the only rational criteria available to us: what our present conventional standards of reflective appraisal tell us sport at its moral best looks like. This means that our rational assessments of moral progress in sport like our rational assessments of everything else in sport, nonmoral and moral alike, are and can only be parochial, provincial ones. But that is no grounds for rejecting them as undeserving of our rational assent. For if philosophy, and presumably moral philosophy, is what G.W.F. Hegel and philosophers after him, such as Bernard Williams and Rorty claim it is, "its own time apprehended in thoughts" (Hegel 1977b, 11), then why should we doubt whether women's and disability sports represent true moral progress? After all, such judgments befit the finite human beings we most assuredly are, despite our more than occasional extravagant pretensions to the contrary.

Notes

INTRODUCTION

1. I have a lot more to say about women's and disability sports and the role played by moral entrepreneurs in the ensuing discussion and, most notably, in the Epilogue.

CHAPTER 1

1. Of course, there is still an undeniable aristocratic sentiment in Samuel Crowther's expression of moral scorn for nonamateurs, since it supports a view of sport most congenial to the aristocratic elite. But, again, one should be careful not to make too much of this, given the middle-class embrace of gentlemanly sport for emergent professional reasons.

2. Of course, it never occurred to them that their good fortune in being able to lead a comfortable amateur life by virtue of their birth and/or university education gave them a distinct and not entirely fair advantage over those excluded from participating in elite amateur sport.

3. That the French had racked up more overall first places than the Americans in the 1896 games, twenty-six to twenty-one, did not sway Americans in the least that they were the best at sport in the world (Dyreson 1998, 69).

4. The English Olympic officials' extraordinary actions on Pietri's behalf did indeed, as the alert reader might have already surmised, have a lot to do with their unabashed nationalism, in making sure the American runner Hayes was denied victory. That fact, of course, only added to the ethical pique of the Americans that they were being treated unfairly.

CHAPTER 2

1. This was Suits's standard view of sport until his 1988 "Tricky Triad: Games, Play, and Sport" essay, in which he distinguished for the first time between "judged" (gymnastics and diving) and "refereed" (football, baseball, etc.) athletic events and claimed that only refereed athletic events are games (he called judged athletic events simply performances). Because I and several others, including Klaus Meier (1988) and R. Scott Kretchmar (1989), regard his standard view more persuasive, I ignore the later retraction of his earlier thesis that all sports are games.

2. I say most but not all analytically inclined philosophers regard Suits's definitional effort as misguided because prominent philosophers such as Thomas Hurka (2007) and Colin McGinn (2012), inspired by what they took to be the success of Suits's effort to define games, have actively agitated for a return to the kind of conceptual analysis Suits pursued. In doing so, of course, they can be understood as rejecting Wittgenstein's "family resemblance" treatment of concepts.

3. This problem is mitigated but not eliminated for Suits because he thinks the ordinary user of language on the street is more so a "working essentialist" than a working Wittgensteinian (2014, 209).

4. As discussed later in the chapter, however, the normative dimension constitutive rules introduced on Searle's account are restricted to evaluative questions about whether one is playing a game. That is because the crucial Y term in Searle's formula creates a new form of behavior by stipulating that, for example, when a player kicks a ball into a net, it counts as goal in the context of a soccer game. The stipulation in question, however, is not an appraisal; that is, it does not call for an aesthetic evaluation of how skillfully the kick was made but rather only whether it was made in accordance with the rules (Searle 1969, 33). For more on this point see Kretchmar 2001, 163. In the case of what David Best (1978) calls aesthetic sports, however, in which an aesthetic judgment is made about how skillfully the goal was achieved, what Searle calls a stipulation includes—indeed consists of—an aesthetic appraisal. Further, the question of a moral appraisal, of whether the kicking of the ball into the net was fairly accomplished, would also seem to figure into the question of whether the game was being played. More on the latter point shortly.

5. One of the authors he cited as guilty of this misinterpretation was yours truly. See Morgan 1987. I am grateful to him for pointing out my mistake.

6. Of course, this observation bears on the definitional utility of formalism as well, but I am presently focused only on the moral payoff of formalism.

7. For a contrary account that argues Searle gets the better of Suits in this regard, see Kretchmar's essay "A Functionalist Analysis of Game Acts: Revisiting Searle" (2001). Kretchmar's defense of Searle's analysis of rules is impressively argued, but I disagree with two of its key points. On the first, Kretchmar contends Searle offers a more convincing functional interpretation of the logical incompatibility thesis precisely because he studiously avoids Suits's logical question of "At what point does a game become a non-game?" in favor of the question of how and why a game ceases to "function effectively" as a game (165). On the second, Kretchmar suggests the way to mark off a greater, more central rule violation from a lesser, more peripheral one is to consider "a gradation in severity in penalties that are . . . themselves constitutive rules" (166). Briefly, my problem with the first point is that Kretchmar's functionalist

reinterpretation of the logical incompatibility thesis is, in fact, an altogether new interpretation of it that is at odds with both Suits's and Searle's interpretive renderings. The point of the logical incompatibility thesis for both of these authors is to tell us when a game ceases to be a game or becomes a different game. It is not normatively equipped to do anything else and certainly not suited to telling us when a game becomes a weaker version of itself. That is why Suits explicitly disclaimed he was trying to define well-played games and why his moral censure of cheaters was restricted to their game-destroying ways. Searle also argued that constitutive rules, specifically the all-important "Y term" in his formula "X counts as Y in context C," are "stipulations" that make new connections between actions but provide no appraisal of those actions (1969, 33). My issue with his second point that we can distinguish greater from lesser constitutive rules by taking note of the severity of the penalty exacted is that it is too broad. That is, it is true that the severest penalty meted out for a rule violation in a game is disqualification and that game players get disqualified when they engage in game-nullifying behaviors (instead of pitching to batters, throwing at their heads, for instance). But it is also true that one can be thrown out of games—indeed, banned from playing for a certain length of time or number of games—for breaking rules that have little or nothing to do with their centrality to the game (for instance, for arguing too vociferously an umpire's call or, as NFL pass-rusher extraordinaire Robert Mathis can attest, for using an unapproved fertility drug in an effort to impregnate his wife).

8. Of course, Delattre might argue that even in officiated games like football, players have an obligation to call penalties on themselves that referees miss or decide to overlook in certain instances (for example, in the closing moments of a game). The problem is, however, that in most cases such self-calls by players would not be recognized and enforced by game officials. Possible exceptions might include, for instance, wide receivers not feigning they have successfully caught passes that actually touched the ground first, that they, in the vernacular of the game, trapped.

9. Delattre's account of when a violation of a regulative rule counts as well as a violation of a constitutive rule is not foolproof, however. Suppose soccer player A, who is not a goalie, uses her hands to advance the ball every opportunity she gets and accepts the penalty for violating the handball rule in every instance. At some point in the game, which will depend on how often she handles the ball, it will become clear to all concerned that she is no longer playing soccer, despite her willingness to abide by the called penalty. At that point it no longer makes sense to penalize her for a simple handball rule violation but to disqualify her for her failure to play the game. In such a case, I think, Delattre's account does not wash. However, because this example is fanciful at best, I do not think it is terribly damaging to his position.

10. For D'Agostino, this counterintuitive feature of formalism is another example of its Platonistic tendencies.

11. The distinction I draw here and the way I develop it is heavily indebted to Geoffrey Brennan, Lina Eriksson, Robert E. Goodwin, and Nicholas Southwood (2013).

12. The general way this distinction is made is that *de dicto* considerations concern what is said about a thing, whereas *de re* ones concern the thing itself.

13. Of course, if the legislative bodies that issue secondary rules are themselves corrupt, the normative authority of these rules would not be credible. Further, if

referees prove to be grossly incompetent, their *de re* normative authority would also be suspect.

14. Because triflers do not deliberately try to win games, they can't be said to deliberately try to lose games.

15. The necessity of discussing other alternative ways teams lessen their chances of winning was impressed on me by Tom Hurka's acute criticisms of an earlier version of this section in private correspondence.

16. Hurka, personal communication, 2015. Hurka argues that something more than a violation of the lusory attitude is in play in this example because the badminton players were doing more than not trying to win; they were actively trying to subvert this game goal. I think he is right about this. But I do not think that formalists like Suits have anything within their formalist arsenal to make such a case, not at least in terms of the four elements of his concept of a game.

17. This counterview might well prevail as contemporary sport becomes increasingly more win obsessed. But one thing that should give us pause is that playoff formats are mostly of the elimination variety (single or double) or the round-robin variety used in the badminton example. And although the latter has its problems, as the badminton case showed, it does have its strengths because every team gets to play every other team at least once. Whereas the elimination-style format takes care of the playing-to-lose problem of round-robin tournaments, it has its own distinct weaknesses, the main one being that a large number of teams are eliminated after one game—hardly a reassuring way of crowning athletic champions.

CHAPTER 3

1. He is certainly not alone in interpreting Suits's definitional achievement as a metaphysical one as well. For a recent example of just such a metaphysical reading of Suits's conceptual analysis of games and sport, see Colin McGin's *Truth by Analysis: Games, Names, and Philosophy* (2012).

2. Russell's claim that the internal principle of sport is rooted in the Aristotelian ideal of human flourishing is one important feature that distinguishes his account of broad internalism from Simon's. Simon (2007) argues that the internal principle not only is, as its name suggests, internal to sport but is unique to sport. That is, he subscribes to what Russell calls the separation thesis, which holds that sport has its own distinctive morality that differs from the morality of most other social practices. Russell, however, thinks the internal principle is internal to sport but not unique to sport. That is, he subscribes to what he calls the continuity thesis, which holds that the internal principle of sport is continuous with moral ideals like human flourishing that inform forms of life outside of sport. He also argues that his second moral principle of sport, the external principle, which he grounds in the Kantian moral ideal of respect for people, is also continuous with forms of life outside of sport that similarly are rooted in this ideal of respect for people. See, in this regard, Russell 2007.

3. An added advantage of the external principle in acts of game violence of this sort is that it is a reliable guide when such instances should be treated as moral transgressions to be handled in-house by the relevant sport authorities and when they should be treated as criminal acts to be handled by external authorities of the law and state.

4. Just how compatible a conceptual analysis is with a coherentist analysis of sport, or of anything else for that matter, will be a major bone of contention in my critical analysis to follow.

5. Two points need to be made here. First, I ignore the important normative function the lusory attitude plays in formalism sketched in Chapter 2 because broad internalists have little if anything to say about it, owing, no doubt, to their preoccupation with the rules of games. Second, in accordance with my main interest in the general normative evaluative prowess of moral theories of sport like broad internalism, I largely ignore the adjudicative slant of Russell's version of broad internalism. That is, I am not interested in the implications of his theory specifically for sports officiating. For those interested in the latter, see Berman 2011.

6. For an argument that similarly questions Russell's categorical dismissal of Martin's strategic ploy in this instance, and more generally argues the moral permissibility of such strategies are an open, interpretative matter, see Berman 2011, 186–187. Berman thinks that interpretative queries like these depend "at least in part on the understanding and practices of participants" (187). I concur, but maintain that such participant understandings depend mostly on larger social and historical considerations and, specifically, conventional norms and standards.

7. This is so despite his declared fallibalism, his concession that he can only claim approximate truth for his moral claims.

8. Suits, of course, was well aware that there is more to language than reference, and thus that he could not ignore usage altogether (2014, 173). But he did clearly think "the chief purpose of definition," his stated interest in the concept of game, "is to make our referential language more exact" (166).

9. That makes it hard to see how Russell's principles can function as anything other than a rubber stamp for most community-backed descriptions of sport.

10. That both the amateur and professional athletic communities broadly subscribed to the perfectionist and voluntarist norms of Russell's internal and external principles does not mean that all such athletic communities in the past did so, or, for that matter, that future athletic communities are fated to follow suit.

11. As I comment on in detail shortly, however, it should not go unnoticed that Russell's use of reflective equilibrium in game adjudication, the historical backward-and-forward-looking he insists game officials are obliged to exercise in rendering their decisions, only figures in the application of his internal and external principles rather than in their generation. That is, the evidence that this historical back-and-forth effort at reflective equilibrium provides is evidence not for these normative principles themselves but for their effective application once they have been divined.

CHAPTER 4

1. It should also be noted that two other compelling reasons might explain why Simon strayed from Rawls's approach to moral discourse. The first is that Rawls's notion of the veil of understanding as a representational device to test our intuitions was specifically designed to develop a conception of justice, one that suited a pluralistic society of a liberal democratic kind, in which its citizens characteristically hold different and often incommensurable conceptions of the good. Because of this, what Rawls calls

a "political fact" about a democratic society arriving at a conception of justice agreeable to all of its citizens was vital to the stability of such a social order (1999, 425). Trying to hold a democratic society together by coming up with a comprehensive conception of the good agreeable to all of its citizens is obviously out of the question, given this "political fact" of pluralism. In the case of sport and other cultural practices, however, we are dealing with a much smaller subset of society and one united by a thick conception of the good particular to these practices. That does not mean sport and the like can do without a conception of justice, but only that the necessity of the priority of the right over the good in the public, political life of a democratic society is appropriately reversed in these particular cases. Second, while in Rawls's earlier book, *A Theory of Justice* (1971), he aimed to justify principles of justice based on the rational self-interests of all human agents, in his later work, he changed course and sought to justify principles of justice based on certain fundamental intuitive ideas mutually shared by the citizens of a democratic society. That is, he dropped the idea of justifying principles of justice to all of humanity in favor of justifying them to a particular historical democratic society.

2. Russell's declaration that sport has "a clear underlying purpose" to demonstrate excellence in overcoming rule-contrived obstacles can be found, among other places, in his 2011 essay on page 265.

3. My initial criticisms of Simon and Dixon can be found in my 2012 and 2013 essays, and Simon's critical responses in his 2014 and 2015 publications.

4. I am quoting an apparently earlier draft of Simon's "Internalism" chapter that was subsequently published in 2015.

5. Of course, this kind of self-referential inconsistency criticism can be an inside critical job as well, as when a proponent of a certain philosophical view of sport, say, points out that a certain conclusion regarding how sport should be ethically governed does not, in fact, follow from its core premises. However, the external critic is the more likely candidate to point out such self-referential inconsistencies if he or she holds no brief for the theory in the first place or finds it objectionable on this and other grounds.

6. I owe this point and example to Rorty (2014, 42). Another helpful example he mentions is the Marxist and Freudian claim that all philosophical explanations are rationalizations, to which the critic replies, must their own explanation of philosophical explanations be mere rationalizations too?

7. Of course, that is not to say that the criticisms did not sting those targeted—only that the criticisms were roundly rejected on both sides as unjustifiable, as rants rather than arguments anyone needed to take seriously enough to change his or her behavior.

8. As it turns out, Dixon's hypothetical was not as hypothetical as it appears; he based the example on the 2002 Winter Olympic Games, in which the judges awarded the gold medal in pairs skating to a Russian couple, even though it was widely believed by the skating community that the Canadian pair had skated better. The judges subsequently awarded an unprecedented second gold medal to the Canadian pair in what amounted to their de facto admission that something was seriously amiss with the judges' initial decision.

9. Moral inquiry into more wide-ranging, thin conceptions of justice, for example, are a different matter. On the international scene, for instance, thinning out our con-

ceptions of justice to reach accord on moral strictures against infanticide, incest, torture, and basic justice are the rational way to go. See Walzer 1994 in this regard. Even questions of political justice within pluralistic societies like our own, as I note in the first endnote above, call for similar general agreement on fair interaction and cooperation between and among its members that go beyond their particular conceptions of the good. As Rawls observes, "It is not true . . . that on a liberal view citizens have no fundamental common aims. . . . But this common aim of political justice must not be mistaken for . . . a conception of the good" (1999, 431, 432).

10. Hurley is actually channeling Wittgenstein here and other philosophers of his persuasion, with whom she disagreed. So this is not her stated view but theirs, and, of course, my adopted view as well.

11. This part of my argument is heavily indebted to Paul Boghossian's (2006) illuminating discussion of this issue.

12. Boghossian raises an important point here, but I think such self-creeping doubt about one's own community's rational justificatory standards and resources is itself a questionable artifact of suspect decontextualized accounts of rationality that promise much more than they can deliver. So I think once we disabuse ourselves of such context-independent notions of rational justification, we will also disabuse ourselves of any concern that local justification is not justification enough, that such particular forms of justification do not have enough going for them to quell any doubts local communities might have regarding their own justificatory practices.

CHAPTER 5

1. I am simply paraphrasing, using slightly different nomenclature, Marmor's (2009, 2) formal rendering of the three features that mark off conventions from other social norms.

2. People may not be motivated to follow conventional norms, which is an especially important feature of what I am calling ethical conventions. For what distinguishes normative from causal and motivating reasons as it applies specifically to conventions, see Letsas 2014, 536–537. Last, the idea that the reasons for following conventions are necessarily normative ones is a controversial one, at least in the case of so-called coordinating conventions. For a criticism in this regard, see Southwood and Eriksson 2011.

3. Marmor provides a more extended account of what counts here as a "conceivable" alternative in his later book (2009, 10).

4. Compliance dependence is only part of the reason why members of a community follow conventions. The other part, of course, is the purposes and values of the convention itself. But, in addition, there may be other reasons for following a convention that have nothing per se to do with the convention itself (Marmor 2009, 12). Such reasons include threats of retaliation or spousal disapproval.

5. My claim that when coordinating conventions come with moral obligations, these obligations are not required by the conventions themselves because they are strictly extraneous is a paraphrase of a claim made by Nicholas Southwood and Lina Eriksson (2011, 201), with one crucial difference. The authors claim that when coordinating conventions come with nonmoral *normative* obligations, they are not entailed

by the conventions themselves. By contrast, I argue that these conventions do indeed have normative entailments but not moral ones.

6. In this latter case, however, the players' defiance of the convention is for a moral reason, and, no doubt, much of the criticism they received from fans was also morally rooted (patriotism). Nonetheless, the playing of and standing for the anthem is a coordinating convention.

7. Interestingly, he credits this last feature of game rules to Thomas Hurka (1993, 126), and not Bernard Suits, whose essays and book he was unaware of at the time of the publication of his last book on the topic in 2009 (Andrei Marmor, personal conversation with the author, 2010).

8. The awareness of the binding force of deep conventions does not mean, as Marmor notes (2009, 7), people are aware that they are conventional norms. People may not know that these norms have an alternative that might have been followed instead. Likewise, players of games and sport might also be mistaken about the arbitrary character of the background norms that make their actions in this domain intelligible.

9. Marmor contrasts such "legislative" codification, which purports to *authoritatively determine* the rules that we typically find, for instance, in rule books, with "encyclopedic" codification, which purports to *report and record* the rules that we typically find, for instance, in grammar textbooks and dictionaries (2009, 50–51).

10. It will be remembered that Suits added the "lusory attitude" to his definition of games to cover just such situations, specifically with respect to game triflers.

11. I later question whether Marmor's answer is, in fact, a persuasive one.

12. It will be remembered that Hart contrasts secondary rules from primary rules that govern the actual conduct that takes place within said practice (2009, 51).

13. To answer it fully would require a detailed analysis of what I am calling ethical conventions. I provide just such an analysis in Chapter 6. For now, however, I am presuming, better hoping, I have said enough to give readers a rough idea, but certainly not a complete one, of what ethical conventions are and do to get my present point across.

14. Thanks go, once again, to Eric Moore, who encouraged me to take another look at Marmor's account of deep conventions.

CHAPTER 6

1. For my gloss on what constitutes a sport practice community, see Chapter 4.

2. As Terry Pinkard argues, "To say that such and such is 'the way things are done' in terms of *Sittlichkeit* is to acknowledge that this idea of 'the way things are done' expresses something like a convention" (1996, 124). And anticipating my argument to come, Pinkard adds, to understand *Sittlichkeit* as a kind of convention is further to acknowledge that "it is nonetheless a *deep* convention, unlike the *mere* conventions of 'driving on the left side of the road' or 'tipping one's hat'" (124; emphasis in original).

3. As Hegel succinctly puts it with respect to the state, "Philosophy . . . must [not] attempt to construct a state as it ought to be. . . . [I]t can only show how the state, the ethical universe, is to be understood" (1977b, 11).

4. In following Hegel's lead in dividing modern society into these three domains, I do not follow him in the dialectical transitions he claims take us from the family to civil society to the state.

5. It was for this very reason that Bernard Williams criticized Koorsgaard's Kantian claim that we can explain the emergence of distinctly liberal values by our general human capacity to confer value. See Williams 2003, 115.

6. I agree with Marmor's criticism that only certain conventions—what I call ethical conventions—create collective subjects, not all conventions, as Gilbert claims. See Marmor 2009, 27.

7. This point holds across the board for all conventions, not just ethical ones, since, as Tyler Burge astutely argues, "people sometimes enter into a convention without knowing that it is conventional—even doubting its conventionality" (1975, 249). One of his main examples is an imaginary small and utterly isolated linguistic community that has not the foggiest idea that there are alternative ways of speaking to their own way of speaking (249–250). But communities of the athletic practice kind and otherwise don't have to be this isolated or incurious to think there are no alternatives to the way they presently do sport and other things, and, therefore, that the way they do these things is not conventional or at least not commonly known to be conventional by some large or small subset of its members.

8. Wittgenstein's further claim is relevant here as well—namely, that to do things like "play[ing] a game of chess, are *customs* (uses, institutions)" (1958 199; emphasis in original).

9. My argument here that attempts to philosophically ground the ethical conventions that I claim are the valid starting points of normative inquiry is further premised on my earlier rejection in Chapter 3 that such philosophical efforts are a way to unlock the normativity that resides "out there" in sport itself. Such efforts, I argue, get us nowhere normatively speaking because the normativity of sport is not "out there" in the world but inside the descriptive and evaluative vocabularies that are the source of our varying historical and social conceptions of sport.

10. That does not rule out, I should say, rival athletic communities trying normatively, as it were, to break bread with one another, trying to find some common points of agreement between them. But all such efforts rest on coherentist grounds—that is, on whether each can find some way to coherently weave the beliefs and norms of the other into its own web of beliefs and norms. I have already stated that disputes like my featured amateur and professional one defy such coherentist reconciliation.

11. Raz claims in this regard that the existence of sustaining social practices is a necessary but not sufficient condition for the existence of cultural values. That is why he argues that his social dependence thesis "does not in any way privilege the point of view of any group or culture. It allows one full recourse to the whole of one's conceptual armoury, information, and powers of argumentation in reaching conclusions as to which practices sustain goods and which sustain evil, or worthless things" (2003, 25). In this book at least, Raz offers no argument for his claim that social practices that birth, as it were, cultural values require for the justification of their status as such a practice-independent, noncontextual normative assessment.

12. I am not alone in criticizing Raz on this normative score. See especially Robert Pippin's critical response to this feature of Raz's account (2003, 91).

13. In Raz's book *Morality of Freedom*, he defends a perfectionist account of the good based on the autonomy of the individual, on the ability of the individual to set his or her own goals and values free of coercion by others. I owe this point to Pippin 2003, 99.

14. The attentive reader will also notice that Marmor's objection that conventional norms only play a mediating role in the governance of conventional practices derives part of whatever persuasive force it seems to have because it features primarily examples of coordinating conventions like the queue. This is also the case for most of the examples Brennan and his coauthors entertain, which are coordinating conventions rather than ethical conventions like those that govern amateur and professional sport. This running together of coordinating and ethical conventions, as I make clear in the ensuing discussion, is the second questionable source of objections raised against ethical conventionalism.

15. That is not to say that when the occasion demands it, this thick morality cannot be thinned out. Walzer cites the example of watching people on television marching in the streets of Prague in 1989 carrying signs demanding the government tell the truth and treat them justly. Because they were not advocating for any particular theory of truth or justice, he noted, we could grasp the point of their protest. But, he hastens to add, if pressed, no doubt, these protestors "would have described a just society in different ways . . . [drawing] on different accounts of history and culture" (1994, 2).

16. What goes for abstract moral ideals here goes as well for conflicting ethical conventions adhered to by rival athletic communities like the amateur and professional ones with one important qualification. Asking members of the amateur athletic community to take on board and abide the ethical conventions of the professional athletic community, or asking professionals to do the same and take on board and abide the ethical conventions of the amateur community, requires each to forsake the moral lives and moral roles that have shaped their very different athletic identities as members of their home communities. Swapping ethical conventions in this way puts members of both communities in the same moral bind as does insisting they honor abstract moral ideals and principles. Both, then, are just not morally plausible ways for members of such communities to conduct their lives. Of course, the difference is that abstract moral ideals fail us because they don't speak to the parochial ethical questions of concern to each community, whereas rival ethical conventional ideals fail us because they speak to the wrong parochial ethical concerns, to the other community's ethical concerns rather than our own.

17. Of course, the morality system itself, in treating, as Hegel notes (1977b), the worth of the individual in himself and herself as its central focus, is guilty of concealing "the dimension in which ethical life lies outside the individual" (Williams 1985, 191).

18. Further, Papineau's claim that conventions govern "matters of no intrinsic importance" runs together what I have been trying to keep separate—namely, coordinating conventions that align with Papineau's claim and ethical conventions that do not (2017, 64).

19. My discussion here is very much indebted to Southwood and Erikson 2011, 205.

20. This part of my account is indebted to David Holley's analysis (1997, 165–167).

21. This is why Hegel in the Berlin edition of his *Encyclopedia Logic* clarifies that what he meant by his oft-quoted phrase equating the rational and the actual does not preempt criticism of the status quo, as if all is well with things as they presently are. As he exclaims, "Who is not acute enough to see a great deal in his own surroundings which is really far from being as it ought to be?" (quoted in Pippin 2008, 95–96).

22. Something like this criticism figures in the second objection I discuss in this section, in which it is claimed that ethical conventions only mediate between abstract moral ideals that do all the heavy moral lifting and their concrete realization. The claim there is that talk of the "done" thing in justificatory terms works only if it involves a suppressed reference to practice-independent moral principles and reasons.

23. This charge of self-contradictory relativism was leveled against my conventionalist ethical theory in a recent article by Eric Moore (2018, 236–237).

EPILOGUE

1. For an illuminating account of norm breaching and its intended purposes, see Brennan et al. 2013, chap. 11.

2. The danger of going completely unconventional in such instances is that they will be regarded by the sporting public as clowns or freaks rather than dissidents—the unkind judgment often rendered, for example, of women bodybuilders.

3. Unfortunately, English's call for new sports tailored to women's bodies and athletic capabilities has so far fallen on deaf ears.

References

Amer, Sarah, and Kristen Dahlgren. 2017. "First Woman to Officially Run Boston Marathon Makes Triumphant Return." *NBC News*, April 18. Available at https://www.nbcnews.com/feature/inspiring-america/first-woman-officially-run-boston-marathon-makes-triumphant-return-n747616.

Anderson, Elizabeth. 2000. "Homo Economicus: New Developments in Theories of Social Norms." *Philosophy and Public Affairs* 29 (2): 170–200.

Baker, Norman. 2004. "Whose Hegemony? The Origins of the Amateur Ethos in Nineteenth Century English Society." *Sport in History* 24 (1): 1–16.

Berman, Mitchell. 2011. "On Interpretivism and Formalism in Sports Officiating: From General to Particular Jurisprudence." *Journal of the Philosophy of Sport* 37 (2): 177–196.

Best, David. 1978. *Philosophy and Human Movement*. London: Allen and Unwin.

Blackburn, Simon. 2018. *On Truth*. New York: Oxford University Press.

Boghossian, Paul. 2006. *Fear of Knowledge: Against Relativism and Constructivism*. New York: Oxford University Press.

Brandom, Robert. 1994. *Making it Explicit*. Cambridge, MA: Harvard University Press.

Brennan, Geoffrey, Lina Eriksson, Robert E. Goodwin, and Nicholas Southwood. 2013. *Explaining Norms*. New York: Oxford University Press.

Brownlee, Timothy. 2015. "Alienation and Recognition in Hegel's Phenomenology of Spirit." *Philosophical Forum* 46 (4): 377–396.

Burge, Tyler. 1975. "Knowledge and Convention." *Philosophical Review* 84 (2): 249–255.

Chappell, Sophie. 2017. "The Objectivity of Ordinary Life." *Ethical Theory and Moral Practice* 20 (4): 709–721.

Collier, Price. 1898. "Sport's Place in the Nation's Well-Being." *Outing* 32:382–388.

Corbin, John. 1901. "Sportsmanship in England and America." *Outing* 39:1–10.

Crowther, Samuel, Jr. 1907. "The Ethics of American Rowing." *Outing* 50:499–502.

D'Agostino, Fred. 1981. "The Ethos of Games." *Journal of the Philosophy of Sport* 8:7–18.

Darwall, Stephen. 2006. *The Second-Person Standpoint*. Cambridge, MA: Harvard University Press.

Delattre, Edwin. 2007. "Some Reflections on Success and Failure in Competitive Athletics." In *Ethics in Sport*, edited by W. J. Morgan, 195–200. Champaign, IL: Human Kinetics.

Dixon, Nick. 2003. "Canadian Figure Skaters, French Judges, and Realism in Sport." *Journal of the Philosophy of Sport* 30:103–116.

Dunning, Eric. 2001. *Sport Matters*. London: Routledge.

Dworkin, Ronald. 1986. *Law's Empire*. Cambridge, MA: Harvard University Press.

Dyreson, Mark. 1989. "The Emergence of Consumer Culture and the Transformation of Physical Culture." *Journal of Sport History* 16 (3): 261–281.

———. 1998. *Making the American Team: Sport, Culture, and the Olympic Experience*. Urbana, IL: University of Illinois Press.

Eichberg, Henning. 2016. *Questioning Play: What Play Can Tell Us about Human Life*. New York: Routledge.

English, Jane. 2018. "Sex Equality in Sports." In *Ethics in Sport*, edited by W. J. Morgan, 355–362. Champaign, IL: Human Kinetics.

Fletcher, George. 1997. "The Case for a Linguistic Self-Defense." In *The Morality of Nationalism*, edited by R. McKim and J. McMahan, 324–339. New York: Oxford University Press.

Frankfurt, Harry G. 2006. *Taking Ourselves Seriously and Getting it Right*. Stanford, CA: Stanford University Press.

Geras, Norman. 2009. "Games and Meanings." In *Hillel Steiner and the Anatomy of Justice: Themes and Challenges*, edited by S. De Wizje, M. H. Kramer, and I. Carter, 185–200. New York: Routledge.

Geuss, Raymond. 1981. *The Idea of a Critical Theory: Habermas and the Frankfurt School*. New York: Cambridge University Press.

Gilbert, Margaret. 1989. *On Social Facts*. Princeton, NJ: Princeton University Press.

Guttmann, Allen. 1978. *From Ritual to Record: The Nature of Modern Sports*. New York: Columbia University Press.

Habermas, Jürgen. 1993. *Justification and Application*. Cambridge, MA: MIT Press.

Hales, Steven. 1997. "A Consistent Relativism." *Mind* 106 (421): 33–52.

Hart, H.L.A. 1997. *The Concept of Law*. New York: Oxford University Press.

Hegel, G.W.F. 1977a. *Phenomenology of Spirit*. Oxford: Clarendon Press.

———. 1977b. *Philosophy of Right*. New York: Oxford University Press.

Hibbard, George. 1900. "The Sporting Spirit: Ancient and Modern." *Outing* 36:601–602.

Holley, David. 1997. "Breaking the Rules When Others Do." *Journal of Applied Philosophy* 14 (2): 159–168.

Holt, Richard. 2006. "The Amateur Body and the Middle-Class Man: Work, Health and Style in Victorian Britain." *Sport in History* 26 (3): 352–369.

Hurka, Thomas. 2007. "Games and the Good." In *Ethics in Sport*, edited by W. J. Morgan, 21–34. Champaign, IL: Human Kinetics.

Hurka, Thomas. 1993. *Perfectionism*. New York: Oxford University Press.

Knowles, Dudley. 2002. *Hegel and the Philosophy of Right*. New York: Routledge.

Koorsgaard, Christine. 1996. *The Sources of Normativity*. Cambridge: Cambridge University Press.

———. 2003. "The Dependence of Value on Humanity." In *The Practice of Value*, edited by R. Jay Wallace, 63–85. Oxford: Clarendon Press.

Kretchmar, R. Scott. 1989. "On Beautiful Games." *Journal of the Philosophy of Sport* 16:34–43.

Kretchmar, Scott. 2001. "A Functionalist Analysis of Game Acts: Revisiting Searle." *Journal of the Philosophy of Sport* 28:160–172.

Laden, Anthony S. 2005. "Evaluating Social Reasons: Hobbes vs. Hegel." *Journal of Philosophy* 102 (7): 327–356.

LaVaque-Manty, Mika. 2009. *The Playing Fields of Eton: Equality and Excellence in Modern Meritocracy*. Ann Arbor: University of Michigan Press.

Letsas, George. 2014. "The DNA of Conventions." *Law and Philosophy* 33:535–571.

Lewis, David. 2002. *Convention*. Oxford: Blackwell.

Manley, Lawrence. 1981. "Concepts of Convention and Models of Critical Discourse." *New Literary History* 13 (1): 31–52.

Marion-Young, Iris. 1988. "The Exclusion of Women from Sport: Conceptual and Existential Dimensions." In *Philosophic Inquiry in Sport*, edited by W. J. Morgan and K. Meier, 335–342. Champaign, IL: Human Kinetics.

Marmor, Andrei. 1996. "On Convention." *Synthese* 107 (3): 349–371.

———. 2006. "How Law Is like Chess." *Legal Theory* 12:347–371.

———. 2007. "Deep Conventions." *Philosophy and Phenomenological Research* 74 (3): 586–610.

———. 2009. *Social Conventions: From Language to Law*. Princeton, NJ: Princeton University Press.

McDowell, John. 2002. "Responses." In *Reading McDowell: On Mind and World*, edited by N. Smith, 269–305. New York: Routledge.

McFee, Graham. 2018. "Occasions for Making Sense of Sport: Celebration of Morgan's View." *Sport, Ethics and Philosophy* 12:435–452.

McGinn, Colin. 2012. *Truth by Analysis: Games, Names, and Philosophy*. New York: Oxford University Press.

Meier, Klaus V. 1988. "Triad Trickery: Playing with Games and Sport." *Journal of the Philosophy of Sport* 15:11–30.

Moore, Eric. 2018. "Against Deep Conventionalism." *Journal of the Philosophy of Sport* 45 (3): 228–240.

Morgan, William J. 2004. "Moral Antirealism, Internalism and Sport." *Journal of the Philosophy of Sport* 31 (2): 161–183.

———. 2012. "Broad Internalism, Deep Conventions, Moral Entrepreneurs and Sport." *Journal of the Philosophy of Sport* 39 (1): 65–100.

———. 2013. "Interpretivism, Conventionalism, and the Ethical Coach." In *The Ethics of Coaching Sports: Moral, Social, and Legal Issues*, edited by Robert Simon, 61–78. Boulder, CO: Westview Press.

———. 2015. "Conventionalism and Sport." In *Routledge Handbook of the Philosophy of Sport*, edited by M. McNamee and W. J. Morgan, 35–52. New York: Routledge.

Mrozek, Donald. 1983. *Sport and the American Mentality*. Knoxville: University of Tennessee Press.

Papineau, David. 2017. *Knowing the Score*. New York: Basic Books.

Pinkard, Terry. 1996. *The Sociality of Reason*. New York: Cambridge University Press.

Pippin, Robert. 2003. "The Conditions of Value." In *The Practice of Value*, edited by R. Jay Wallace, 86–105. Oxford: Clarendon Press.

———. 2008. *Hegel's Practical Philosophy: Rational Agency as Ethical Life*. New York: Cambridge University Press.

Posner, Richard. 1999. *The Problematics of Moral and Legal Theory*. Cambridge, MA: Harvard University Press.

Putnam, Hilary. 1981. *Reason, Truth and History*. Cambridge: Cambridge University Press.

Quine, Willard Van Orman. 1960. *Word and Object*. Cambridge, MA: MIT Press.

Rader, Benjamin. 2004. *American Sports: From the Age of Folk Games to the Age of Televised Sports*. Upper Saddle River, NJ: Prentice Hall.

Rawls, John. 1971. *A Theory of Justice*. Cambridge, MA: Harvard University Press.

———. 1999. "Kantian Constructivism in Moral Theory." In *John Rawls: Collected Papers*, edited by S. Freeman, 303–358. Cambridge, MA: Harvard University Press.

Raz, Joseph. 2003. *The Practice of Value*. Oxford: Clarendon Press.

Rorty, Richard. 1989. *Contingency, Irony, and Solidarity*. New York: Cambridge University Press.

———. 1991. *Objectivity, Relativism, and Truth*. New York: Cambridge University Press.

———. 1996. "Who Are We? Moral Universalism and Economic Triage." *Diogenes* 44 (173): 5–15.

———. 1998. *Truth and Progress: Philosophical Papers*. Vol. 3. Cambridge: Cambridge University Press.

———. 2000. "Existential Necessity and Kantian Unconditionality: A Response to Harald Koehl." File 468, Richard Rorty Digital Research Files, 1992–2002, University of California, Irvine, Libraries.

———. 2014. "The Limits of Reductionism." In *Mind, Language, and Meta-Philosophy: Early Philosophical Papers*, edited by S. Leach and J. Tartaglia, 39–54. New York: Cambridge University Press.

Russell, John S. 1999. "Are Rules All an Umpire Has to Work With?" *Journal of the Philosophy of Sport* 26:27–49.

———. 2004. "Moral Realism in Sport." *Journal of the Philosophy of Sport* 31 (2): 142–160.

———. 2007. "Broad Internalism and the Moral Foundations of Sport." In *Ethics in Sport*, edited by W. J. Morgan, 51–66. Champaign, IL: Human Kinetics.

———. 2011. "Limitations of the Sport-Law Comparison." *Journal of the Philosophy of Sport* 38 (2): 254–272.

———. 2012. "Does Metaethics Make a Difference in the Philosophy of Sport." Paper presented at the Pacific Division of the American Philosophical Association, Seattle, Washington, April 7.

———. 2018. "A Critique of Conventionalist Broad Internalism." *Sport, Ethics and Philosophy* 12:453–467.

Searle, John. 1969. *Speech Acts: An Essay in the Philosophy of Language*. Cambridge: Cambridge University Press.

———. 1995. *The Construction of Social Reality*. New York: Free Press.

———. 2010. *Making the Social World: The Structure of Human Civilization*. New York: Oxford University Press.

Sellars, Wilfrid. 1968. *Science and Metaphysics*. New York: Routledge and Kegan Paul.

Silvers, Anita, and David Wasserman. 2007. "Convention and Competence: Disability Rights in Sports and Education." In *Ethics in Sport*, edited by W. J. Morgan, 451–459. Champaign, IL: Human Kinetics.

Simon, Robert. 2004. "From Ethnocentrism to Realism: Can Discourse Ethics Bridge the Gap?" *Journal of the Philosophy of Sport* 31 (2): 122–141.

———. 2007. "Internalism and Internal Values in Sport." In *Ethics in Sport*, edited by W. J. Morgan, 35–50. Champaign, IL: Human Kinetics.

———. 2014. "Theories of Sport." In *The Bloomsbury Companion to the Philosophy of Sport*, edited by C. R. Torres, 83–97. New York: Bloomsbury.

———. 2015. "Internalism and Sport." In *Routledge Handbook of the Philosophy of Sport*, edited by M. McNamee and W. J. Morgan, 22–34. New York: Routledge.

Southwood, Nicholas, and Lina Eriksson. 2011. "Norms and Conventions." *Philosophical Explorations* 14 (2): 195–217.

Suits, Bernard. 1988. "Tricky Triad: Games, Play, and Sport." *Journal of the Philosophy of Sport* 15:1–10.

———. 1989. "The Trick of the Disappearing Goal." *Journal of the Philosophy of Sport* 16:1–12.

———. 2007. "The Elements of Sport." In *Ethics in Sport*, edited by W. J. Morgan, 9–20. Champaign, IL: Human Kinetics.

———. 2014. *The Grasshopper: Games, Life, and Utopia*. 3rd ed. Ontario: Broadview Press.

Taylor, Charles. 1985. *Philosophical Papers I: Human Agency and Language*. Cambridge: Cambridge University Press.

———. 1992. *Multiculturalism and the Politics of Recognition*. Princeton, NJ: Princeton University Press.

———. 1995. "A Most Peculiar Institution." In *World, Mind and Ethics: Essays on the Ethical Philosophy of Bernard Williams*, edited by J. Alltham and R. Harrison, 132–155. Cambridge, MA: Cambridge University Press

Turbo, Jason, and Michael Duca. 2010. *The Baseball Codes*. New York: Anchor Books.

Velleman, J. David. 2013. *Foundations for Moral Relativism*. New York: Open Book.

Walzer, Michael. 1987. *Interpretation and Social Criticism*. Cambridge, MA: Harvard University Press.

———. 1994. *Thick and Thin: Moral Argument at Home and Abroad*. Notre Dame, IN: University of Notre Dame Press.

Whitney, Caspar. 1907. "The View-Point." *Outing* 50:485–492.

———. 1908a. "The View-Point." *Outing* 52:761–766.

———. 1908b. "The View-Point." *Outing* 53:244–249.

———. 1909. "The View-Point." *Outing* 53:643–646.

Williams, Bernard. 1981. *Moral Luck*. Cambridge: Cambridge University Press.

———. 1985. *Ethics and the Limits of Philosophy*. Cambridge, MA: Harvard University Press.

———. 2003. "Relativism, History, and the Existence of Values." In *The Practice of Value*, edited by R. Jay Wallace, 106–118. Oxford: Oxford University Press.

Withington, Lothrop. 1914. "When Harvard Won at Henley." *Outing* 65:95–106.

Wittgenstein, Ludwig. 1958. *Philosophical Investigations*, 3rd ed. Upper Saddle River, NJ: Prentice Hall.

"The World of Sport." 1912. *Outing* 59:637–639.

Index

Abrahams, Harold, 94
Aiken, Henry, 126–127
Amateur-professional sport divide, 27–28, 148–149, 159
Amateur sportsmanship, 11–18; beliefs of, 106–109, 119; and beliefs of professional community, 92; evaluative schemes of, 145–146; and game officials, 17; instrumental reason, strategy, and specialization in, 14–17; lethargy of, 22; and past conceptions of sport, 108; on purpose of sport, 194; on right thing to do in sport, 116; Russell on normative divide of, 77; winning from amateur perspective, 13–14. *See also* English
American Olympic Committee, 25
Americans: versus English in Olympic Games, 23, 25, 27; and idea of fair play, 175; version of professional sport by, 3, 9, 23, 27, 112, 117. *See also* United States
Aristotle, 68, 69, 206n2
Athletic endeavor: complex moral terrain of, 2; conceptions of, 9, 15, 77; human interests in, 78; point and purpose of, 4, 9, 61, 76, 81, 145, 161, 168, 174; reconceptualization of proper aim of, 19–21; spirit and integrity of, 68
Athletic excellence: aim of sport as achievement of, 67; demonstration of, 58, 61, 68; determination of, 56; as enshrined in Russell's internal principle, 76; maintenance and fostering of, 169, 170; pursuit of, 19, 21, 49, 68, 69, 77, 194; undermining of, 26; understandings of, 1–4, 105–106, 107; unprecedented levels of, 18
Athletic performance, enhancement of, 3, 14, 15
Athletic specialization, 16, 24, 26

Baker, Norman, 11, 13
Baseball, invention of, 82
Berne, Eric, 79
Best, David, 204n4
Boghossian, Paul, 122–123, 209nn11–12
Bootstrapping, 126, 179, 181–182, 186
Boston Marathon (1967), moral disobedience in, 196–197
Brandom, Robert, 168
Brennan, Geoffrey, 126, 176, 179, 205n11, 212n14
Brett, George, 60–61, 74–75, 77, 86, 88, 102, 147
Broad competence, valuing of, 16
Broad internalism: as compared to formalism, 6; discourse version of, 96–123; metaphysical version of, 62–95; as one of two moral theories of sport, 4, 5; shortcomings of, 6; variants of, 5–6

Brownlee, Timothy, 164
Burge, Tyler, 211n7

Chappell, Sophie, 157
Chariots of Fire (film), 94
Coherence, importance of, 171–172
Coherentism, 71–73, 87, 92, 93
Collective subject, 161
Collier, Price, 14
Compliance dependence, 127, 128, 167, 209n4
Constitutive (surface) conventions, 137–145, 167. *See also* Deep and surface (constitutive) conventions
Constitutive rules: distinction between regulative and, 29; formalism and, 48–49; Marmor on, 135, 138, 140, 141, 144, 148, 149–151; Searle on, 33–44, 53, 149–151, 204n4, 204–205n7; Suits on, 33–44, 53, 149–151, 204n4, 204–205n7
Consumership of commercialized sports, 22
Convention (Lewis), 129
Conventionalist ethical theory of sport, 155–192, 193; as unlike coordinating, deep, or surface conventions, 7, 124–154
Conventional norms: ethics and, 184, 187, 188, 190, 197, 209n2; Hegel on, 157; Marmor on, 128, 175, 210n8, 212n14; as practice-dependent, 126–127, 207n6; rules versus, 139; validity of, 189
Conventions: arbitrariness of, 127–129, 132–133, 135, 137, 143–144, 149–150, 160, 165–167, 178–181, 184; moral conventions, 8, 176, 180; ubiquity and general features of, 124–129. *See also* Constitutive (surface) conventions; Coordinating conventions; Deep and surface (constitutive) conventions; Ethical conventions
Coordinating conventions, 129–133, 159; constitutive conventions as distinguished from, 141, 142; deep conventions as compared to, 135; with moral obligations, 209–210n5; playing and standing for anthem as, 210n6; queueing practice as, 212n14; rational calling card of, 143; and reasons for following conventions, 209n2; use of term, 6, 123, 124
Corbin, John, 20
Crowther, Samuel, 12, 57, 203n1
Curry, Wesley, 101

D'Agostino, Fred, 29, 39–42, 43, 44, 45, 46, 47, 57, 58
Darwell, Stephen, 163
Davidson, Donald, 106
De dicto normative attitudes, 46, 47, 48, 205n12
Deep and surface (constitutive) conventions, 133–137; case against, 124–154; use of terms, 6, 123, 124, 189
Deep conventions, 146. *See also* Deep and surface (constitutive) conventions
Delattre, Edwin, 44, 45
De re normative attitudes, 46, 47, 48, 205n12
Descriptive relativity, 80
Dialogical inquiry, 98–100
Disability sport, 1–2, 198–199, 200, 201
Discourse, restrictions on, 97–98
Discourse ethics, 97–98, 100, 102, 103, 107, 108, 113, 123
Discourse version of broad internalism/interpretivism, 96–123
Dixon, Nick, 62, 63, 80, 95, 96–107, 110–118, 120, 123, 208n8
Dworkin, Ronald, 62, 71, 72, 73, 88, 89, 93, 94, 146
Dyreson, Mark, 10, 12

Eichberg, Henning, 136
Encyclopedia Logic (Hegel), 213n21
English: versus Americans in Olympic Games, 23, 25, 27; and idea of fair play, 175; as practicing amateur sportsmanship, 27; version of gentleman-amateur sport by, 3, 9, 10, 14, 16, 18, 20, 112, 117
English, Jane, 199
Equality: new conceptions of, 1; role of, in professional sportsmanship, 22
Eriksson, Lina, 183, 205n11, 209–210n5, 212n19
Ethical conventions: amateur versus professional, 172, 212n16; arbitrariness of, 165–167; and collective subjects, 211n6; context-dependent, 147; and community, 161–165; coordinating conventions versus, 124, 129–133, 159–160, 209n2, 212n14; crucial role of sport play and, 9; deep and surface conventions versus, 124, 133–145, 148, 160–161, 167–169; Hegel and, 155–158, 162–165, 174; language and, 169–171; moral entrepreneurs and, 197; and moral theory bias, 174–175; normative force of, 145, 146, 156–159, 161–162, 165, 168–174, 211n9; objections to, 174–192, 213n22; overview of, 6, 7, 8, 123; practice-dependent status of, 156, 161, 163; and *pro tanto* reasons to play sports, 167
Ethics and the Limits of Philosophy (Williams), 174

"The Ethos of Games" (D'Agostino), 39
Evaluative vocabularies: community and, 92, 111, 121–122, 169, 173; descriptive vocabularies and, 81, 82, 86; impartiality in, 113; in-house, 170; and normativity of sport, 211n9; transition from, 194; Wittgenstein on, 115
Excellence: athletic (*see* Athletic excellence); standards of, 23, 85, 104
External principle: advantages of, 206n3; critique of, 90–93; Russell on, 5, 69–73, 76–78, 81, 83, 89, 91–93, 206n2, 207nn10–11
Extra-community perspective, 113, 115, 118, 119, 120, 195

Fairness: Americans' understanding of, 25; as central to genuine athletic accomplishment, 1; justice as, 175; new conceptions of, 1; role of, in professional sportsmanship, 22; in Russell's metaphysical view, 63–64; as virtue of amateurs, 14
Financial remuneration for athletic engagement, 11–12, 13, 17, 23, 109, 187
Fletcher, George, 175
Formalism: broad internalism as compared to, 6; conceptual analysis of, 30–32; defense of, as moral theory of sport, 39–56; definition of sport and, 32–38; as family of theories of sport, 29; as inadequate moral theory of sport, 30; as moral theory of sport, 38–39; as one of two moral theories of sport, 4; rebuttal of, 56–61
Foucault, Michel, 7
Frankfurt, Harry G., 84
Freud, Sigmund, 208n6
"A Functional Analysis of Game Acts" (Kretchmar), 204–205n7

Galarraga, Armando, 47–48
Game officials: amateurism and, 17; as charged with calling and enforcing rules, 45; decisions of, as interpretative judgments, 72–73; disqualification of, 53; errant calls of, 46, 47–48; and inconsistent enforcement of rules, 152; professional sportsmanship on, 26–27; and self-calls by players, 205n8; and theory of adjudication, 59, 72, 88, 89, 207n11
Games: according to Suits, 31, 32, 65, 66–67, 78–79; according to Wittgenstein, 31, 66–67; locating value of, 51–52
Games People Play (Berne), 79
Gentleman-amateur sport: genealogy of, 10–11; and moral standards, 3, 4; versus professional conception of athletic endeavor, 9. *See also* Amateur sportsmanship
Geras, Norman, 31
Geuss, Raymond, 188
Gilbert, Margaret, 161
Goals: lusory, 32–33, 52, 53, 54, 68; pre-lusory, 32–33, 51, 52, 68, 140; trivial, 51
Goodwin, Robert E., 205n11
The Grasshopper (Suits), 49, 50, 79

Habermas, Jürgen, 97, 179
Hard cases, 4, 85, 116; D'Agostino and, 41; Dixon on, 107, 115; lusory attitude and, 58; Russell on, 60, 72, 73–74, 76–77, 82–83, 86–88, 90–92, 101–102, 105; Simon on, 108, 115, 119
Hart, H.L.A., 29, 30, 37, 38, 125, 144, 149, 151, 153
Hayes, John, 27
Hegel, G.W.F., 7–8; on community, 162–165; *Encyclopedia Logic*, 213n21; ethical conventions and, 123; on ethical norms, 188; on morality, 174, 180, 186, 201, 212n17; *Philosophy of Right*, 154, 157–158, 210n3; and *Sittlichkeit*, 155, 157
"Helping Out at Home" case, 73–74
History in moral essentialism/realism, 94–95
Hoak, Don, 74
Holley, David, 185, 212n20
Human flourishing, 68, 69, 206n2
Hume, David, 126
Hurka, Thomas, 49, 51, 204n2, 206nn15–16, 210n7
Hurley, Susan, 118, 209n10

Inquiry view of dialogical inquiry, 98–99, 100
Instrumental reason, 15; amateur sportsmanship on, 15; professional sportsmanship on, 24–25
Intellectual cogency, 98, 101, 103, 104, 107, 110, 111, 112, 114, 115
Internal principle, 5, 6; criticisms of, 177, 191; Russell on, 68–70, 74, 76–78, 88–90, 101, 104, 105, 206n2, 207nn10–11; sport actions and, 178
Interpretive theory of law, 62, 93, 94
Interpretivism, 4, 62–63, 73, 93, 95, 96, 98

James, William, 78
Jotto, 139
Joyce, Jim, 47–48
Judged athletic events, 204n1
Justice, theory of, 103

Kant, Immanuel, 26, 69, 97, 156, 160, 163, 164, 170, 172, 180, 183
Koorsgaard, Christine, 161, 164, 210n5
Kretchmar, R. Scott, 37, 204n1, 204–205n7

Laden, Anthony, 173
Language, 31, 64, 79, 80, 115, 125, 169, 192, 207n8
Language-games, 80, 83, 84, 86, 112, 169, 170, 171, 193–194, 197, 199
LaVaque-Manty, Mika, 1, 22
Letsas, George, 129
Lewis, David: classical analysis, 138–139; *Convention*, 129; on coordinating conventions, 6, 7, 123–125, 127–132, 145, 154; on games and rules, 141
Lusory attitude, 38, 39, 48–56, 57, 58–59, 60, 62, 101, 206n16, 207n5, 210n10
Lusory goals, 32–33, 52, 53, 54, 68

Mackie, John, 64
MacPhail, Lee, 60, 61
Marion-Young, Iris, 198
Marmor, Andrei: on alternative conventions, 128, 209n3; on arbitrariness, 167; on collective subjects, 211n6; on compliance dependence, 127; on constitutive conventions, 138, 139–140, 141–142, 144–146, 147–148; on conventional norms, 212n14; on conventional practices, 175, 176, 177; on deep and surface conventions, 6, 7, 123, 124, 134–137, 145–146, 160, 161, 169, 189, 210n8; on "generally recognized" reasons, 131; institutionalization thesis, 149; on "legislative" codification, 210n9; on Searle, 150–154
Martin, Billy, 75, 77, 86, 102
Marx, Karl, 208n6
Mathis, Robert, 204–205n7
McDowell, John, 192
McFee, Graham, 191–192
McGinn, Colin, 204n2
McPhail, Lee, 74–75
Meier, Klaus, 34, 36, 204n1
Metaphysical version of broad internalism, 62–95
Money: financial remuneration, 11–12, 13, 17, 23, 109, 187; influx of, in sport, 13; worry regarding corrupting power of, 21
Moore, Eric, 6–7, 210n14, 213n23
Moral change, 197, 199, 200
Moral conventions, 8, 176, 180
Moral disobedience/defiance, 195, 196–197, 210n6
Moral entrepreneurs, 8, 197–200
Morality of Freedom (Raz), 212n13
Morality system, 175–186, 188, 212n17
Moral principles, 179; criticisms of, 191; Dixon on, 96–99, 101, 103–106; Dworkian, 146, 155; Russell on, 5–6, 64–67, 71, 94, 206n2; Simon on, 96–99, 101, 103–106; validity of, 182–183, 184; Williams on, 177
Moral progress, 9, 28, 193–194, 195–201
Moral realism: according to Russell, 64–67; according to Simon and Dixon, 96–123; basic tenets of, 63; basic tenets of discourse realist moral theory of sport, 97–100; broad internalism as version of, 5; versions of, 63
Moral reasons, 63, 96, 142, 175, 176, 179, 181, 182
Moral vocabularies, 8, 111, 181, 193, 194, 195, 197, 199, 200
Mrozek, Donald, 24

Nagel, Thomas, 97, 118
Non-reductive ethical naturalism, 63
Normative attitudes: *de dicto*, 46, 47, 48, 205n12; *de re*, 46, 47, 48, 205n12
Normative principles: in game adjudication, 89; internal and external, of sport, 67–76; principal drawback of, 169; proponents of, 62–63; Russell on, 86, 87, 90–94, 207n11
Norms: arbitrary character of background norms, 210n8; conventional, 126–128, 139, 157, 175, 184, 187–190, 197, 207n6, 209n2, 210n8, 212n14; reasons as constituting, 135–136

Objectionable bootstrapping, 179, 181–182, 183–184
Officials. *See* Game officials
Olympic Games: conceptions of sport in 1896–1924 games, 2–4, 9–28; founding idea behind modern revival of, 51; 1908 marathon finish, 27; 1912 Stockholm Games, 117; purpose of inauguration of modern ones, 12; 2002 Winter Olympic Games, 208n8; 2012 London Games women's badminton doubles, 53, 54, 55, 56

Papineau, David, 159, 181, 212n18
Paralympics Games, 199
Peirce, Charles Sanders, 171
Penalties, self-called, 205n8
Penalty-bearing rules, 33–34, 36, 37, 40, 41, 45
Philosophy of Right (Hegel), 154, 157
Pietri, Dorando, 27

"Pine Tar Incident," 60–61, 74–75, 77, 86, 88, 102, 147
Pinkard, Terry, 210n2
Pippin, Robert, 211n12
Platonism, 40, 41, 42, 43, 44, 45
Playoff formats, 56, 206n17
Posner, Richard, 8, 197
Practical reasoning about sport, 171, 172–173
Pre-lusory goals, 32–33, 51, 52, 68, 140
Primary rules, 29–30, 37, 46, 47, 154, 210n12
Principles. *See* External principle; Internal principle; Moral principles; Normative principles
Professional coaches, use of, 3, 16, 18
Professional sportsmanship, 20–23; beliefs of, 106–109, 119; and beliefs of professional community, 93; evaluative schemes of, 145–146; genealogy of, 18–20; instrumental reason, strategy, and specialization in, 24–26; moral norms of, 3; and past conceptions of sport, 108; as pitted against gentleman-amateur sport, 9; on purpose of sport, 194; on right thing to do in sport, 116; Russell on normative divide of, 77; strenuous life of, 21, 22; winning from perspective of, 23. *See also* Americans
Pro tanto moral obligation, 132
Pro tanto reasons, 127, 131, 135, 136, 142, 167, 185
Putnam, Hilary, 120, 190, 191

Queueing practice, 176–177
Quine, Willard Van Orman, 80

Rational dialogue: Dixon on, 63, 100, 103, 112–114, 123; independent standards of, 99; inquiry view of, 98; moral arguments in, 117; Simon on, 100, 103, 110–111, 112–114, 120, 121, 123; starting point of, 97, 102, 107, 116
Rawls, John, 71, 87–88, 93, 103–104, 111, 175, 178, 179, 207–208n1, 208–209n9
Raz, Joseph, 173, 211n11, 212n13
Refereed athletic events, 204n1
Referees: amateurism and, 17; professional sportsmanship on, 26–27
Reflective appraisal, 98, 99, 102, 106, 121, 200
Reflective equilibrium, 71, 87, 88, 89, 91, 92, 93, 94, 207n11
Regulative rules, 29, 33, 34, 35, 36, 37, 40, 41, 42, 44, 45, 54, 205n9
Respect view of dialogical inquiry, 98, 100
Rorty, Richard: on beliefs, 181; on definitional inquiry, 30, 78; on moral ideals and principles, 177; on moral philosophy, 201, 208n6; on purpose, 158; on redescription, 197; on rivals, 122; on skyhooks, 172; on "vegetarian sense of aboutness," 84; on vocabularies, 118–119, 120–121, 195
Rules: according to Hart, 29–30, 33, 37; according to Suits, 33; addition of, 59–60; arbitrariness of, 149, 150, 151, 152; changes in, 152; constitutive, 29, 33–44, 48–49, 53, 135, 138, 140, 141, 144, 148, 149–151, 204n4, 204–205n7; formalism as privileging of, 61; fringe, 42; gaps in, 59; indeterminacy of, 72; interpretation of, 60; loopholes in, 119; means-limiting function of, 25, 50; as not self-interpreting, 60; penalty-bearing, 33–34, 36, 37, 40, 41, 45; primary, 29–30, 37, 46, 154, 210n12; problems with, 4–5; regulative, 29, 33, 34, 35, 36, 37, 40, 41, 42, 44, 45, 54, 205n9; rule-centered dilemmas, 148; Russell on strict adherence to, 61; secondary, 29–30, 37, 39, 46, 47, 48, 144, 149, 151, 153, 154, 205–206n13, 210n12; spirit of, in amateur and professional sportsmanship, 22; strategic approach to, 25–26; trivial, 42; unpunished violations of, 61
Russell, John: on broad internalism, 62, 104, 207n5; Dworkian moral principles employed by, 146; on internal and external principles, 206n2, 207n10; on moral principles, 6; on moral realism, 5; on normative theory of sport, 63–95, 97, 100–101, 102, 105, 162, 207n9; on professional rules, 59–61; on purpose of sport, 208n2; on reflective equilibrium, 207n11; rule-centered dilemmas raised by, 148; on validity of moral view, 99

Sandlot sports, 144, 150, 151, 152
Science: enlistment of, in improving athletic performance, 15; as important element of professional sport, 24
Searle, John: on "brute" facts, 82; on constitutive rules, 29, 33–37, 42, 149–151, 204n4; on D'Agostino's Platonism objection, 43, 44; on feminist objection to "ladies" and "gentlemen," 80; on formalism, 38; on institutional facts, 84; on regulative rules, 29, 33–37
Secondary rules: formalists on, 39, 46–48, 205–206n13; Hart on, 29–30, 37, 144, 149, 153, 154, 210n12; Marmor on, 151
Secret practices in professional sportsmanship, 25
Sellars, Wilfrid, 111
Silvers, Anita, 138

Simon, Robert: on broad internalism, 62, 80, 95–115, 118–123, 206n2; Dworkian moral principles employed by, 146; on formalism, 29; on moral discourse, 207–208n1; on moral realism, 5, 6, 63; rule-centered dilemmas raised by, 148; on shift in rules, 26
Sittlichkeit, 7, 8, 154, 155, 157, 174, 210n2
Skating community, Dixon's hypothetical example of, 114, 116, 117, 118, 208n8
Social class, 3, 10, 11, 18, 103
Social dependence thesis, 173, 211n11
Southwood, Nicholas, 183, 205n11, 209–210n5, 212n19
Specialization, 16, 24, 26
Sport: avocational take on, 3; as bona fide species of conventional social practices, 144; changes in already instituted sports, 82; conventionalist ethical theory of, 155–192, 193; defined, 32–38; disability sport, 1–2, 198–199, 200, 201; ethical conventions of, 155–192; ethos of, 58; formalism as moral theory of, 38–39; as form of human flourishing, 68, 69; four main elements of, 32–38; influx of money in, 13; institutional and natural properties of, 83–84; invention of new sport, 82; as moral laboratory, 1–2; moral progress in, 195–201; moral realist theory of, 90; need for comprehensive moral theory of, 4; normative analysis of, 92; as paradigmatic perfectionist practice, 104; purpose of, 115–116, 194; purpose of, according to Russell, 76; purpose of, according to Simon, 107; rationalized scientific approach to, 14–15; as rule-governed activity, 107; rules of, as not exhaustive, 4; Russell's conceptual analysis of, 71, 87, 91, 94; as social artifact/practice, 65–66, 81, 83–84, 104, 111, 172–173; Suits's conceptual analysis of, 31–32, 65, 66, 67, 73, 76, 78–79, 85, 93, 204n2, 206n1
Strategy: amateur sportsmanship on, 16; place of, in sport, 75; professional sportsmanship on, 25–26; recent ramifications of, 54
Suits, Bernard: on athletic distinction, 69; on athletic excellence, 68; conceptual analysis of sport by, 65–67, 73, 76, 78–79, 85, 87, 93, 94, 104, 204nn1–2, 204–205n7, 206n1, 207n8; on constitutive rules, 40, 43, 140; on D'Agostino, 41–42; on formalism, 29–37, 46, 58, 206n16; on game rules, 39, 45, 204n3; on lusory attitude, 38, 48, 49–56, 62, 210n10; on regulative rules, 40, 44
Sullivan, James, 25
Surface conventions, 135, 161. *See also* Constitutive (surface) conventions; Deep and surface (constitutive) conventions
Switzer, Kathrine V., 196–197

Taylor, Charles, 162, 165, 180
Technological interventions in sport, 15
Theory of justice, 103
A Theory of Justice (Rawls), 87–88, 207–208n1
Training, 2, 10, 14, 24, 25, 81, 117
Trick plays, 25
"Tricky Triad" (Suits), 204n1
Trollope, Anthony, 13, 58
Turnen (calisthenics) movement, as alternative sport practice, 136

Umpires: amateurism and, 17; professional sportsmanship on, 26–27
United States: focus of, on track and field in Olympic Games, 23; people of, as considering themselves consumers more than producers, 21–22; successes in Olympic Games by, 25. *See also* Americans
Utilitarianism, 156, 163, 178, 180

Veil of ignorance, 103, 178, 179
Veil of understanding, 207–208n1
Velleman, David, 111, 116
Vocabularies: community use of, 81, 92–93, 111, 113, 168, 181, 193–195, 197, 199, 200; descriptive, 82, 86, 211n9; evaluative, 82, 86, 122, 169, 170, 173, 211n9; overview of, 5, 8; Rorty on, 119, 121; Suits on, 79; Wittgenstein on, 31, 80, 115

Walzer, Michael, 108, 117, 177, 181, 208–209n9, 212n15
Ware, Edmund, 18
Wasserman, David, 138
Whitney, Casper, 21, 26
Williams, Bernard, 12, 174–175, 177, 178, 179, 180, 181, 183, 201, 210n5
Winning: amateurs' approach to, 13–14; as the be-all and end-all of athletic competition, 2; professional sport's approach to, 21, 23, 25, 26; as too valued in sport today, 53
Wittgenstein, Ludwig, 31, 66–67, 80, 115, 169, 189, 192, 204n2, 209n10, 211n8
Women's sport, 1–2, 196–197, 198, 199, 200
Word and Object (Quine), 80

William J. Morgan is Professor Emeritus, Division of Occupational Science and the Annenberg School for Communication and Journalism, University of Southern California. He is author of multiple books, most recently of *Why Sports Morally Matter*, co-editor of the *Routledge Handbook of the Philosophy of Sport*, and editor of *Ethics in Sport*, third edition.